Glimpses
of an
Uncharted Life

Glimpses *of an* Uncharted Life

RICHARD H. SHRIVER

GLIMPSES OF AN UNCHARTED LIFE

In the final two years of the Soviet Union, there was great tension in the three Baltic republics. The Soviets used tanks and special troops to attack and kill people in Vilnius, Lithuania, and in Riga, Latvia. In Tallinn, the capital city of Estonia, the Estonians erected this sign saying No Tanks! on the road to their parliament building. (Cover photo by author)

iUniverse books may be ordered through booksellers or by contacting:

iUniverse
1663 Liberty Drive
Bloomington, IN 47403
www.iuniverse.com
1-800-Authors (1-800-288-4677)

ISBN: 978-1-5320-0967-9 (sc)
ISBN: 978-1-5320-0968-6 (hc)
ISBN: 978-1-5320-0969-3 (e)

Library of Congress Control Number: 2016917873

Print information available on the last page.

iUniverse rev. date: 02/10/2017

To Barb, without whom virtually none of the stories told in this book would have happened—or, in the unlikely event that they did, would have happened without the laughs.

To Rich and Andrew, who learned to work hard and with integrity.

CONTENTS

PREFACE

In 2006, I developed a college-level, one-semester course titled Global Issues. I taught this course twice, once at the European College of Liberal Arts–Berlin and once for a class of seniors at the US Coast Guard Academy. The course addressed matters that I thought college students should understand before they were ushered out into an unruly and untidy world, and I started writing an academic book on these topics. It soon became obvious, however, that I could not do justice to such a project. Instead, in 2011, I began writing this book, one I could construct almost entirely from memory, with little need to seek permission from anyone.

After graduating from college in 1956, I worked nonstop for the next fifty-three years. Then *poof*—I was seventy-five years old. During that period, my wife, Barb, and I lived in or visited fifty countries, almost all in the course of our work but a few times as curious visitors. I recall taking a vacation longer than one week only twice in that time.

The work, in fact, was mostly mine, but Barb definitely played a part. She assembled and published an award-winning coffee table book of drawings by the pencil-sketch artist Volodymyr Shagala illustrating Ukrainian culture. In Berlin, she developed the archives for the college, which turned out to be quite useful when the school changed hands.

This is a book of reminiscences and reflections by someone who enjoyed the best of opportunities this remarkable country has to offer.

For starters, I was lucky to be born in Maryland to a Protestant family that achieved decent means and to live the first six years of my life in my grandfather's farmhouse with the farm's dairy in our basement. Augie Deller, the milkman, walked the five miles from Pikesville every morning, seven days a week, 365 days a year as near as I can recall, arriving at five o'clock to milk the cows. Then, with much clanging and banging, he brought the five-gallon cans of fresh warm milk to our basement, where it was placed in quart bottles or was separated by the Danish De Laval machine into cream and skim milk. Once a week, cream was churned into butter. Cooling was done not with a refrigerator but with fresh cold water pumped into the dairy from a nearby spring. Every morning I awoke to the magical sounds, smells, and results. I was probably four when I learned that the best way to clean milk and other dairy products from pots and pans and glasses was with cold water. Growing up in a place where food was produced was not a bad beginning for someone destined to try to help developing countries.

In the great lottery of birth, things could have been—and, given the odds, should have been—far worse.

I could have been born on the garbage dumps of Cebu in the Philippines of equally respectable and caring but chronically poor parents. My mother might have been a thirteen-year-old, and my father might have had to scavenge for the family to survive, with earnings well below subsistence, even for the Philippines. A formal education would have been unthinkable. The life expectancy for the hundreds of people who called the dumps home in 2010 was less than thirty years.

That's not what happened, however. At forty-three years old during the height of the Cold War, I was offered an appointment in the Office of the Secretary of Defense as director of telecommunications and command-and-control systems. I had a great long-standing desire to see from the inside how our government functioned, so I sold my interest in a successful company I'd started and took the plunge. This book is mainly about the consequences of that decision.

Barb and I lived fifteen years overseas, long enough to absorb the local and national cultures of Sweden, the Netherlands, Ukraine, and Germany, in that order. We made lifelong friends in every country and community where we lived.

Today, I volunteer much time mentoring young people who are beginning to chart their careers. I'm a fine one to talk since I did little to nothing to map out my own career beyond taking action to survive. By almost any comparison, my career was uncharted. After accepting a political appointment, I soon found myself adrift on the open seas of business ventures and government and international opportunities, with no compass other than a calendar that told me what I would be doing for the next few days.

After more than thirty years in technology, I was suddenly unemployed in 1989 with a fair severance package from McGraw-Hill. I used this money to invest in an entirely different and new career: economic and legal development in newly independent countries. I worked first in those countries emerging from the darkness of Soviet communism in the 1990s. Then it was on to the failed state of Afghanistan. In 2002 I traveled there to persuade the powers that be to let Americans and their organizations help build a modern system of laws to attract foreign capital to this once-great country and to develop commerce there. Finally, Barb and I moved to Berlin, Germany, in 2003 where we helped establish a need-blind, English-language college that attracted students from all over the globe.

This book's accounts are not in chronological order. The first section, "Foreign Affairs," starts with the beginning of the end of the Cold War. The second section, "Domestic Affairs," is about my experiences with the federal government and offers observations about government in my state, Connecticut. The final section, "Tapering Off," is about what happens when a calendar that was full for more than fifty years suddenly goes blank. It is a collection of stories that might amuse others who have had, or will have, similar experiences and who find their most productive years being subtly replaced with the infirmities of age.

Barb and I have had a unique adventure that others might enjoy vicariously—and without the travails.

A B B R E V I A T I O N S

CAJEF: Christian A. Johnson Endeavor Foundation. I met its president, Julie Johnson Kidd, in 1987.

CIME: Center for International Management Education. My wife, Barb, and I established this 501(c)(3) nonprofit in the spring of 1990 "to promote democracy and free enterprise inside the Soviet Union." Julie Kidd provided CIME major support in its international work. Russ Deane joined CIME in 1991 and led its ten-year effort to develop the rule of law in Estonia.

ECLA: European College of Liberal Arts–Berlin. This experiment in liberal arts education was started by German academic entrepreneurs who had seen and had valued the US form of liberal arts education. The ECLA began in 2000 as a six-week summer program. The CAJEF took over the school in the fall of 2002 when forty-nine students arrived to take a full-year college program. The school (now known as Bard College Berlin) was located in the eastern part of Berlin and occupied eight former embassies that operated in the former German Democratic Republic (communist East Germany). Classes were taught in English, and the college was need-blind, thus attracting students from all over Eastern Europe, the former Soviet Union, and Asia. Germans were outnumbered by Romanians, there was only an occasional student from the rest of Western Europe, and there were never more than two Americans at the college at the same time.

IESC: International Executive Service Corps. It was established by order of President Lyndon Johnson in 1964 principally through the efforts of David Rockefeller and Sol Linowitz.

IMI-Kiev: International Management Institute–Kiev. The institute, started in September 1990, was the first Western-style business program in the Soviet Union.

LCG: L'viv Consulting Group. Founded by CIME in L'viv, the largest city in western Ukraine, this Ukrainian consultancy helped more than one hundred Ukrainian entities become established or thrive, leading to the creation or preservation of more than ten thousand permanent jobs.

PSDTFA: Private Sector Development Task Force for Afghanistan. The group, which operated in 2002, was established as an informal collection of businesses and was cochaired by Ishaq Shahryar, Afghanistan's ambassador to the United States, and me. At the time, I was executive vice president of the IESC. The PSDTFA had unlimited access to the political leadership of Afghanistan; the group made three presentations to Afghanistan's president Hamid Karzai (two in Kabul, one in New York City) and met with key ministers as needed.

RSA: R. Shriver Associates. I started this business in 1966 with $5,000, enough to carry us for six months. The company offered consultancy services in mathematics and computers to businesses throughout the United States and to some extent to international industry. The firm employed fifty consultants and support staff in 1976 when I sold it to the employees, agreeing to be paid over time, and joined the Department of Defense.

USAID: United States Agency for International Development. This agency provides American assistance wherever needs exist and the United States has political, national security, economic, or humanitarian interests.

Dick and T-28

Imagine being paid to fly this bad boy, the 800-horsepower variant of North American's T28, a plane that was in service in the United States mainly as a pilot training aircraft from 1949 until 1994. I was on active duty in the US Air Force from 1957 until 1960. My contemporaries and I, members of the Silent Generation that followed the Greatest Generation, were eager to do our part for our country. Alas, our service time coincided with one of the most peaceful times in American history; we were too young for World War II, in college during the Korean War, and had left the services before the Vietnam War. It is probably no coincidence that a large percentage of civilians serving in the Pentagon during the Ford administration in 1976, at the height of the Cold War, were quite close in age. Those of us in this group may have suffered guilt because we never came under enemy fire, and so we felt an unfulfilled obligation to our country. (Photo by author)

Part 1

Foreign Affairs

————◦◦◦————

In Joseph Conrad's 1911 novel *Under Western Eyes*, the character Peter Ivanovych, speaking about the Russia of 1900, says that "at this moment, there yawns a chasm between the past and the future. It can never be bridged by foreign liberalism. All attempts at it are either folly or cheating. Bridged, it can never be! It has to be filled up."

Conrad, one of the great English-language novelists, was born Jozef Teodor Konrad Korzeniowski in Poland. A Slav and a member of a politically active family, he may have understood Russia better than many Russians did. He was born a Russian citizen in Polish-controlled Ukraine and grew up hating Russia and distrusting democracies at the same time. English was his third language after Polish and French; the Russian language was apparently not part of his repertoire, though the Slavic connection and his interest in history and politics helped him understand much about the Russian psyche. This excerpt from his book offers a view of the Russian mentality that may have resonance well into the twenty-first century.

1

A Life-Changing Impromptu Speech

March 1990

"Meester Shriver, in fifteen minutes could you give a one-hour presentation on how democracy works?" The time: March 10, 1990. The place: Tbilisi, Georgia. The speaker: the Georgian chairman of a UNESCO conference ostensibly about agriculture. Other attendees, about fifty in total, represented perhaps thirty countries, including only one other democracy that I knew of for certain, France. It occurred to me that if I hesitated, this opportunity would be offered to the Frenchman. I quickly replied, "Of course."

The UNESCO meeting showed me firsthand why President Ronald Reagan had withdrawn US support for this branch of the United Nations. With the exception of the Frenchman and me, the attendees were from countries run by tyrannical regimes, some from Africa but a plurality from republics of the Soviet Union. The topics at this conference centered not on UNESCO's mission of education and culture but on government-managed, collective agriculture as part of a command economy. The senior UNESCO representative at the conference was a hard-core communist, a woman from Cuba whose main function was to see if the Georgians were worthy of future UNESCO funding.

So what was I, a former member of Reagan's administration, doing at this conference? In September of the preceding year, at the final meeting of the McGraw-Hill International Advisory Council, I had been invited to go to Ukraine to teach at the first and only Western-style MBA program in the Soviet Union, the International Management Institute (IMI-Kiev). This McGraw-Hill group, which included luminaries such as future European Union president Romano Prodi, also included Bohdan Hawrylyshyn, a Ukrainian Canadian academician who had been head of a business school in Switzerland, IMI-Geneva.

Hawrylyshyn was excited, as he had just succeeded in registering the IMI-Kiev, no small accomplishment considering the intractable bureaucracy in one of the more conservative of the fifteen Soviet republics. Since we had been casual friends and I was departing McGraw-Hill, Hawrylyshyn asked if I would teach at his new school. I was eager to see the Soviet Union from the inside, having learned a great deal about it from the US side of the ongoing Cold War.

I told Hawrylyshyn I'd do it—for two weeks. Then, in November, the Berlin Wall was torn down. The phone rang days later. The call was from the school in Kiev. The topics on which I was to teach—trade, marketing, and free market economics—had become more interesting. Could I stay longer?

Barb and I spent the entire 1990 school year in Kiev, with a twelve-week break in the summer. The first thirty-one students arrived at the IMI in January. They were mainly from Ukraine. In addition, there was a woman from Uzbekistan, a man from Belarus, and a young woman from Moscow. Virtually all had been sent to the IMI by their employers. The youngest was Tanya Kindrat, twenty-two-year-old daughter of the Soviet Union's deputy minister of oil and gas pipelines, and the oldest was Arkady Arzanov, a forty-nine-year-old engineer with the massive Antonov aircraft design plant near Kiev.[1]

In February 1990, the IMI received a call from the agricultural institute in Tbilisi, Georgia, to see if it could send someone to a UNESCO conference to speak about international trade, marketing, and finance, the core subjects I was teaching in Kiev. I was asked to go. Yuri Poluneev, deputy director of the IMI, and I went to Tbilisi and were met at the airport by our host, Koba Arabuli, in the traditional way, with flowers, a shot of vodka, and the fair Vika (for Viktoria), a translator assigned to us by the Georgian KGB.

Koba was a product of Georgia's Komsomol, the Communist youth group between the Young Pioneers and the Communist Party, for which a few years in Komsomol was a prerequisite. (I was surprised to learn that becoming a member of the Communist Party before the age of thirty was the exception rather than the rule.) Koba was also a proud member of the Hefsurs, one of the more than forty tribes in Georgia. The Hefsurs had been the traditional protectors of kings through the ages and, much like US Secret Service agents, were trained to put themselves in harm's way to protect the sovereign.

Koba was a nonstop rambling encyclopedia of Georgian history, culture, and folklore. He had worked for Edouard Shevardnadze, then foreign minister of the Soviet Union and a favorite of the United States.

---

[1] I observed during this period that if you were from one of the fourteen non-Russian republics, one way to get ahead in the Soviet Communist Party was to demonstrate that you could be harsh on the citizens of your native republic. An attempted coup by the "gang of eight" hardliners at the top of the Communist apparatus failed on August 21, 1991, and one of the leaders was Boris Pugo, a Latvian who headed the Soviet Ministry of Interior. This ministry had nothing to do with parks and forests; it was the national police force, something that fortunately does not exist in the United States. Rather than face his fellow Latvians and other Baltic citizens in a newly freed society, Pugo killed himself the next day.

He introduced me to a great many of the hundreds of Georgian wines and to the traditions of wine drinking and toasting in Georgia.[2]

On Monday, I gave my talk on trade, finance, and marketing. So far as I knew, I had no further responsibilities at the conference, which was to last through Friday. Yuri was eager to return to Kiev. We asked our hosts Monday evening if we could have our passports and tickets for the return trip. We were told that wasn't possible. Our tickets and passports were being held by the chairman of the conference, and there was no way to get them back until he was ready to give them to us. He had other plans for me, which unfolded during the week. Still, I was glad to have the opportunity to learn more about this fascinating country.

As it happened, the conference had no official agenda—merely a list of participants and an array of topics. At a quarter to eleven the next day, Tuesday, March 10, 1990, the moderator nudged me and asked if I would be so kind as to give an hour talk about democracy.

Fifteen minutes was just the right amount of time to prepare a talk on how democracy works. More time might not have been helpful. With Vika translating, I prattled on about individual freedoms, paraphrased quotes from our founding fathers, and noted differences between what I had observed in my first two months in the Soviet Union versus the United States, especially the empty consumer markets and the absence of a climate for entrepreneurs and private business.

My life began to change immediately after my talk. Two Lithuanians asked if they could have a word with me. Since my Russian was poor and my Lithuanian nonexistent, we conversed in French, a language we all understood equally well. This had another advantage: we didn't need Vika, the KGB agent, to interpret.

The Lithuanian leader was Petras Tvarionavicius (tv-AR-eeon-NA-vichus). His was the first of many tongue-twisting Lithuanian names we

---

[2] Three years later, as head of the US assistance program for the former Soviet Union at the International Executive Service Corps in Stamford, Connecticut, I hired Koba to be the IESC's director for Georgia.

were to learn. He asked if I could come to Lithuania. I thanked him and asked what he would like me to do. He replied, "We want you to give that speech all over Lithuania." Petras and I exchanged the necessary information on that second day of the conference.

At the beginning of the third day, March 11, 1990, the chairman of the conference announced that Lithuania had declared its independence from the Soviet Union. (I began to sense my new career inch forward.) The attendees were stunned, all except the two Lithuanians, as I later learned. After an awkward pause, there was a ripple of tentative, polite applause, the kind of feigned approval one might hear after a four-cello ensemble performed a work by an ultramodern German composer. Later that day, I asked Petras if the deal was still on for me to visit Lithuania. He said, "Yes. We're leaving the Soviet Union. They'll have to shoot every one of us."

So, under Mikhail Gorbachev, the Soviet Union was coming unglued before my eyes. Many sovietologists later said the change occurred because of his two famous accommodations in the face of widespread civil and nationalist unrest throughout the empire, *perestroika* (economic restructuring) and *glasnost* (political openness). I think he couldn't stop the process and made the best possible moves to keep the Soviet Union afloat. Those who thought he was too soft on restive states urged a return to Stalinist tactics—short of the mass murders, of course. In 1990, however, calls for Stalinism were heard less and less.[3]

---

[3] I worked throughout Russia in later years, from Saint Petersburg to Vladivostock and much in the vast in-between. I often asked Russians, "How do you feel about Ukrainians?" They would invariably say something like, "They're like family. We've had our spats from time to time, but we're all members of the same family." I would then ask true Ukrainians, who spoke Ukrainian as their first language, how they felt about Russia and Russians. More often than not, their response was something like, "Three hundred years of mass murders, enslavement, dismissiveness, and forced starvation was enough."

The great hetman of Ukraine, the leader of the Cossacks, Bohdan Khmelnitsky, had driven the Poles from Ukraine in 1650, thereby establishing the first serious Ukrainian nation. Khmelnitsky remains a hero to Ukrainians to this day. He was

The Soviet Union, the hegemon on the other side of the Cold War in which I had been a civilian combatant for a time, was crumbling, and I had just been invited to help with its demise. Gorbachev had let the camel stick its nose under the tent, and now the camel was beginning to lift up its head and rip the tent off its poles.[4]

Before Yuri and I headed for the airport in Tbilisi to return to Kiev, we visited a wine shop on the city's grand boulevard, Rustavelli Street, where we purchased nearly four dozen bottles of wine, the varieties Koba had shown us during the week. In particular, we favored Kvanchkara, Minavi, and Stalin's favorite, Kindzmaruli. We were lugging all this wine toward the plane when I remarked to Yuri that we must look pretty silly, "like a couple of immigrants." Yuri countered, "If you left Georgia without this much wine, *then* you'd look silly."[5]

---

concerned, however, that Poland would retaliate, and so he signed a twenty-year mutual defense treaty with Russia at Periaslav in 1654. Russia planted military installations around Ukraine in accordance with this pact, and Khmelnitsky died shortly thereafter. Russia ignored the expiration date of the Treaty of Periaslav and remained master over much of Ukraine up until Soviet times. So the transition from czarist Russia to the Soviet Union meant little change for Ukrainians. Indeed, as World War I was ending, Ukraine declared itself independent of Russia, elected a president, and declared L'viv as its capital. The new independent Ukraine was short-lived, however.

[4] One of the accommodations of glasnost was to allow the flags of the republics to be flown. The first symbols of the breakup of the Soviet Union were these flags of pre-Soviet domination. During 1990, we saw the red, green, and yellow of Lithuania; the red and white of Georgia; the blue and yellow of Ukraine; the red and white of Latvia; and the blue, white, and black of Estonia. We never saw the red, white, and blue of Russia that year, however, just the red flag with the yellow hammer and sickle of the Soviet Union, which had become synonymous with nationalist unrest. These flags were the most visible symbols of patriotism in an otherwise unpatriotic Soviet Union. They were proudly displayed and gave people hope that their desire for freedom might one day be realized.

[5] I had anticipated questions about the United States and about US agriculture in particular before we departed Kiev. Furthermore, since I was attending a UNESCO conference, I thought I should seek the counsel of the agricultural attaché at the US embassy in Moscow before going to Tbilisi. In those days, the embassy had nine incoming phone lines but no rollover. If one number was busy, you had to try the other numbers one at a time. The reason for this technical

Barb and I made plans to meet Petras in Vilnius toward the end of April. The details were daunting, and we had to make arrangements on our own. I spoke by phone with our friends in Vilnius to clarify the means of getting there.

"How do we get a visa?"

"No visa—come by train."

We could travel by train anywhere in the Soviet Union without having to show our passports. There were no official borders, and virtually all train travelers, other than the occasional itinerant American professor, were Soviet citizens. If we flew, however, we would need invitations and passports, with no guarantee that we would reach our destination. An educator on the loose in this hostile environment just might succeed, however, so we opted for the train and no visa.

As a precaution, I sent word through my one Russian student, Tanya Kindrat, to her father, Stepan Kindrat, the Soviet deputy minister for oil and gas pipelines, about our plan to visit Lithuania. Over the course of several weekends in Moscow, Stepan and I had become good friends. Stepan advised us, "Don't go. This is a strange and unpredictable country."

Barb and I were eager to go, however, his counsel notwithstanding. If only we knew how to get tickets for the train. We did not want to buy them through the school and thereby let the whole world in on what we were planning. As luck would have it, after I gave a talk at

---

anachronism was to make it easier for the Soviet KGB to tap calls going into and out of our embassy. The Thursday before the Saturday when Yuri and I left for Tbilisi, I tried calling the embassy. I tried all nine numbers several times and got a busy signal for close to an hour before giving up. First thing Friday morning, I asked the school secretary to dial those numbers periodically until someone answered and to give me a call when she got someone. She contacted me around two Friday afternoon. I ran to the phone and asked to speak with the agricultural attaché. The operator connected me. He came to the phone, but as I started to speak, he interrupted and said, "I'm really busy at the moment. Please call back in fifteen minutes." Click. So much for advice from the United States beforehand.

Kiev's Polytechnic Institute some weeks earlier, the only student in the room approached me and said, "Mr. Shriver, my name is Alexander Ponomarenko, and I want to come to the United States."

Alex, or Sashko, made a good impression. I gave him my phone number, and one evening he called and asked if there was anything he could do for us. I asked, "If I give you the money, can you get us two tickets for the train to Vilnius on April 26?"

Sashko was at our door within the hour. I gave him the money, and he returned with the tickets a couple of hours later. The night we left, he met us at the station with a basket of food and drink for the trip.

We arrived in Vilnius without incident at two on the morning of April 27, 1990. Petras greeted us with his huge smile. Even at that hour, we were exhilarated after escaping the oppressive and depressing environment of Ukraine. We were relieved that the trip had ended and were ready to go to work. Petras had reserved rooms for us at the Vytautas Hotel. The next day we met with members of the Lithuanian government, including several ministers. On the following day, I was scheduled to meet with Lithuania's prime minister, Madame Kazimiera Prunskiene.

At about three in the morning, however, Barb and I were awakened by a roar. I thought a plane was crashing nearby. Barb said it sounded like tanks. She was right. Russian T-72 tanks were racing past the hotel on the highway below. The Soviet army was taking over Lithuania's only oil refinery, intending to withhold fuel to compel the breakaway republic to knuckle under.

The tanks sped through the streets in the middle of the night to strike fear into the Lithuanians. As we were to learn, however, the Russians couldn't easily intimidate them. When we reached the prime minister's office the next morning, she had just flown to Norway to negotiate for oil products.

I subsequently gave speeches to freedom-hungry Lithuanians in Vilnius, the capital city of Kaunas, and the port city of Klaipeda, Hitler's last territorial acquisition by diplomatic pressure before World War II. Then we met with business and educational groups. Petras had found a translator, and when she showed up for our first business seminar, he asked if she had ever translated business or political topics. She said no, and Petras moaned, "We're doomed." But Egle Jakubenaite (YA-ku-ben-AY-etya) proved to be more than equal to the task and would help us with many matters over the next few years.

Before we left Lithuania to fly to the United States via Moscow (in those days, as I recall, the only public-transport planes flying in or out of the USSR were from Moscow), my fledgling career took another leap forward. Prime Minister Prunskiene sent word asking if I could organize a conference in the fall for her ministers and deputy ministers on their role in a democracy. This invitation led directly to work on foreign economic and legal development over the next twelve years in more than a dozen countries.

Barb and I flew out of Vilnius in the rain. The plane was delayed, so the pilot and the crew got off the plane for coffee while we mere customers remained in our seats. We arrived late in Moscow and saw our Pan Am flight departing. Getting another flight proved no small matter. On top of the airport workers' rudeness, a characteristic common to almost everyone dealing with lowly consumers throughout the communist world, there were no information desks to help stranded foreigners. If you didn't know how to deal with the system, too bad. If you didn't speak Russian well enough, those in charge had no time for you. I wandered through the upper floors of the airport looking for open offices with the names of airlines on the doors. Most were closed since it was Sunday. The British Airways office was still open, however; the employees spoke English, were polite, and had a flight leaving in two hours. I bought tickets, and after the obligatory indignities at customs and every other station along the way to the plane, we were finally on board and took off for London.

Aeroflot was *the* Soviet airline at the time. It was so huge that when the Soviet Union broke up, the airline also came apart, initially dividing into more than a hundred smaller ad hoc airlines. Aeroflot had a two-tiered pricing system—one price for foreigners like us and a vastly lower price for Soviet citizens who had an official need to fly. Since fuel, flight crews, and airplanes were essentially free in Marxist economics, Soviet citizens whose trips were authorized could fly for practically nothing—maybe ten dollars for the trip from Moscow to the UK versus five hundred dollars for foreigners like us. (One trick was that Soviet citizens paid in rubles, a nonconvertible currency, whereas foreigners had to pay in a so-called hard currency, such as dollars.) Hence, there were no Soviet citizens on this British Airways plane. All passengers were foreigners, each with his or her own reasons for being thrilled to leave the USSR.

About an hour into the trip, the pilot came on the PA system and with a cheery British accent said, "Don't know if anyone cares, but we have just left Soviet airspace."

The plane erupted. Everyone cheered, clapped, and laughed—and stewardesses were as busy as bees handing out gin and tonics. We would experience the same feeling each time we left Soviet airspace on dozens of trips in the years to follow.

We returned to our home in Connecticut in May 1990, exhausted but awestruck over our experiences, with enthusiasm for, but little comprehension of, the adventures that lay ahead. My first task: to plan a three-day conference on democracy for the Lithuanian prime minister and her cabinet.

In the twelve years I worked in and around the former Soviet Union, I had many unexpected and interesting experiences such as this one. Georgia's minister of defense, Tedo Zaparidze, asked me to meet with him on New Year's Day 1991. At the time, the United States had no embassy in Georgia, and he was eager to get an American's view on Georgia's issues with Russia. Even though I had many Russian friends, I was no fan of Russia, which monopolized virtually all governmental power throughout the USSR. I was a fan of countries like Georgia that were trying to extricate themselves from decades or even centuries of Russian domination. (Photo by author)

———◦◦◦———

2

Diora: One Young Woman's Clash of Civilizations

Summer of 1990

The hamburgers were nearly cooked when the phone rang. It was my friend June, a professor of English as a second language at the University of Delaware, on the line. She was in great distress and could barely speak.

"My mother just died," June said. "I'm in Kentucky for her funeral, and Diora is in jail in Washington."

I immediately told June not to worry; I would take care of the matter. Little did I dream what new lessons about life under communism lay ahead.

Diora Klimkova was a Tatar, a Muslim student in my class at IMI-Kiev, the newly minted Western-style graduate business school in Ukraine. Diora had a PhD in sociology from her hometown of Samarkand, Uzbekistan, and was one of fifteen students from IMI-Kiev who had been assigned to the University of Delaware for the summer of 1990. (The other half of the class was at York University in Toronto.)

Diora had fallen in with a married American man who had put

her up in a hotel in Washington for the weekend. She went shopping at Woodward & Lothrop, and when she emerged, alarm bells went off. The store's security guards found $800 in Woodward & Lothrop finery stuffed inside her clothes. Diora had never seen such security systems in Samarkand, but that was no excuse. Her salary in Uzbekistan, even with a PhD, was probably less than $1,000 a year, so the vast array of wonderful things unavailable in her country doubtless took a momentary toll on her integrity. The security guards turned Diora over to the Washington police, who put her in jail that warm Saturday evening.

I delegated responsibility for the hamburgers to another family member and called Woodward & Lothrop. I told the manager that what the young lady had done was clearly wrong but that she was from a foreign country and was one of my students, in fact. If the store would drop the charges, I would arrange to have her leave the United States. The manager agreed to drop the charges but added that I would have to go through the security office of W&L's parent, Strawbridge & Clothier, in Philadelphia. I called Philadelphia. The people there had received word of our arrangement, but there was nothing they could do until Monday when they would drop the charges before a judge. Diora was going to spend at least two nights in jail.

Jeb Magruder, a former acquaintance of mine from Richard Nixon's reelection committee, had described the inside of a Washington jail to me as "not pleasant" with "very bright lights." I called the jail and asked the desk sergeant if I could speak with Diora.

He replied firmly, "No. She already made her one call."

"Can you tell me who she called?" I asked.

"The Soviet embassy."

I cringed. That should have been precisely her last choice of places to call since this would guarantee that the school in Ukraine would be informed immediately. I had hoped to get Diora back into the Soviet Union without the school learning of her misconduct. After all, the charges against her were being dropped, which meant that technically she had not committed a crime and had no criminal record in the United States.

Diora was released Monday morning. We had a friend meet her at the jail and escort her to the Eastern Airlines shuttle bound for La Guardia Airport. Barb met her there and drove her to JFK Airport, handing her a ticket for the next Aeroflot flight to Moscow.

When Barb and I returned to Kiev in late August to finish out the final term, the first thing that caught our attention was that our room at the Communist Party's Hotel October was not available and that our belongings, left there for the summer, were now heaped on the floor. The hotel administration, prompted by someone else, clearly wanted us out.

I asked to see the manager with whom I had established a cordial relationship. This relationship was no more. Nyet, nyet, and more nyet. We were tired from the trip. It was late. Hotel rooms in Kiev were virtually impossible for a foreigner to obtain. We staged a sit-down strike in the center of the lobby. Soon the manager came by again. I told him we were not leaving. Would he please give us a room? He stuttered and stammered, but to my surprise, he relented and escorted us to a tiny room, a kind of penal broom closet in which we lived for the next few months.

The next day, I was invited to discuss Diora with the chairman and founder of the school, the Ukrainian-Canadian academician Bohdan Hawrylyshyn, and the school's rector, Oleg Bilorus, who would later be named Ukraine's ambassador to the United States. Eventually I realized that it was not only Diora with whom they were angry. They were also furious with me for helping her.

I explained the technicality that meant Diora was officially innocent, that under US law she had committed no crime, and that there was no record of the incident. That was the problem, they objected; I should have let her rot in jail. Hawrylyshyn was the more politic of the two, but it was clear that I was now persona non grata. They both said Diora should be expelled. Since I was a volunteer without portfolio, they had no obligation even to listen to my opinion and could have done what they wanted to do. If they had had a replacement for me handy and the funds to hire such a replacement, I would surely have been fired.

One difficulty for the two school leaders was that I was the only teacher working full time on the substance of the entire MBA program to help make the first year of the school's existence a success. I had joined with several volunteer guest lecturers in Kiev at my behest to cover free market economics, international marketing, international trade and finance, international banking, merchandising, and even laws of business.

A possibly larger barrier to my ouster may have been money. Given that I was a volunteer and was even paying my own travel expenses, any replacement might have cost serious money, presenting these two leaders with a dilemma typical in communist societies: better quality of education versus a bigger share of the pie for other, doubtless less virtuous purposes.

Diora was not permitted to attend class while she awaited her fate. She had pleaded with Bilorus to mete out any punishment he wished but to let her complete the semester. If she went home in disgrace, she would surely lose her job, and her husband might lose his job. She probably feared even worse in her traditionally restrictive Muslim society, especially as she had been privileged to be the only woman— indeed, the only person—from Uzbekistan permitted to attend IMI's program. I saw terror in Diora's eyes.

At Diora's request, I arranged for her to address her fellow students. She stood bravely before the class, apologized sincerely and completely, and asked for mercy to let her finish the term and get her degree. Remember that she had committed no crime, not even a misdemeanor.

She then left the room while the students debated the matter. I half expected a consensus that she should stay, albeit with some penalty. I could not have been more wrong. The five other women in the class of thirty-one spoke first.

"She should be expelled."

"She always has her hand in my purse."

"She's a Tatar." This was a bigoted slur referring to Muslim Turkic people descended from the Mongolian invaders.

Some of the male students chimed in and also argued for her ouster with often viciously discriminatory comments, no doubt because she was Muslim.

This continued until one of the older students, a Christian, chided the largely atheist group, saying, "Let he who has not sinned cast the first stone."

In their report to the rector, Bilorus, the students voted almost unanimously for Diora's expulsion.

I met once more with Bilorus and Hawrylyshyn on the Diora matter. The three of us finally agreed that Diora should be allowed to withdraw from the school for medical reasons. This conclusion was supported by the fact that she had lost considerable weight as a result of her ordeal. She must have weighed less than ninety pounds. This resolution meant she would be spared the fate of being a disgraced Muslim woman in a backward society known for its oppressive treatment of women.

The following weekend, one of my guest speakers, longtime friend Jim Schoff, and his wife, Joanna, arrived in Kiev where Jim was to lead three days of seminars on merchandising. Jim was not new to the merchandising game, having been, some years earlier, president of Bloomingdale's department store in New York City. Of course the school (Hawrylyshyn and Bilorus) had seemingly forgotten to arrange a hotel room for our friends, an embarrassment that was never rectified. The Schoffs wound up in a noisy second-rate hotel built with ultrathin walls and teeming with prostitutes.

The next morning, I accompanied Jim to the school in northern Kiev. As we entered the vestibule, we saw a woman being carried out of Bilorus's office through the obligatory double leather-covered doors, a typical sound barrier for communist bigwigs. Despite having agreed to discharge Diora for reasons of health, Bilorus had expelled her, after which she fainted. I knew precisely what had happened but told Jim I would have to explain later.

Diora visited us in our apartment shortly after, looking frightened and even thinner, if that was possible, as she prepared to return to Uzbekistan. She thanked us for trying to help. She gave us a chess set from Uzbekistan and disappeared into a Soviet miasma, which has been equated with Dante's inferno.

The Russian journalist Andrei Loshko recently shed light on what had happened to Diora and me in 1990: "Lawyers say that to be arrested in Russia means more or less the same thing as being convicted. Here's how it works. The courts accept about 90 percent of applications for confinement under arrest, meaning that a rejection is considered a serious incident, resulting in professional competence checks and reprimands. A verdict of 'not guilty' after an arrest is an incident even more serious, as it indicates that a court made a mistake and improperly deprived the accused of his freedom. And that's a scandal. The accused will demand compensation, and who needs that?"

I've often thought of how I might have handled this situation differently and to a better end for all, but nothing has come to mind.

Note: names and places in this story have been altered to protect the innocent.

Schoffs and Shrivers at school 51

Jim and Joanna Schoff came to Kiev as our guests. At my request, Jim conducted a three-day seminar on merchandising for my class at IMI-Kiev. Jim knew something about this topic since he had spent his entire career in merchandising, eventually becoming president of Bloomingdale's department stores. Joanna, coming from a Dutch American Quaker family, grew up in a strong entrepreneurial, free-enterprise, anticommunist environment. Arriving in Kiev was such a cultural shock that she briefly felt the understandable urge to escape Ukraine's oppressive atmosphere. As we took in an opera and a concert or two, Joanna relaxed and began to enjoy her stay, and it was a learning experience worth speaking about when she returned home. The four of us are shown with a class of seniors at the number one high school in Kiev, School 51. This was the school for the children of the most important party members based in Kiev. The more than fifty students we met with were fluent in English. More than that, they had studied international affairs, obviously with Soviet experts, and had strong and knowledgeable opinions about the United States and its foreign policy. I don't recall much propaganda in their training. They asked great questions. Most had had a semester in high school somewhere in the United States. It was like being in a room full of young Henry Kissingers. (Photo by author)

3

When the Money Stopped Coming

O ur visit to the former defense plant in western Ukraine was supposed to begin at ten in the morning but was delayed until eleven. It was a gray, cold day in a long series of gray, cold days that we had dubbed "two-sock days," so cold that if you didn't wear two pairs of socks, your feet would freeze. For the same reason, none of us took off our coats during the meeting. It was February 1996, about five years after the money from Moscow had stopped coming. That included money for fuel to heat the buildings.

The meeting began with vodka and small plates of *salo s'chesnikom.* Salo is the fat of a pig, basically lard, which has a near-religious significance in Ukraine. Salo was one of the main means of sustenance for Ukrainians during World War II. In peacetime, however, it is edible only when accompanied by garlic (*chesnikom*) and especially by the traditional shot of vodka. Our hosts poured the vodka time and again, insisting in increasingly demanding tones that we accept it as the shots began to take effect. The flow from aperitif into lunch was seamless. The vodka was supplemented by several bottles of wine and beer in case anyone was interested.

It was like this every day at the plant. Members of the management team met in the morning when they were all reasonably sober, but things fell apart rather quickly thereafter. Nothing constructive was even attempted after lunch. Sooner or later, everyone drifted home, with no visible work having been done. The days had been like this for much of the time since the USSR had dissolved. Many workers had left, but many still came to the plant. Their monthly stipend had been reduced to a bag of groats and a bottle of cheap wine from Moldova.

Our visit, to determine if we could help the plant find new business, was a failure. We met with people from more than fifteen hundred plants and other businesses in Ukraine from 1995 to 2002 and found only one hundred directors with whom we could work.

The collapse of communism took a toll on men especially. Women had been placed in what were deemed the less important jobs, such as retailing, food, and banking. Now that defense plants were basically shut down, women found themselves in charge of much of what remained of the economy, while men had little to do but drink. Many men died prematurely of alcoholism. The life expectancy of males in Russia (I assume the same was true for Ukraine) dropped from sixty-four in 1990 to fifty-eight by 1995, almost a statistical impossibility. (Statistics in the USSR were notoriously unreliable, however, sometimes deliberately so.) Their useful lives had ended when the Soviet Union collapsed. Few of the older, more senior managers wanted to learn how to function in a market economy. When the money stopped coming from Moscow, they tried to steal what they could from the system. They cheated their employees. Their employees cheated on expense accounts. Whenever we arrived at a train station, there were always men asking for our ticket stubs so they could turn them in to be reimbursed for phony travel expenses. What few orders came to the plant were accepted only after the two sides had agreed upon the amount of the bribe.

The more we Americans rely on money from the government, the harder we will fall when the money stops coming from Washington. The national debt stood at $19 trillion at the start of 2016, with many financial experts predicting the eventual demise of the dollar as the world's main, or reserve, currency. They are also recommending investments in commodities such as gold and silver, the value of which would provide protection against the declining value of the dollar, a development akin to less money coming from Washington. Can't happen here? Would you please pass the lard?

Russian Ambassador to the U.S., IESC CEO Tom Carroll, Dick Shriver

Tom Carroll once confided in me that he enjoyed running the IESC more than being the CEO of Unilever US. In 1994, we received a request from the Russian embassy in Washington to design and offer a course in market economics to the entire embassy staff. I believe there were more than four hundred employees; approximately one hundred attended our course. In this photo, Tom and I are shaking hands with Yuli Vorontsov, the Russian ambassador to the United States, after agreeing to develop and conduct this program. Tom pulled out all the stops to get some of the most practical and successful business leaders in America to give lectures as part of this program. (Photo courtesy of the Russian embassy, Washington, DC)

4

Standing in the Middle of the End of the Cold War: Baltic Breezes Pale Next to Nuclear Windstorms

1990–91

American foreign policy toward the Soviet Union during the last eighteen months of its existence was being pulled in many directions. Fortunately for everyone, US-Soviet relations were 100 percent under the control of the two heads of state, Mikhail Gorbachev and George H. W. Bush. The two men agreed to work together to keep the Soviet Union intact despite many countercurrents, especially in the three Baltic republics—Lithuania, Latvia, and Estonia. Ironically, Bush's support for Gorbachev helped bring about the very thing these two men were working to avoid, the collapse of the Soviet Union. Here's how it happened, at least from my viewpoint as an observer inside the Soviet Union during most of that period. After Lithuania declared its independence from the Soviet Union in March 1990, some in the US Congress, notably New York Senator Al D'Amato, thought the United States should recognize that independence. After all, following World

War II, America had never recognized the illegal annexation of the three Baltic countries by the USSR.

Lennart Meri, Estonia's minister of foreign affairs, was particularly outspoken on this point. He and I had become rather good friends in the early months of 1991. When he came to the United States with his wife in June 1991, Barb and I invited them to join us for dinner in New York.

Meri, who would soon become a free Estonia's first president, told us about his visit to Washington earlier that day with Secretary of State James Baker. He said that Baker led him under the nearly two hundred flags overhead in the lobby of the State Department building and pointed up toward the black, white, and blue flag of Estonia, noting proudly, "You see, Mr. Minister, your flag has been hanging here since 1939." Looking up at his country's flag hanging limp far above them, Meri replied, "Yes, Mr. Secretary, but there's no wind!"

It is fair to say that no one, not even Soviet or American experts on relations between the two countries, could have confidently predicted the final outcome for the Soviet Union between August and December of 1991. It is also fair to say that if Bush had not supported Gorbachev's efforts to keep the Soviet Union alive, the USSR might not have died so quickly or so peacefully.

There was much sentiment in the US national security establishment to keep the Soviet Union alive. Bush's ultraconservative national security adviser, Brent Scowcroft, feared a breakup of the Soviet Union would result in three additional nuclear states whose aims might have been inimical to our own. In addition to missile sites in Russia, there were enough missiles in Kazkhstan, Belarus, or Ukraine to destroy the United States. The missiles in Kazakhstan and Belarus were almost certainly under the control of Russian rocket troops; as for Ukraine, however, which may have controlled its own rockets, some joked that if the Soviet Union broke up, Ukraine was more likely to retarget its missiles toward Russia.

Incredibly, after the country had spent trillions of dollars to counter the Soviet threat during the Cold War, some top-level US policy makers wanted America to help prop up the failing Soviet Union.

In late July 1991, when Ukraine was among six or seven restive republics, including the Baltic states, seeking freedom from the yoke of Soviet, or Russian, communism, President Bush accepted an offer to address the Ukrainian parliament. He did not mince words. He said the United States would not "aid those who promote suicidal nationalism." This led William Safire to write an opinion piece in the *New York Times* a day or so later titled "Bush's Chicken Kiev Speech." My initial reaction to Bush's speech was akin to Safire's. Those of us favoring US recognition of Lithuania enthusiastically supported freedom for three million people who had suffered enough under tyranny.

Bush's speech was more for Gorbabchev's benefit, however, than for his Ukrainian audience. In fact, had Bush added fuel to the fire as Ukraine pushed for independence, this would have strengthened the case one month later for the leaders of the still-secret, and subsequently failed, Soviet coup being plotted by Minister of Defense Dmitri Yazov and KGB chief Vladimir Kryuchkov. Neither Bush nor Gorbachev could have seen that coming at the time, however.

Nor could one have foreseen that Bush's support for Gorbachev ultimately helped free more than three hundred million people from the iron grip of Soviet tyranny. These included the three million Lithuanians as well as 150 million Russians and another 150 million in the remaining republics.

Bush's close relationship with Gorbachev was not universally applauded in the United States, especially by neoconservatives who felt America should let the USSR collapse. I was also of that opinion at the time. One must be careful about second-guessing important presidential decisions, however. Only those present when the decision was made, viewing the same information the president and his advisers had at that precise moment, could know all the ramifications of that choice.

In 2011 at a *National Journal* conference titled "Nunn-Lugar at 20,"

National Journal senior editor James Kitfield summed up the situation in the summer of 1991: "We had an empire crumbling, which frequently leads to other wars throughout history. But this was the first time you had an empire crumbling that had thirty thousand nuclear weapons, sixty thousand nuclear bombs' worth of material, forty thousand tons of chemical weapons, smallpox (biological weapons of mass destruction), and tens of thousands of scientists who suddenly didn't have a paycheck but had a lot of nuclear know-how."

The fear of a Soviet collapse was thus widespread in late 1990 and early 1991. Harvard Professor Graham Allison and Soviet economist Grigory Yavlinsky quickly coauthored a book and an op-ed piece touting a "grand bargain" that could bring democracy to the Soviet Union. Their proposal, in early 1991, was that for a modest $30 billion, the United States could help Gorbachev keep the Soviet Union from collapsing.

This was unbelievable. Would we really try to rescue a regime that had threatened over the previous four decades to bury us? Once it was back on its feet, might it not try to do so again? President Reagan's simple strategy toward the USSR was "We win; they lose." Nine years after he signed National Security Decision Directive NSDD – 32, the purpose of which was to topple the USSR by any and all means, the USSR was toppling. Then, in early 1991, we were afraid the USSR really would fall and began to consider how we could keep it upright.[6]

I was far from all this debate, however, back in the spring of 1990 as

---

[6] NSDD-32 emerged as the ultimate classified strategic policy of the United States toward the Soviet Union. The purpose of this document, signed by President Reagan on May 20, 1982, was to lay out a broad set of actions to push the USSR over the financial cliff in every way and not to assist it inadvertently in any way. The eight-page document sought to develop and to integrate "a set of strategies, including diplomatic, informational, economic/political, and military components." According to my friend Tom Reed, who was at the table (along with George Shulz, James Baker, Caspar Weinberger, William Clark, and Harry Rowen), Reagan asked, "Why can't we just push them over?" Rowen told the president that yes, this was possible. This conversation led to NSDD-32, which has since been largely declassified.

our train from Kiev, Ukraine, pulled into the Vilnius station in Lithuania shortly after two in the morning on April 17. Barb and I saw our host, Petras, smiling broadly on the platform.

I noticed in what international news we could get that there was some debate in the United States over whether America should recognize Lithuania. The Soviets had seized Lithuania in 1939. Then came the Germans, who annihilated all the Jews along the way. Then the Soviets returned, forcibly taking over Lithuania once again in 1944. The illegal annexation of the three Baltic republics was never recognized by the United States.[7]

Once Barb and I had returned to Kiev, I put the question of US recognition of Lithuania's independence to my class of thirty-one communists in late April 1990. My questions were related to the decisions about Lithuania faced by President George H. W. Bush and Mikhail Gorbachev, leader of the USSR and general secretary of the Communist Party of the Soviet Union. The students enjoyed this diversion from what might otherwise have been a relatively dull and commonplace discussion of the General Agreement on Tarrifs and Trade, or GATT. They quickly concluded that if the United States recognized Lithuania's independence, the USSR would not react with violence. Such a decision would, however, destroy Bush's meticulously developed and highly valued relationship with Gorbavchev. The students also felt that if Lithuania gained US recognition, Gorbachev would have to retaliate internally in some way to avoid a coup d'etat. My students had sized up the geopolitics of the situation accurately as events showed eighteen months later.

When a student mentioned that Gorbachev might fear a coup d'état, I suddenly recalled that I was a guest in the Soviet Union. I brought

---

[7] A good friend, Tony Grina, who was born in Lithuania around 1930, often joked about having been bombed first by the Germans, then by the Russians, and then, while imprisoned in Germany toward the war's end, by the Americans and the British.

the session to a close, quickly folded up the charts, and headed home, knowing the class communist would have to report my digression from market economics. (I had those original charts from 1990 before me as I wrote this chapter in 2016.)

In October 1990, almost a year before the Soviet coup attempt, the CIME organized a three-day conference in Lithuania at the request of its prime minister, Kazimiera Prunskiene. She wanted her ministers and deputy ministers to understand their role in a democracy, and we were retained to put together this conference. After the conference, as we were about to depart Lithuania, Prunskiene invited Barb and me to breakfast. Revealing that she had not abandoned all her communist habits, she said she knew we had other plans (two days of hot mud baths at the nearby spa of Druninskiene), but her driver would pick us up in two hours. She said her driver would take us to Riga, capital city of Latvia, where we would meet a man (his name is lost) who would take care of us and introduce us to various Latvian government executives. We would remain in Riga overnight, and then her driver would take us to Tallinn, Estonia, where we would meet the minister of the economy, Jaak Leimann. Word had spread about our conference in Vilnius, and it appeared the other two Baltic countries wanted the same.

The three Baltic republics, especially Lithuania and Latvia, were punished by Soviet troops for their nationalist behavior. Tragically, Soviet troops gunned down, ran over, and otherwise killed several dozen people at the main radio and TV towers in Vilnius and Riga in January 1991. These acts of recidivist violence were not lost on the rest of the non-Russian republics.

Finally, on August 18, 1991, the leaders of the Soviet military and the KGB, the two most powerful agencies in the Soviet Union, placed Gorbachev under house arrest. As I read subsequently, instead of resisting arrest, Gorbachev in essence said, "Now, fellas, let's not do anything rash. Have a seat and let's discuss this matter." Good host that he was, I'm sure he also poured large tumblers of vodka for the gentlemen who controlled two of the most powerful organizations in the world. In any event, the coup fizzled, but Gorbachev and the Soviet Union had been mortally wounded politically. President Bush quietly shifted his weight in the direction of Boris Yeltsin, a former communist who now opposed the party and was president of the Russian republic. In December, Yeltsin arranged a secret meeting with the presidents of the other three nuclear republics—Ukraine, Kazakhstan, and Belarus—in a forest in Belarus, and the four agreed secretly to bring the Soviet Union to an end.

The collapse of the Soviet Union meant the end of the Cold War— for a while, at least. Thus one of the most frightening confrontations in history was over, without a shot or casualty on either side, following a standoff of more than forty years in which the stakes grew to Mutually Assured Destruction.

Our work in the ensuing decade was mainly to assist the newly independent republics in developing new legal and economic regimes and political structures and to offer training to help them transition from the tyranny of communism to more democratic, market-oriented structures. In 1995 Barb and I moved to western Ukraine where we opened the first office for private-sector development in that country. On one of our first days there, I announced to a group of Ukrainians with whom we would be working that our new organization would obey the country's laws. One Ukrainian fell to the floor laughing. "If you want to obey every law in Ukraine, you might as well lie down right now and die." I guessed it wasn't going to be easy.

Russ in Estonia

Russ Deane answered the call in February of 1991 when Yuri Raidla, Estonia's minister of justice, invited him and the CIME to propose a rule-of-law development program for Estonia. The CIME won out over Germany's Truehand (essentially, Germany's USAID) and Herman Kahn's Hudson Institute out of Indianapolis. Russ engaged Georgetown University's Law Center, which contributed the time of three professors and six law students over an extended period for this effort. Russ's leadership, with the complete support of Estonia's top officials, resulted in arguably the best rule-of-law program in any of the former Soviet republics. The system is often credited with Estonia's economic success in the early years after the Soviet collapse. For his efforts on behalf of Estonia over more than a decade, for which he accepted no compensation, Russ was awarded Estonia's highest honor for a foreigner, the Order of the White Star, by Estonian president Lennart Meri. (Photo by author)

Ivars Godmanis and Dick

Ivars Godmanis was prime minister of Latvia from 1991 to 1993 and held several other government positions in the ensuing years. In early 1991, he invited the CIME to organize a three-day conference in Riga for members of his cabinet. He moderated the entire conference as cochair with me. Latvia had unique problems with Russia and still does to an extent.

Following the Soviet collapse, it was hard to know whom one could trust anywhere, especially in the Baltics. Latvia had a 40 percent Russian population—Russians who had been imported to replace Latvians deported and killed by the Soviets after World War II. By contrast, Lithuania had only a 5 to 6 percent Russian population at that time. Estonia's population was 35 percent Russian, but these people were mainly sequestered in a secret city in Estonia's northeast, whereas the Russians in Latvia were assimilated throughout the country.

Latvia has had perhaps the most difficulty of the three Baltic republics in establishing a country independent of Russia. NATO membership makes Latvia especially vulnerable to Russian incursions under President Vladimir Putin. As in Crimea, he might perceive the cost of a Russian takeover to be very low versus the value of testing NATO's fifth tenet: that an attack on one member is an attack against all. (Photo by author)

Team Lithuania ... RHS, Doug Costle, Bob Marik, and David Willey

The CIME's first government conference in the Baltics was held in Vilnius, Lithuania, in November 1990. The team included Bob Marik, a former executive with the Office of Management and Budget; Douglas Costle, administrator of the Environmental Protection Agency under President Jimmy Carter, and David Willey, a former vice president of the New York Federal Reserve. At one point, I was asked to meet with the two top leaders of the Lithuanian Ministry of Interior. I asked Doug if he could join me. (The Vilnius police reported to the Lithuanian police, which reported to the Soviet Ministry of the Interior in Moscow.) Our two hosts led us into a room where eighty uniformed police officers came to attention, rather sloppily, I thought. The two represented the entire leadership of Lithuania's national police force. It occurred to me that this ministry was likely to have more spies loyal to the USSR than almost any other ministry did. Among other issues, these folks wanted to know how police were organized in the United States. The concept of local police reporting to mayors and selectmen, elected officials usually with no law enforcement experience, was incomprehensible to them. They were loaded for us with their communist baloney. At one point, Doug began a lecture on the founding of the United States. At the time, he was dean of the Vermont Law School, so he had this speech at the ready. It was one of our finest moments in Lithuania, a country where I enjoyed working over the next decade. (Photo by author)

Team Latvia: Jay Peake, Russ Deane, Bill Morrill, Frank Widener, Dick Shriver

The team for the CIME conference in Latvia in the spring of 1991 consisted of Junius "Jay" Peake, a capital markets expert; Russ Deane (rule of law); William Morrill, a consummate government administrator and an innovator; Frank Widener (domestic governance); and me. On a walk through one of Riga's parks, we heard a bird singing, and Frank casually mentioned, "That's a northern warbler." None of the rest of us knew enough about the subject to argue. Frank explained that before he realized he might have to earn money, he had planned to make a living as an ornithologist. With its large Russian population, Latvia had the most difficult time of the three Baltic republics recovering from fifty years of communism. The CIME conducted two conferences in Latvia in 1991 but had little involvement in the country thereafter. (Photo by author)

Team Estonia: Hans Jalasto (our Estonian host), translator, Clark
Abt, Russ Deane, Jay Peake (Dick Shriver taking photo)

The CIME's first conference in Estonia took place in February 1991. Of the dozen
or so programs organized by the group in the former Soviet Union, the conference
in Tallinn had the greatest impact, resulting in a ten-year CIME program of
legal reform for the country. Russ Deane led this program in collaboration with
Estonia's minister of justice, Yuri Raidla. Shown here, from left to right, are Hans
Jalasto, professor of economics at Tallinn University, and his translator; Dr. Clark
Abt, founder of Abt Associates, entrepreneur, social scientist, teacher, and author;
Deane, an attorney with a gift and a passion for introducing the rule of law to
emerging democracies; and Junius "Jay" Peake, a capital markets expert who left
the Estonia conference for St. Petersburg, where he advised Anatolie Sobchak,
the city's mayor and a legal scholar. Sobchak was a mentor to Vladimir Putin and
Dmitri Medvedev, Russia's last two presidents. During Peake's first night in St.
Petersburg, his hotel caught fire on the two floors below him. He was unable to
leave his eighth-floor room, having no idea which way to turn in the dense smoke.
After calling his wife in the United States to say good-bye, he heard a tap at the
bottom of his door. He opened it a crack, and the floor lady, or *dezhurnaya*, came
in with a wet towel for his face and led him as they crawled on the floor to safety.
(Photo by author)

Don Rumsfeld and Jaak Leimann

Former Defense Secretary Donald Rumsfeld joined several CIME conferences, three in the Baltic republics and one in L'viv, Ukraine. His wife, Joyce, joined him for the Ukraine conference. Rumsfeld is speaking here with Estonia's minister of economy, Jaak Leimann, the key organizer of the CIME's work in Estonia. (Photo by author)

Doug and Betsy Costle came to Kiev to conduct seminars at IMI-Kiev just days before the CIME's first conference in Lithuania in October 1990. Doug had been director of the Environmental Protection Agency under President Carter and at the time was dean of the law school at the University of Vermont. Betsy was a member of Vermont's Banking Commission. They gave seminars on their respective areas of expertise. The Costles then joined Barb and me as we went by train through Belarus to Lithuania for the first CIME conference in support of democracy inside the Soviet Union. (Photo by author)

Dick Shriver, Algirdas Brazauskas, Kazmiera Prunskiene

While under the thumb of the Soviet Union, Estonia worked diligently to achieve some measure of economic autonomy. In this, it was helped greatly by its cultural and geographic ties to Finland. Lithuania, on the other hand, sought political freedom above all else. In this regard, Lithuania was unique among the Soviet republics. Prime Minister Kazimiera Prunskiene was one of the leaders of the move to declare Lithuania's independence from the Soviet Union in March 1990. Her deputy prime minister, soon to be the first directly-elected president of a free and independent Lithuania, was Algirdas Brazauskas. Brazauskas and I co-chaired the CIME's first conference on the role of government executives and agencies in a democracy. Brazauskas, whose mentality remained locked in communist ways, but whose heart was solidly in the corner of freedom and liberty, eventually became prime minister in 2002. (Photo by author)

5

Vignettes from L'viv

1996

I served with the International Executive Service Corps (IESC) from 1992 to 1995. During that time we opened some twenty offices in ten former Soviet republics, providing these countries with $12 million annually in American volunteer expert assistance by 1995. I had a relatively secure position, and the future appeared bright. Nonetheless, I was concerned that neither we at the IESC nor the US government knew if we were working for the right people and the right causes. Were we helping future oligarchs? We were. Were we helping organized crime? Probably. Were we helping future autocrats reassert themselves over a helpless populace? Without a doubt. Only in the three Baltic states was our work going in the right direction, but that was because those countries wanted to turn toward the West, while the other twelve republics equivocated, demurred, and slid backward toward autocracy.

In early 1995, I applied to Julie Kidd at the CAJEF for a one-year grant so that Barb and I could relocate inside the former Soviet Union and establish a private-sector development office to attract Western capital for worthwhile projects in Ukraine. Julie accepted our proposal, enthusiastically, I think. I believe she shared our view that we needed to know more about the region in which we were working. The first year of the seven we spent in L'viv, the largest city in western Ukraine, involved a series of daily cultural lessons. Here is a sampling.

Privation: We opened our last box of raisin bran. I had memorized all the nutrition information and recipes on the box. In the spring we had bought three cases with twelve boxes each of cornflakes, Honey Crunch, and raisin bran as we were not fond of the Ukrainian alternatives. Our preferences showed, however, since we still had all the cornflakes and Honey Crunch, and these had to be consumed before we reordered. It would be a long winter.

McDonald's: The first McDonald's opened in L'viv, and normally such an event would not have been big news. In the United States we entered such places only under duress, but we waited outside in the snow for an hour just to get in line for the grand opening in L'viv. The standard fare seemed vastly superior to McD's back home. In addition, a swing band on the upper deck played "Yellow Submarine" and other tunes from North and South America. The joint was jumpin'. When we arrived home, we saw the McDonald's fireworks show, which was better than the fireworks display for the presidential campaign a few weeks earlier.

Moving up: We abandoned privation that year in favor of nineteenth-century Austro-Hungarian elegance. We moved into an apartment built in 1897. Mindful that a country that could privatize dwellings could also reappropriate them, we were reluctant at first to buy an apartment. The problem with rented apartments, however, was that we could do little to protect ourselves. With our own apartment, we could invest in safety features such as steel doorjambs, window grates, and motion detectors to alert the police and the successor to the KGB if we were being robbed. We paid $200 a month for this protection after buying the apartment. Barb gutted the place and presided for the next ten months over a crew of several hundred Ukrainians equipped with toothpicks, sharp twigs, and dull butter knives. This was one of Barb's finest creations.

Where is the Humane Society?: I was asked to visit a meat processing factory not far from town on what we called a "cold plant tour." This was any plant visit between November and March when the offices were colder than the temperature outside. The cows were being herded by their peasant owners along the last hundred yards to their doom. The road was cold and slippery, and the cows weren't built for ice. Their legs splayed as they struggled to stay aloft. Many fell, breaking limbs, and were left to wait until a tractor dragged them away. This went on all day. Ukraine would not squander sand to keep animals from hurting themselves.

Lest we forget where we are: Some time earlier, like most Ukrainians, we entered a phase of denial about the atrocities of the German and Soviet occupations. I seldom inquired about those times anymore since everyone had a horror story, though some had happy endings. For example, one local Jewish man working for the Soviets knew which families would be forcibly loaded on the next train to Siberia. The train was made up of old boxcars. Before the train left for Siberia, blood was dripping from the sides of the boxcars as people killed themselves rather than face torture and slow, almost certain death. The Jewish man managed to hide many Ukrainian neighbors. After the Germans drove out the Soviets in 1941, a Ukrainian family returned the favor by hiding his family from the Germans at huge risk until the war ended.

Free to criticize but not for long: Georgi Gongadze, a Georgian who was a popular Internet journalist in Kiev, disappeared. He had published articles critical of Ukraine's president, Leonid Kuchma. A few weeks after the disappearance, Gongadze's body was found in a shallow grave near Kiev, beheaded and partly eaten by animals. Evil people do this sort of thing to intimidate. Perhaps we've not heard the last of this crime.

Health: It is the practice in Ukraine to introduce your good friends to your favorite doctor. One of my friends offered to have his doctor take a look at my finger, which had incurred a nasty infection. It would have been a mild insult to have said no, so I thanked my friend and agreed to see his doctor. When the doctor arrived, we conversed with the help of a translator. The three of us were crammed into my tiny bathroom. The doctor glanced at my finger and then asked me to take off my shirt. He explored a bit and then announced that the problem was not with my finger (the open infection notwithstanding) but with my shoulder. He pulled hard on my arm, resocketing it in the process. Then he offered his prescription: each night I should put honey on my shoulder and cover it with a large cabbage leaf and a hot compress. It wouldn't hurt to do both shoulders, in fact. Then he spied a protruding vertebra in my back and said if I came down to his office, he could fix it in a jiffy. I politely declined, but based on another friend's advice, I soaked my finger each night in a tea made from the root of willow.

Meeting of the regional government: About sixty members of the L'viv regional parliament showed up along with one hundred guests. I was the only non-Ukrainian present. The governor of the L'viv region (an area about the size of Connecticut) raised the first issue for the group: electricity. L'viv was not getting its pro rata share of electricity, said the governor, an appointee of Ukraine's president. It was being discriminated against by larger, more powerful cities.

"Where is the prosecutor?" he asked.

No one stood up.

"It's very bad that the prosecutor is not here. We should sue the national government. No more telephone rule," he said, referring to the communist days when judges would receive phone calls from special people telling them how they should decide cases.

The regional leader for energy matters got in about three minutes of mindless finger-pointing before members seized the microphone from him and began shouting, "We can't take the government to court. We'll stand out. It won't help. Hospitals and schools can't pay for electricity anyway."

The governor said, "Save up and buy generators!"

The meeting went downhill from there. On the one hand, I felt privileged to be invited inside the government apparatus; on the other hand, I was embarrassed for these people, watching this pathetic spectacle so reminiscent of their seventy years on the dark side. When the powers that be turned off the electricity in L'viv, which they often did, the area felt like the dark side of the moon.

Morality and medicine: Obstetricians, stem-cell researchers, midwives, medical doctors, young girls seeking abortions as a means of birth control, and government-run orphanages provided ample opportunities for mischief. A scandal in L'viv when we first arrived involved medical professionals telling new mothers that their children had been born dead when they had not. Such babies were sold for organs and tissues or kept alive and held captive for other lucrative markets.

LCG Partners

Partners of the L'viv Consulting Group worked with more than one hundred clients over seven years. Hundreds of potential clients would not accept our conditions for working with them. Despite the obstacles, the LCG's work gave rise to a merger that produced the largest bottled-water company in Ukraine. The organization also helped recover $5 million in grain stolen by the Ukrainian government from a US entrepreneur. The LCG helped create the largest franchised pizza operation in the country, with more than one hundred outlets. Our group worked hard to turn around a complex of five hotels at a famous spa with five thousand employees. In its early days, the LCG produced a thirteen-page business plan that brought a $250,000 investment to a textile company. The firm was then able to hire more than two thousand women for permanent jobs. The LCG was also retained by a German manufacturer of wire harnesses for automobiles, such as Mercedes-Benzes, to help develop the supervisory staff to hire and manage more than four thousand workers, almost all women. (Photo by author)

Julie Kidd with Mikhail Horyn

Julie Kidd and her son Wilmot visited L'viv in 2000. Speaking with her in this photo is Mikhail Horyn, one of Ukraine's most famous dissidents from the Soviet era. Marta Kolomayets, the best Ukrainian-English translator in L'viv, has her back to the photographer. When we retained her to translate for an investment project, she made the project sound better than it was. Horyn is shown here giving Julie a tour outside the prison where he spent twenty-seven years for publishing what he thought about the Soviet system. I learned one important lesson from him: if you must be a dissident, be a good one. That way you will develop a public following (as Horyn did), and although the goons may imprison you, they are less likely to torture or kill you, because of the anti-Soviet reaction that would result among your supporters. (Photo by author)

RHS and Kiev Atlantic Ukraine

This $25 million project was the first to bring modern facilities to Ukraine's dilapidated agriculture infrastructure. It was the brainchild of David Sweere, a Dutch American farmer from the Midwest. He put the project together with a large loan from the European Bank for Reconstruction and Development. One season before the project was completed, the Ukrainian government seized $5 million of Sweere's grain from state elevators. He had placed it there because his own storage silos, shown here, were not yet completed. It was not uncommon for the government to steal from farmers when the national harvest failed to yield enough grain to meet the nation's annual target. The L'viv Consulting Group contacted US officials to pressure the Ukrainian government, and Sweere was reimbursed by Ukraine. The reimbursement took place shortly after a deputy prime minister for agriculture was told his visa for a trip to the United States would be forthcoming only after Sweere received his $5 million. (Photo by author)

Barb Shriver, center, being honored for a book she
compiled and edited on Ukrainian Culture

Barb spent two years assembling, translating, and publishing a coffee table book
of sketches of Ukraine's rural culture. The sketches were the life's work of an artist
from Stare Sambyr, an old town in the far western region of Ukraine. The CIME
bought the rights to Volodymyr Shagala's fifty years of drawings of churches,
harvests, wars, architecture, and nature. The book won prizes in L'viv and Kiev.
(Photo by author)

6

Steve Demchuk and the Ukrainian Diaspora

Entering the drab Hotel Rus lobby in Kiev one evening in June 1991, I spotted Jon Gunderson, the newly sworn-in US consul general in Ukraine. He was explaining to two Americans that his main activity since arriving in Kiev a couple of months earlier had been getting a dead American out of Ukraine and returning him to his family in the United States. Jon was in the middle of his story, so I walked over and listened. He said a Ukrainian American had come to Kiev to teach, and when he went to the lectern for his first lecture, he had a heart attack and died. A chill shot up my back.

When he finished, I queried, "Jon, you're not talking about Steve Demchuk, are you?"

Jon was dumbstruck. "How did you know?"[8]

---

[8] The two persons with Gunderson were Michael Mandelbaum, head of the US Council on Foreign Relations, and Strobe Talbott, *Time* magazine's editor at large. Both men would soon become high-level Clinton appointees. Talbott was destined to become deputy secretary of state for relations with, and economic assistance to, the soon-to-be former republics of the late Soviet Union. The two men were on a reconnaissance trip to Ukraine and the Baltics as part of Clinton's preelection advisory team on international affairs. I had taught at the

Steve and I had met in 1990 at gatherings of the Ukrainian diaspora in the United States and had become friends. He had fled Ukraine in the late forties as a boy when the Soviets were slaughtering their own people, especially western Ukrainians, after World War II. In L'viv during the late thirties and again during 1946 and 1947, Stalin's police arrested people for no reason other than that they may have been important educators or owned large houses. People were also imprisoned on suspicion of collaboration with the Nazis, a charge that could be leveled at anyone. During the late forties, just down the street from our apartment in L'viv, the police killed one hundred or so on an average day. The bodies were then laid out along the streetcar tracks for families to sift through to find dead husbands, fathers, uncles, or brothers. One survivor told us that when the police were about to shoot a hundred victims, they thoughtfully revved up the trucks in the lot surrounding the building so that the shots and the screams (if there were any) would not be heard.

Steve had not been back to Ukraine since he fled the country in 1946. In 1990, when we first met, he was working for PepsiCo in its beverages division. He had several family members in Ukraine whom he had not seen in more than forty years, including his brother, who had been in a wheelchair for a long time. Steve confided in me that he had had serious heart problems similar to my own, so I knew something about his health situation.

I was aware of all this when Steve called me excitedly in early 1991. He had been invited to spend two weeks lecturing at IMI-Kiev, the business school where I had just finished teaching. "Do you think I should go?" he asked. I took my time answering since I had not offered medical advice to anyone before.

Immediately following World War II, Ukrainians left Ukraine by

International Management Institute in Kiev the previous year. This was where Steve Demchuk died.

the millions. At war's end, many wound up in Germany in labor camps, prison camps, or camps for displaced persons. They rarely returned to Ukraine unless compelled to do so by the US Army. Dwight Eisenhower, true to his word to Josef Stalin, had inadvertently sent many Soviet prisoners of war in Germany to their doom by returning them to the Soviet Union. In Stalin's view, if they were captured, they might now be spies. If they were so weak as to get captured, they deserved to die. This mentality, unthinkable in the United States, was standard fare under Stalin.

Ukrainians who came to the United States and Canada established their own schools and camps in an effort to preserve their culture, especially their language and customs. They did this in the faint hope that one day Ukraine might be independent after more than three hundred years of Russian domination.

Those returning to a miraculously free Ukraine in the early nineties brought gifts, money, and know-how, from dentistry to marketing and finance. In addition, they brought ideas, especially about how Ukraine should be run. Soon after Ukraine gained its independence in 1991, the Ukrainians who had stayed behind and lived through more than fifty years of communism under Moscow began to resent the arrogance of their returning brethren. In the midnineties, Ukraine passed a law making it a criminal act for returnees to engage in political affairs such as elections.

To be sure, a number of Ukrainian Americans returned and were able to leverage their advantages of market or technical know-how, staying away from politics. Some made substantial fortunes in fields like agriculture and commodity exports.

Some returned to Ukraine purely to do good. Bohdan Kurylko was such a person. His father and other members of his family had been killed by the Soviets. Bohdan had escaped, and after a successful career as chief financial officer of a large international ad agency, he retired to Switzerland. He often drove from there to Ukraine, his vehicle loaded with items that young people could use. He once brought several thousand pairs of shoes for children. Not trusting orphanage officials, he put hundreds of pairs of high-quality new shoes (unobtainable in Ukraine) on the children himself. He also contributed computers to the high school in L'viv that he had attended as a boy. Bohdan would not take credit for his charity, and I never detected any bitterness toward those who had killed his family.

Other expatriates came to Ukraine for brief visits and then stayed. I inadvertently helped one Ukrainian American do just that. Cathy Chumachenko had an MBA and in her late twenties had had much experience in commerce, trade, and capital markets. I recruited Cathy as a member of a US team participating in a June 1991 conference in Kiev titled "Capital Markets." The CIME bought her a ticket from Washington to Kiev. Little did we or anyone else know that the Soviet Union would exist for less than two more months.

The conference, at least thirty years ahead of its time, was cosponsored by the CIME and Rukh, a Western-leaning political, social, and economic movement with headquarters in L'viv in western Ukraine.

Cathy gave her talk on the second day of the conference and vanished into the Ukrainian culture. Katje (a.k.a. Cathy) resurfaced some years later as the wife of Victor Yushchenko, head of the Ukrainian National Bank at the time. Yushchenko served as prime minister from 1999 to 2001 and as president of Ukraine from 2005 to 2010. He is remembered worldwide for his disfigured face, which appeared on magazine and newspaper covers after he had been poisoned by dioxide in his soup. Dioxide is a concoction similar to Agent Orange, the poisonous defoliator used in Vietnam. It was one of the dozens of poisons used by the KGB for assassinations. One cup of the soup could have killed Yushchenko. Because the US military had had much experience curing people exposed to Agent Orange, Yushchenko met in Vienna with a group of American medical experts who helped him recover.

But back to Steve Demchuk and his question to me: "Do you think I should go?"

I do not recall giving anyone medical advice up to that moment. I made an exception in this case. I said, "Steve, if I were you, I wouldn't do it. Preparing and giving lectures can be stressful on those of us who are not professional teachers, not to mention the emotional impact of visiting with your Ukrainian family." I spoke for myself, knowing how nerve-racking it had been to prepare and deliver lectures in general, let alone in Ukraine. Steve at least could speak the language.

Furthermore, I told him about the extraordinary emotional traumas I had seen when Ukrainian expatriates returned to visit relatives they had not seen in forty or fifty years. Communism had taken a huge toll on these people physically, spiritually, emotionally, and psychologically. Years of perfunctory correspondence would not prepare returnees for a face-to-face reunion. I concluded, all things being equal, that I might not survive the experience that Steve was considering for himself.

I could sense that Steve was not likely to heed my advice, which I regretted giving. I never heard from or about him again until my encounter with Jon Gunderson at Kiev's Hotel Rus months later.

Subsequently, while living in L'viv during the late nineties, I received several calls from Ukrainian Americans in a short period. They were all Jewish and living in Florida or New Jersey. They sought my advice about whether they should make a nostalgic return visit to L'viv or Ternopil or Ivano-Frankivsk. They had all lived somewhere in the Pale of Settlement, a fenceless prison for Jews created by Catherine the Great and officially abolished after World War I. Many Jews were forced into the Pale, a region in western Ukraine, eastern Poland, and southwestern Belarus. Jews living in the Pale were easy victims of many pogroms, or mass executions. Anatevka, the fictitious town in *Fiddler on the Roof,* was located in the Pale. Jews concentrated in this region were targeted for annihilation in Hitler's Final Solution.

When I received such calls, I always asked about the person's age and health. Everyone who called was more than eighty and in questionable health. No longer mincing words as I may have with Steve, I explained to them that their homes were long gone, that there was only one synagogue remaining in L'viv, and that there would be no tombstones or graveyards. I said that 100 percent of the Jewish families in virtually all of western Ukraine had been erased by the Nazis. The radio messages went directly from the local commanders to Hitler himself: "Ternopil ist Judenfrei" (Ternopil is free of Jews). I told them that a visit to Ukraine could be such a depressing experience that it might affect their health. To my knowledge, none of those with whom I spoke traveled there.

Oksana, Viktor Petrenko, and Barb

Something good from Ukraine. The country had a bad reputation in the West, aided and abetted by Russian propaganda, Ukraine's own criminal leaders, and fears emanating from the 1986 Chernobyl nuclear disaster. Here, however, are two migrants to the United States representing the best of Ukraine: professional figure skaters Oksana Baiul and Viktor Petrenko. They are chatting with Barb at a rink in Simsbury, Connecticut. Coming from Dnipropetrovsk, one of the toughest regions of Ukraine, Oksana was officially an orphan. Petrenko recognized her ability, and she became a ward of his coach and began skating professionally. She was an overnight sensation in the West, winning an Olympic gold medal in 1994. Instant fame, fortune, and freedom took a brief toll on her behavior, perhaps understandably, but she quickly adapted. Viktor Petrenko won a gold medal at the 1992 Olympics, skating with what was called the "unified team" of the former Soviet Union. He beat out American Paul Wylie for this honor and is perhaps best known in Ukraine for his US-style philanthropy. He raised funds and invested his own money to create the Viktor Petrenko Neonatal Intensive Care Unit in Odessa, Ukraine, a medical facility that deals with birth defects in children from Chernobyl, who were victims of the worst nuclear accident in history. (Photo by Barbara B. Shriver)

7

Shriver's Guide to Moscow

1996

Dear Fellow Travelers:

Many have observed that after seven years of traipsing through parts of what was, at the outset, the Soviet Union and is now the former Soviet Union, Barb and I must have gained much valuable experience that we could pass on to the benefit of friends thinking about traveling there. I thought we should start with Moscow, which I have now visited more than a dozen times, and Barb at least half that. The suggestions that follow are based on our most recent trip there, spanning about four weeks in October and November 1996.

Get a visa: This may seem obvious. Actually, the first few times we visited Moscow, we traveled by train from Ukraine for which we had a visa. We didn't need a special visa for Russia since the Soviet Union was one country. For a World Bank project in Moscow in 1996, however, I was to go from L'viv to Moscow for a few days and then return to Ukraine. A week after that, Barb and I were to visit Moscow for a couple of weeks. The project was on again, off again but finally came together just a few days before I was to fly to Moscow. Not one of us, including the host organization, which would normally have issued an official invitation, ever gave a thought to the visa since I was coming from Ukraine.

When I reached the L'viv airport early on Sunday morning to catch the Moldavian Air Lines shuttle to Moscow, I was asked for my visa for Russia. Uh-oh. I asked if I could at least fly to Moscow and perhaps solve the problem there. The L'viv gendarmes said okay, and off I went, a normal flight in the Yak 42 jet aircraft. When we arrived at Vnukhovo Airport in Moscow, we were debarking when a six-foot-three woman in fatigues, with considerable armament protruding from parts of her anatomy, appeared at the exit door and asked for visas.

When I handed her my passport, she said, "No visa?"

I said, "Right."

She said firmly in Russian, though it could have been in any language, "Sit down!"

I countered weakly that a friend was waiting inside and doubtless had my invitation, and perhaps I could purchase a visa on the spot.

Again, in Russian: "Not on your life, fellow. You're going back to Ukraine—just sit down and shut up."

Barb was surprised to see me again later that day, one that had its ups and downs.

Know where you live: This may also seem obvious or even trivial. It is if you're staying in a hotel, but we were staying in an apartment. We suggest you immediately write your address on a piece of paper and put it in your wallet (two wallets if there are two of you). You should also put your apartment phone number and any codes necessary to enter the building on that piece of paper. It could be helpful as well to add the street name in Cyrillic; this way, you can show a taxi driver where you live in a language he understands.

We did none of these things. On our first day in the apartment, we could open the door to the building simply by pushing a button in the upper right-hand corner of the code panel. Having been lulled into complacency, I returned home late the next night to find that the single button no longer did the job after dark. Time to use the code panel. But what was the code? I had put it out of my mind, thinking I had to push only one button, easily found in the upper right-hand corner. This button was visible even in the dark. The same could not be said for the numbers on the regular buttons with which I now had to contend. Unable to see the numbers and not knowing the code, I pondered spending the night in the marrow-chilling vestibule while Barb was upstairs in the warm apartment. She would soon begin to worry, I thought, unaware that I was so close. Of course, I could run out and find one of the ubiquitous phones and call her. Or at least I could have if I had put the phone number in my wallet. By accident, I discovered I had left a small flashlight in my jacket some months earlier. Remembering at least part of the code, I was able to enter after some trial and error. I hope this story is helpful, especially the part about the flashlight.

Ride the Metro: We met several Americans who had been living in Moscow for a year or more and had never been on the Metro. The possible violation of international labor laws during its construction notwithstanding, the Moscow Metro is one of the best public transportation systems in the world. Being an old hand at using public transit in the former Soviet Union, I sidled up to the pay booth and asked the 150-year-old woman inside for a *myesets bilyet*, a monthly ticket. Barb, who would not be going to work every day, chose to travel one token, or ride, at a time. At this point, I realized that I had outsmarted myself, because the monthly ticket was not the expected bargain. At ninety thousand rubles for the monthly ticket versus fifteen hundred for a token, I would have to go to work forty days a month to pay for the thing.

Ah well, I was heavy into negotiation by this time. Russia could use the extra ten bucks, so I purchased my ticket, which to my surprise had a magnetic stripe down one side. This suggested I would have to use a machine rather than flash the monthly pass to the 150-year-old woman at the gate. Sure enough, there were now machines for both tokens and tickets. Barb stuck her token in and walked through. I put the monthly ticket in the slot, retrieving it when it came back out, and attempted to hurry through the gate to catch up. Whango! A metal frame spurted out from each side of the gate and pinioned my knee in a killer grip. The noise woke up the old woman, who ran out shouting. The commotion also roused a slovenly but well-armed guard I hadn't noticed before. I protested and held up my monthly ticket. The woman kept saying, "Zaftra, zaftra," or "Tomorrow, tomorrow," the meaning of which finally dawned on me. It happened that this was the first use of the magnetic ticket at this station, and I had bought one of the first tickets, which was good for the month of November. However, it was still October 31. Barb handed me a token over the barrier, the woman pressed a button to release my knee, and I limped through the proper gate.

Plan city trips well in advance: Moscow is a big city with many peculiarities such as constantly changing street names, no street names, single addresses for more residents than Scranton, buildings separated by long distances but with the same street name and number, and multiple buildings having the same address. No problem, of course, for veterans like us. We were invited to dinner at a friend's apartment and proceeded via the Metro. Surfacing at the proper stop, we searched for the right street. After twenty-five minutes of futile wandering, we quietly and calmly discussed exactly who was in charge of planning this excursion. We finally found the street and then the right number. At last! But the inhabitants were not our friends. Since the neighborhood was somewhat hostile, Barb won the toss and got to go into the heavy-duty gangster restaurant by herself and make the phone call. We were still half a mile away but were less than an hour late.

Have a contingency laundry plan: Laundry and cleaning services for the Russian public are business opportunities with big potential. I had learned this long before, especially in Jalalabad, Kyrgyzstan, in

1993 where I invented the two-day shirt. Our Moscow apartment came equipped with a clothes washer (driers are another opportunity) designed as a freshman engineering project by the same man who, weeks later, would design the Chernobyl nuclear reactor. Consequently, we couldn't operate the device. Shortly before dawn on November 14, 1996, I invented the three-day shirt. When I tried to have my idea patented I was told the Russians were way ahead of us.

The next time we travel to Moscow, we plan to be guided by Lonely Planet.

8

Svitlana

First lady Hillary Clinton visited L'viv in 1997 to give a speech. Barb and I were living there at the time. The US embassy in Kiev asked if we would serve as ushers at the opera house where Mrs. Clinton would be speaking. We agreed.

Mrs. Clinton had visited Ukraine's capital city on a previous trip to Ukraine with her husband, President Bill Clinton. On this trip, however, she was traveling on her own (with two 747s, her own bed, and dozens of White House staffers and other employees of the US government). Prominent among her passengers was Melanne Verveer, her chief of staff. Verveer was a Ukrainian American and reputedly had great sway over Mrs. Clinton's decision to stop in only one Ukrainian city on this trip, L'viv.

I'm guessing that Verveer's grandparents had come from L'viv or elsewhere in western Ukraine around 1900, as so many Ukrainians followed that route.[9]

---

[9] By 2015, following a successful career in government, Melanne Verveer had become executive director of the Georgetown Institute for Women, Peace and Security at Georgetown University and a founding partner of Seneca Point Global, a global women's strategy firm.

On the first day of the visit, Mrs. Clinton and Ludmila Kuchma, wife of Ukrainian president Leonid Kuchma, unveiled a monument to the victims of communism. This monument stood at a prominent intersection that we could see from our nearby third-story apartment. The monument was erected just one hundred feet from the prison where, in the late 1940s, a hundred or so innocent L'viv residents were killed each day and laid out on streetcar tracks that still ran alongside the memorial. This was said to be the first monument to victims of communism erected in the former Soviet Union. This was hardly surprising since many former communists opposed such monuments, some to the point of violence.

The next day the two first ladies were scheduled to make speeches before one thousand or so spectators, mostly Ukrainians, but also a number of Americans from the Peace Corps and the US embassy in Kiev along with others working in western Ukraine. Mrs. Clinton's speech was noteworthy because she became the highest-ranking American to shed light on the massive illegal trafficking of Ukrainians, mostly young girls. She said the number of young girls who had disappeared from the former Soviet Union in the five years following its collapse was an astounding four hundred thousand. "We want to help those women who have fallen into danger," Mrs. Clinton said.

Barb and I had known one such young woman. Svitlana (Svita, informally, a Russian and pan-Slavic name that means "light," "blessed," or "pure") worked at IMI-Kiev in 1990, the year I taught there. She was a bright kopek among the members of the school administration. Svita was pleasant and enjoyed a good time. Whenever students, faculty, and other members of the school went to the woods for relaxation around a campfire and cooked up kebabs and mushrooms, Svita made sure all the necessities for the party were provided. She was also the first to dance when the musicians broke out their instruments. These were heady moments when people could escape the suffocating control of state-controlled management over their everyday lives.

We later heard that Svita had announced plans to go to Yugoslavia for three months. She was earning about $400 per year at IMI-Kiev. She said she would work as a prostitute in Yugoslavia, where she had been told that she could earn $5,000, before returning to Kiev. Her parents, both working, were earning a total of about $1,500 a year, so $5,000 was a big sum to bring home to her family. She was lost along with the four hundred thousand other people, mostly young women, who were deceived and forced into slavery of some sort. To our knowledge, Svita was never heard from again.

Trafficking in people for whatever purpose is not exclusive to backward countries. It is a problem in Connecticut and throughout the United States, though not to the same degree as in Ukraine. Eliminating trafficking in one part of the world, however, will aid in eliminating it in others.

9

Toto Talitarianism

S hortly after we began a seven-year stint in western Ukraine in 1995, I wrote to a friend, a scratch golfer who had made a career selling for Scott Paper. I invited him to come to Ukraine, suggesting he take over the local toilet paper factory and make golf clubs there. Even though there was no golf course in Ukraine, at least no one would get hurt.

Good old-fashioned Western toilet paper is made mainly from wood pulp, linen, and old rags. Chemicals are blended in with the wood pulp for softness. On the other hand, it seemed like Soviet toilet paper was made from used sandpaper, scrap metal, and broken glass.

Soviet toilet facilities were among the more difficult cultural differences to which Americans had to adjust. I pictured a man standing at the end of the Soviet toilet assembly line with his four-kilo maul and smashing every toilet seat as it came by. They were always broken. Every time I entered a friend's restroom, I assumed I would have to do something with the seat to make it useful.

Turning on the hot water for a shower often caused a small explosion in the energy-conserving *kalonka*, a primitive automatic water heater, the flame of which might singe your eyebrows.

Holes in the floor were often there in place of toilets. In the best of places, these holes were adorned with colorful ceramic tiles that also showed where to place one's feet.

Toilet facilities smelled awful. The sanitation was enough to make a CITGO gas station manager blush.

We could take showers in L'viv from six until seven in the morning and from eight until nine at night. The restriction was imposed to save electricity. With pumps shut down twice a day, pressure outside of the main pipelines caused toxins in the soil surrounding the pipelines to infiltrate the clean water. The old pipelines installed by the Austro-Hungarians, who had built most of L'viv, were made of cast iron, a metal that did not corrode and thus did not leak. The Soviet pipelines, on the other hand, were made of stainless steel, a material impervious to rust but not to electrolysis, an indiscriminate corroding environment. The infiltration caused the foulest water imaginable, smelly and having the color of weak tea, with particles suspended in a colloidal dispersion. The toxins included gasoline, oil, metals, and many food poisons, from salmonella to E. coli.

While hot water for showers and water clean enough to drink were issues, they were problems that could easily be solved. One needed only a few hundred dollars to pay for the necessary infrastructure, but this amount was out of sight for the vast majority of Ukrainians. As for toilet paper, we brought it with us when we flew into Ukraine.

In December 1993, I flew out of Ukraine to attend a meeting in London at the European Bank for Reconstruction and Development (EBRD). This institution was known among insiders as "the house that Jacques built," Jacques being Jacques Atelier, the French banker who had been the EBRD's first president. Unfortunately, the lavish edifice he created in downtown London became one of the reasons he lost his job. I thought this to be all in my favor, however, when, during a break in my meeting at the bank, I repaired to the restroom. At the proper time, I reached into one of the polished, chrome-plated toilet paper holders that Jacques had placed in the stalls. The holder was empty. Mild panic, but Jacques had spared no expense, and there was a second polished, chrome-plated toilet paper holder. I rolled back the cover, and (gasp) this one was empty as well.

Life's darkest moment. What to do? I reached into my pockets and found some Ukrainian money that I had brought with me on the plane from Kiev. I had thirty-five bills worth one thousand karbovanets each. Ukraine was just emerging from possibly the worst inflation of any country in history, including that suffered by Brazil in the 1980s and Germany's Weimar Republic in the late twenties.

Ukrainian friends of ours who were living in Germany bought a used Mercedes in late 1992. They drove it to Ukraine, sold it for Ukrainian currency worth about $2,000 at the time, and put the money in a Ukrainian bank account. At the end of 1993, they closed the account and received enough money for one of their daughters to purchase a single pair of silk stockings.

A quick calculation in the EBRD restroom told me that the thirty-five thousand karbovantsi in bills in my hand, worth more than $5,000 not long before, were at that moment worth less than two dollars, or about the same as a packet of Kleenex tissue.

On that day, December 14, 1993, Ukraine's currency reached a new bottom.

10

Nikolay

Nikolay, a Ukrainian from Kharkiv, the largest city in eastern Ukraine, had translated secret American documents for the KGB, but we became friends in 1992 despite the fact that we had worked on opposing sides during the Cold War. Nikolay was fluent in English and had been helpful to us at the International Executive Service Corps (IESC) where I was responsible for developing a US-funded assistance program for the former Soviet republics. Fifteen new countries were spawned following the Yeltsin-inspired breakup of the unworkable economic, geographical, ethnic, religious, and political sprawl known as the Soviet Union. The USSR had been cobbled together beginning eighty years before by a combination of military force, corruption, internal espionage, a unitary national police force, and an abundance of sycophants who operated out of fear or a desire for self-preservation. Nikolay had visited the IESC headquarters in Stamford, Connecticut, where he impressed everyone as being somehow different from the typical Soviet apparatchik. Should we not hire him to develop and run an IESC office in Kharkiv?

From Nikolay's standpoint, I had spent time at a high level in the Office of the Secretary of Defense, which to Ukrainians translated as, "He's CIA."

Nikolay's wife, Lena, was equally impressive. She was lovely and kind but in fragile health at the time.[10]

Since Nikolay would report to me, I was curious as to his loyalties. To what degree could an American organization trust someone from the Soviet environment? Nikolay likely had his own suspicions given the position I had held at the Pentagon during President Ford's administration, which was public knowledge.

As we were having tea in Kharkiv one day, Nikolay must have decided to let me know indirectly where he stood vis-à-vis Soviet communism. I was to be engaged in similar discussions many times in the years that followed.

Nikolay began. His grandparents were Ukrainian and had lived near the Ukrainian border in southern Russia, black-earth farming country that was really an eastern extension of Ukraine into Russia. They were there in the early thirties, a time when Josef Stalin had been frustrated in his efforts to compel or persuade the farmers of Ukraine and southern Russia to collectivize. They were independent farmers and refused the orders from Moscow to form collective farms. To force the farmers to see things his way, Stalin created one of the largest and deadliest artificial famines in modern history.[11] The Soviet grain harvest in the fall of 1932 was stored in state-controlled silos, and the meat from slaughterhouses was stored in state-controlled refrigeration plants. In short, all food supplies were gathered up by the state and were then withheld from the rural people of Ukraine and southern Russia.

There was little mobility in the countryside of Ukraine and southern Russia. People had no place to go and no way to escape since

---

[10] Today, Lena is well, and their two children, bright and fluent in English, live in Sweden where they had been invited, complete with academic scholarships.

[11] In his 2010 book *Mao's Great Famine: The History of China's Most Devastating Catastrophe*, Professor Frank Dikoetter documented a Mao Zedong–inspired famine in China from 1958 to 1962 in which forty-five million people died; Mao is quoted as saying, "When there is not enough to eat people starve to death. It is better to let half of the people die so that the other half can eat their fill." The leaders of overbearing governments can afford to think that way.

transportation was also controlled by the state. They had nothing to eat where they lived and couldn't move.

As the fall of 1932 turned into the winter of 1933, millions of Ukrainians were starving to death. In sum, in 1932–33, Stalin deliberately killed eight million of his fellow citizens through starvation, more than the number of Jews killed by Hitler. This was his way of enforcing his ideology and destroying peasant resistance to collectivization.[12]

Nikolay's grandmother was looking after her three sons, all ten years of age or less, during that awful winter. One evening at dinner, she placed a single rationed potato on each plate. One boy ate his potato and, starving, reached over and stabbed the potato on a brother's plate and gobbled it up. His mother rapped the boy on the head with her wooden spoon, and the weakened child dropped dead. It was just the start of a long, cold winter. His mother placed the boy's body outside in the cold, away from animals; the other two boys made it through the winter, unknowingly with the sustenance reaped from their dead brother.

We Americans are often told how lucky we are. We are told this by our parents and grandparents as well as by foreign visitors. But we are not reminded enough, and our children are protected from such unpleasant real-life stories, ultimately to their detriment in terms of understanding the world. Our kids can take it, and they should know how the rest of the world lives and how people around the world less fortunate than we have lived throughout history. This would help them in choosing their studies and their careers.

Today, twenty-five years after we heard this story, Nikolay and Lena remain two of our closest friends.

---

[12] News of the famine (the Ukrainians use the word *holodomor*, or "sorrow") was suppressed. There were several Western news reporters in Moscow, including Walter Duranty of the *New York Times*. Duranty knew of the famine but never wrote about it because to do so would have cost him his position as one of Stalin's favorite reporters. Tyrants always seem to know how to use the American press to their advantage. To this day, Ukrainian expatriates are working to have Duranty's Pulitzer Prize rescinded.

Yakimenko, Anders, and Hoffmann

The IESC's Nikolay Yakimenko, William Anders (lunar module pilot of Apollo 8, the first manned circumlunar flight; US ambassador to Norway; CEO of General Dynamics), and former secretary of the army Martin R. Hoffmann. After the Soviet Union collapsed, there was much political turmoil over the nuclear weapons targeted on the United States in underground sites in Belarus, Kazakhstan, Ukraine, and Russia. One response was a bill sponsored by US senators Richard Lugar and Sam Nunn to pay for the transfer to Russia or the demolition of all such missiles, silos, and warheads in the three smaller countries. Nunn-Lugar funds were also used by the Department of Defense to help Soviet defense plants in those countries convert from making military weaponry to commercial products for the economically starved civilian sector. Ashton Carter, the deputy to Defense Secretary William Perry, was himself named secretary of defense in 2015. Carter was our principal contact for this work.

We arranged for a recently retired head of Combustion Engineering, and new IESC volunteer, to greet his friend Perry at a demonstration of defense conversion opportunities in Russia. In Kiev, we held a three-day conference on defense industry conversion for which our two principle speakers were Anders and Hoffmann. Anders had held a number of industrial, space-related positions before becoming CEO of General Dynamics. He recalled that as head of General Dynamics in 1989 and 1990, he tried to buy key weapons systems. His competitors wouldn't sell, so he sold off pieces of his company. He then remitted the profits from the sale of these assets to the shareholders as a substantial one-time dividend. In his letter to shareholders he said in effect, "You know how to spend this money better than we do." Anders understood defense industry conversion. During the conference in Kiev, the Ukrainians were eager to have Anders visit Kharkov. We flew there in an Antonov 28, a high-winged twin-turbo prop plane. On the return trip, the pilot invited Anders to take the controls. Anders sat in the pilot's seat of a strange Russian plane, flew the three hundred miles to Kiev, converting meters to feet in his head, and greased the landing in Kiev. (Photo by author)

Perry and Worcester

Bill Perry, secretary of defense from 1994 to 1997, was perhaps President Clinton's most astute cabinet appointment. He is shown here, to the left, with the IESC's country director for Ukraine, Bruce Worcester, and a Ukrainian general at a social gathering in Kiev. The gathering took place during the IESC's defense industry conversion conference there. It was not easy to persuade the so-called red directors of former Soviet defense plants that their companies should make goods for the civilian sector or simply shut down obsolete operations. The money to operate almost all defense plants had stopped coming from Moscow. The mentality needed to operate in the private sector is dramatically different from the mentality needed to compete for a share of the public budget. Most companies could not adapt to the rough-and-tumble of free markets, but the Defense Department's effort was a welcome gesture by the United States, and there were enough successes to make the effort worthwhile. One of the best defense conversion ideas was associated with a tank factory in Bratislava, Slovakia, which, in the midnineties, was finishing the last part of an order for Soviet T-72 tanks for Syria. The European Union had big plans to invest in superhighways connecting Western Europe with newly opened Eastern Europe. Although the military market was shrinking, the need for a massive pan-European public highway might fill the vacuum. We contacted the Raytheon Corporation, which owned the Cedar Rapids Company, which in turn controlled the Herrmann Equipment Company. It turned out the footprint on the factory floor for a T-72 tank was almost identical to the footprint for a Herrmann Equipment road paver. (Photo by author)

Dr. Yakov Eisenberg and Thomas C. Reed

Tom Reed, scientist, politician, and US national security expert, went to Kharkiv, Ukraine, with his wife, Kay, on an IESC defense conversion assignment. The client was the B. Verkhin Institute for Low Temperature Physics. The comparably brilliant Dr. Yakov Eisenberg was the director of the plant. As it happened, in the sixties Tom had started a for-profit business engaged in low-temperature physics, a Texas company called Supercon, so named because its product was filament-thin superconducting wire for use in space at temperatures close to absolute zero. Armatures made from such wire, especially beryllium, could produce much power with little size or weight, an important factor in space projects. As the temperature of the motor or generator approaches absolute zero (minus 273 degrees Celsius), the resistance in the wires also approaches zero, so small, light motors can deliver a lot of power for their weight. While in Kharkiv, Tom somehow made his way into the top-secret Kharkiv aircraft plant, which, as former secretary of the air force, he knew to be one of the Soviet Union's premier military plants. (Photo by author)

11

I've Got a Horse Right Here

1994

The Russian audience in a large hall in the city of Vladimir, northeast of Moscow, waited patiently for the presentation by the IESC's financial and accounting expert. These people were stunned by a PowerPoint presentation on the Vladimir tractor factory's profit-and-loss statement and balance sheet based on international accounting standards (which are pretty close to generally accepted accounting principles). They were astonished by the numbers, which showed a good profit. The Soviet chart of accounts had no word for *profit* in it and no reasonable way to calculate a profit.

The presentation also showed that this new way of producing financial information could be helpful in making business decisions or in placing a value on a business, two things impossible to do when using Soviet accounting methods.

We at the IESC were helping to convert the Vladimir tractor factory's systems and operations to prepare it for privatization.

Privatization refers to the process by which the government sells or otherwise transfers assets into private hands. This was a massive task in the former Soviet Union since virtually every business of consequence had been owned and operated by the government. To privatize a business and to arrive at a fair sale price, it was necessary to place a value on the business. One common way of doing this was via financial performance, especially profits measured according to international standards, measures not possible using Soviet accounting rules. The Vladimir tractor plant was to be a model for how to do this.

In Moscow the next day, we reviewed the results of this presentation with the Russian Ministry for Privatization and its principal deputy, Maxim Boyko. (The minister of privatization was the flamboyant Anatoly Chubais.) A junior economist met us and began the conversation as we waited for Boyko. A short while later, another seemingly more junior person joined us silently, even shyly, and sat to one side as we continued the discussion. This turned out to be Boyko himself, who, after Chubais, was the most influential person engaged in the privatization of Russian industry, a project of vast and immeasurable size, complexity, and opportunities for chicanery.

Privatization started out as a modest success with the help of the International Finance Corporation, an arm of the World Bank. This organization was influential in developing the rules for privatization for the ancient city of Nizhny Novgorod. A few thousand small entities were successfully privatized under this project.

Unfortunately, some of the most brazen, corrupt, and immoral, if not illegal, takeovers of Russia's prime industries soon followed. These involved manufacturing companies, but the major scandals were in commodities such as iron and steel, oil, gas, aluminum, and related industries. These were the most crooked takeovers since the days of America's own robber barons such as J. P. Morgan, John D. Rockefeller, and Andrew Mellon. At least those were the examples Russians liked to cite when defending the excesses of the privatization process. When it came to insider trading of securities, the main engine of oligarchs' wealth, there may have been an element of truth in the comparison.

The Russian privatization scandals were notable for their enormous scale. Time after time, unregulated offers went out to workers in major industries, often cheating the poor out of their inheritance from the breakup of the Soviet Union by swindling or coercing them into selling their company shares at ridiculously low prices. These deals were lining the pockets (or more precisely, the Cyprus bank accounts) of the growing class of Russian oligarchs. Even hapless Western giants such as British Petroleum were not spared the excesses of the Wild East. The level of bullying, threats, and even assassinations was beyond the comprehension of most Americans.

One unwritten rule for the oligarchs by 2000 was that the government (i.e., President Vladimir Putin) would turn a blind eye to irregularities as long as the new billionaires stayed out of Russian politics. The test case came when Mikhail Khodorkovsky grew rich, popular, and powerful with his oil giant, YUKOS, thus becoming a potential political threat to Putin. Khodorkovsky felt he was bulletproof because of his wealth (an estimated $15 billion at its peak) and the bodyguards and level of protection that he could purchase for his safety. His popularity was growing in Russia because of his philanthropic activities. Nonetheless, he was arrested at an airport and spent eight years in prison before being pardoned in 2013. Putin's message was not lost on the remaining oligarchs.

Soviet bookkeeping, with its single-entry accounting, a practice eliminated in the West a century ago by Scottish accountants, was not designed to aid in the management of firms. It was designed to control money, to ensure payment of withholding taxes, and to make it difficult to steal—officially. This system led to a staggering array of thefts, subterfuges, and under-the-table transactions, likely a principal reason for the pervasive corruption today, the very disease the system was designed to prevent.

Working with Ukrainian companies in the late nineties, we saw the effects of Soviet accounting on many occasions. The Primy farm near

L'viv stands out in my memory. Our visit took place around 1996. Primy had more than fifty acres of greenhouses containing enough cucumbers and tomatoes to feed almost a third of the country. Primy's director told us that Mikhail Gorbachev had visited the farm in the late 1980s and was so impressed that he asked the director if there was any one thing he would like. The director asked Gorbachev for an export license. He had the license within a few days. This enabled the farm to open an account for foreign (hard) currency at the Vneshekonom Bank in Moscow, the only bank permitted to handle transactions involving foreign currencies.

The director said his accountant came to him a year later and announced the farm had more than a million US dollars in the Moscow account.

"Wow. That's a lot of tomatoes and cucumbers!" I exclaimed.

"Oh, we didn't sell any vegetables," the director said. "We sold some scrap iron and steel for a while. Then we sold, into Western Europe, two horses that were on our balance sheet. The transaction was a bit tricky from an accounting standpoint, and the horses didn't disappear from our balance sheet after they were sold. So we bought two more horses at Ukrainian prices and sold them into Western Europe at European prices for a very large profit. Again, the original two horses remained on our books. We sold those two horses seven hundred times."

12

"Operatzie? Tak, Operatzie"

1996

I did not need to understand much Ukrainian to realize that the three doctors at L'viv's main hospital were planning to operate on Barb. I panicked and quickly asked my L'viv Consulting Group partner and translator Dmytro to ask the doctors which one was in charge. When they hesitated for an instant, I intervened and asked Dmytro to make it clear to the doctors that I was in charge. I instructed them to do their best to stop the internal bleeding and said I would be back at six the next morning to take Barb to the airport.

The head of the hospital, one of the three doctors conferring about the matter, responded with concern that flying would be too dangerous. When Barb got to higher altitude, he explained, the decrease in atmospheric pressure would cause her to bleed even more. He had a point, but I assured him that we fully understood the risks and that I would return at six in the morning. A second opinion in L'viv was not in the works.

The main hospital in L'viv had fourteen hundred beds. Four hundred were occupied. Half of the four hundred occupants were sick. The other two hundred souls had no better place to live.

This was our first and only experience with a Soviet-style hospital, the ultimate result of decades of pure single-payer health care. The best health care in the USSR, which I understood was not bad in certain fields, was reserved for top government and party officials. An ideology that would not discriminate on the basis of ability clearly discriminated in favor of political rank and influence. Hospitals also served as refuges for those in temporary political trouble. The media reported that a person was in the hospital when he or she was avoiding indictment. It was considered bad form, if not illegal, to arrest someone in the hospital. Coroners were also involved in the game. If a politician was assassinated by the KGB, the cause of death was listed simply as "His heart stopped."

The hospital wards were spartan. A funnel and a rubber tube hung from hooks at each bedside in Barb's ward. Stomach pumps were the only visible technology in the hospital. The main function of this two-hundred-year-old technique was to clean out the stomach after a person had consumed a poison or too much alcohol or drugs. Today, modern stomach pumps are used in the United States as a routine alternative to dieting. In Ukraine at that time, however, they appeared ready for a deluge of citizens who had consumed poisoned mushrooms, for hordes of alcoholics or drug addicts, and for a lot of poorly diagnosed patients who wouldn't suffer from a good pumping-out. The doctors even used a stomach pump on Barb to determine if her internal bleeding had stopped.

After I had left for the evening, the doctors brought out a new device from Japan, a camera of which they were very proud. The camera was designed to be inserted down the throat to peer around the stomach to find the source of bleeding. We are familiar with such devices in the United States and with the numbing technique used so that patients don't feel the device going up and down their throats. Barb told me about this experience the next day. The only problem was that the doctors didn't have or didn't use any numbing substance.

When Barb and I boarded the Antonov 28 bound for Kiev the next day, the head of the hospital was several seats ahead of us. We exchanged greetings, and when we landed in Kiev, he and Barb gave each other a thumbs-up since she had survived the trip.

In Kiev, we were not much better off than we had been in L'viv. We had to go to Kiev, however, because one could generally leave Soviet territory only from such capitals. The doctor we met there, however, quickly recognized that Barb's condition exceeded his capabilities and the institution's and recommended that we fly to Geneva. All this took several days. Finally, we boarded a plane for Geneva with a stopover in Vienna. We somehow got the name of a respected doctor in Vienna and elected to debark from the plane there to get Barb to a competent medical examiner without further delay.

After about thirty minutes, a Dr. Ferenczi concluded that based on her story and the blood tests, Barb's problem had to do with her liver. He had her admitted to the eighteenth floor of Austria's main hospital, the Allgemeine Krankenhaus. These good people correctly diagnosed Barb as having sclerosing colingitis, a degenerative liver disease caused by her autoimmune system. (Several years of participating in copious Soviet vodka toasts could not have helped matters.)

Barb wasn't operated on until 2004, eight years later. We were living in Berlin at the time. She had flown to Pittsburgh and went to the Thomas Starzl Transplantation Center at the University of Pittsburgh Medical Center (UPMC) for a routine checkup while I remained in Berlin. Our friend John McLaughlin, the political talk show host, had previously called the US secretary of health and human services, Donna Shalala, on Barb's behalf. She referred Barb to Dr. John Fung, head of organ transplants at UPMC.

The protocol for getting an organ transplant in the United States was in flux at the time. Baseball hero Mickey Mantle had died in 1995 following a liver transplant some months earlier. A controversy developed when people alleged that doctors had shown favoritism to Mantle because of his fame and had moved him to the head of the waiting list for an immediate transplant. Thus, when Barb checked in at UPMC in 1997, she was placed in line and had to wait until she was judged the sickest person in the Pittsburgh region before receiving a liver transplant. In February 2004, after she had experienced a moderate but steady decline in her health, imaging technology in Pittsburgh revealed a lesion that proved cancerous, and she shot to the top of the list. (It is possible, if not likely, that Mantle also went to the front of the line because he was desperately ill and that he was not shown undue favoritism.)

I was at work in Berlin and headed immediately for Pittsburgh. While I was on the way, Barb phoned and told me she had met two complete strangers, Annie and Herb Ferguson, who had invited us to live with them. Miraculously, our L'viv partner, Dmytro, had lived with the Fergusons a few years earlier as a Rotary exchange high school student. Because we might have to wait several months for a matching liver, I had decided I would thank Herb and Annie profusely but decline their generous offer to live with them. When I stepped out of the cab at Herb's house, however, he immediately launched into his speech. "We have an apartment downstairs where you and Barb will be on your own," he said. "We will hook you up to our Internet. You can come and go as you wish, but stay as long as you like. Full stop!" We did precisely as instructed.

Herb had just retired as head photographer for the University of Pittsburgh. He showed us the surprisingly large array of magnificent sights around Pittsburgh. We lived comfortably with Herb and Annie from mid-February until shortly after Barb's transplant operation on April 15, 2004.

During the two-month waiting period, which seemed much longer, the hospital called us four times to come in for an operation that didn't occur. Each time, Barb was prepped for the operation and was wheeled into a preop room where she was told that for one reason or another she would not get the liver and that she could get dressed and go home. The stress was palpable as we kept our mobile phone charged and always at hand to receive the next call to report to the hospital.

Donated livers come from people who have indicated on their driver's licenses or other documents that should they die, they wish to donate their bodies to medicine. When UPMC received word from a regional medical facility that it had a liver available for transplant, a UPMC surgeon would be dispatched to remove the transplantable organs from the cadaver, pack them in ice, and bring them back to UPMC. The organs would be usable for about eighteen hours, so time was always of the essence.

When we raced to the hospital after receiving the first alert, the surgeon in charge declared the liver "too fatty, unfit for a transplant." After the second alert, Barb was told that someone in intensive care needed a new liver immediately or he would die. At the third opportunity, the surgeon declared the liver had been damaged when it was removed from the donor. Neither Barb nor I can recall the reason for the fourth false alarm.

The fifth call was the charm. Early on a Sunday morning, Barb went into the operating room and was there for about fourteen hours. A huge advantage that UPMC has over other liver transplant sites in the United States is the large number of professionals who can form teams of doctors, nurses, anesthesiologists, and so on and who can remain on their feet for such a long time. (Except for the two chief surgeons, others could leave at the end of a shift.) At the time, UPMC performed two hundred liver transplants a year. When we lived in the UPMC Family House to which Barb was discharged seven days after her operation, we met people waiting for combinations of organs like an esophagus and a stomach or a small intestine and a pancreas. Our fellow guests included the sickest people in the world. Barb received her new liver at what is arguably the best institution anywhere for such a procedure. We were lucky.

Ukraine will not have a health system capable of such miracles at any time in the foreseeable future. Ukrainians who can afford it will go to France or Germany for such care; those who can't will die prematurely. I hope the US system will be maintained and will continue to improve on the amazing capabilities we enjoy today.

13

"Za Ruth Lundin!"

During the fifth and final round of the Russian sauna routine, an ice-cold swim followed by vodka and hors d'oeuvres, the deputy mayor of Volgograd (formerly Stalingrad and before that, also Volgograd) raised his glass in a toast to Ruth Lundin. She was the IESC's regional director for volunteer assistance along the Volga River. When men toast a woman in such a situation, it is the last and most important toast, and the men must stand, which Victor Tchelistchev, the IESC's country director[13] for Russia, and I and a half-dozen Volgograd officials did. Also, in accordance with Russian sauna tradition, all eight of us were stark naked.

The tribute to Ruth took place while she remained with our other

---

[13] In the IESC's jargon, a director oversaw an office that covered a specific area, often an entire country. We had six offices in Russia, given its importance and large geographical size. Such an office was responsible for writing consulting proposals mainly for local businesses and occasionally for a government client. The director also oversaw all matters related to clients' acceptance of consultants suggested by the IESC, handling travel and lodging and providing reports on the results of their work. In Moscow, the nation's capital, the director of that office, known as a country director, had additional responsibilities for providing consolidated reports to the USAID office in that city.

IESC colleagues at a three-day workshop involving all of the IESC's offices in the former Soviet states. Only Victor and I had been invited to join this male-chauvinist contingent.

Ruth had been an engineer in Oklahoma before coming to work as regional director for the IESC in Volgograd. Ruth, who spoke with a southern drawl, was fluent in Russian, a more-than-desirable qualification for managing the IESC volunteer program in that part of the world. Ruth did so well in this capacity that Volgograd's top officials soon worshiped her, as the toast made clear.

As head of the IESC's program for the former Soviet Union in 1994, I decided to invite the managers and the deputies of our sixteen offices in the former Soviet republics to Volgograd for a three-day conference. What's more, I wanted to hold this meeting in the dead of winter, in February, so that we could better appreciate what conditions must have been like during the Battle of Stalingrad in World War II.

Beginning with a German offensive to take the city on September 3, 1942, this monumental battle lasted for 152 days, ending with the surrender of the German Sixth Army on February 2, 1943. This army, led by the highly respected Wehrmacht general Friedrich Paulus, fought its way into the center of the city and beyond, only to be brought to a standstill and eventually surrounded.[14]

The Sixth Army had no chance of survival by December 1942. Hitler ordered Paulus not to surrender, and he had obeyed well beyond the measured duties of an honorable soldier. Hitler intended that what remained of the Sixth Army would all die fighting or commit suicide.

---

[14] The Battle of Stalingrad is generally viewed as the turning point of the war in the East. The Germans launched one more major offensive near the town of Kursk on the Russian-Ukrainian border the following July. The Battle of Kursk was the largest armored battle in the history of warfare, involving an estimated three million soldiers, six thousand tanks, and almost as many aircraft on both sides. After Kursk, where they were badly defeated, the Germans never again went on an important offensive in the East. They retreated steadily for nearly two years until the war in Europe ended on May 8, 1945.

To encourage this grisly end, he had promoted Paulus to the highest military rank, field marshal, telling Paulus that surely he would not wish to be the first Wehrmacht field marshal in history to surrender. In the end, Paulus did surrender, famously declaring, "I have no intention of shooting myself for this Bohemian corporal."

The top floor of our hotel for the IESC conference looked down on the frozen Volga, and we could see paths across the ice on which people commuted and traded.

We visited the Vladimir Military Museum, dedicated to the Battle of Stalingrad. It was unusual for a Soviet military museum in that its account of the war was extremely well presented and was not loaded with the usual Soviet propaganda. The museum tallied the number of killed, injured, or captured at three hundred thousand for the Germans (only six thousand of the original three hundred thousand crack troops made it back to Germany) and an astounding 1.3 million killed on the Soviet side. No matter the correct number, the Battle of Stalingrad was arguably the costliest in human history, a multiple of the number of US casualties during the entirety of World War II on both fronts.

Here we were again in the Soviet Union where stunning atrocities had been routine, a part of everyday life. All that was now in the past, rarely discussed, but ever present in our minds by way of contrast with our simpler life at that time.

The sauna to which Victor and I had been invited was nearing its end with the final toast of the evening. The five rounds of vodka had taken a toll on our sensibilities. We were all in a highly congenial state when the deputy mayor raised his glass and bellowed hoarsely, "Za Ruth Lundin!" With that, all of us stood up in one motion around the perineum-high table, revealing a cornucopia of male genitalia at the table's rim. When we described this scene to her later that evening, Ruth was so proud.

Koba and Nancy

At the IESC Volgograd/Stalingrad conference in February 1993: Koba Arabuli
was the IESC's country director in Tbilisi, Georgia. Koba was a Georgian patriot
and a descendant of the ancient Hefsur tribe (one of more than forty tribes
in Georgia) that protected the king, much like the US Secret Service protects
the president. Koba had worked for Edouard Shevardnadze, then Soviet foreign
minister and a favorite of US Secretary of State James Baker. Next to Koba is
Nancy Lindborg, the IESC's country director in Almaty, Kazakhstan. Nancy left
the IESC to join the Mercy Corps where she rose to its presidency. She was later
named USAID's assistant administrator with a $12 billion budget for the Bureau
for Democracy, Conflict, and Humanitarian Assistance. Today she is president of
the Washington, DC–based United States Institute for Peace, which describes itself
as an "independent, nonpartisan institution established and funded by Congress to
increase the nation's capacity to manage international conflict without violence."
(Photo by author)

IESC's young tigers

The IESC's main resource, as far as the outside world was concerned, was its skills bank of some twelve thousand retired American experts and executives eager to volunteer their time in developing regions of the world. Behind the scenes, however, were regional and country directors, American and indigenous managers who worked for a salary, as well as a crew of recent college graduates who worked in the Stamford, Connecticut, office to help nail down projects, aid in the selection of volunteers, and steer the process from the selling of a project through health, travel, and living issues, to follow-up reports. These were some of the brightest, hardest-working people I ever had the pleasure of working with. Their future careers reflected their competence as they moved into important careers with the World Bank, the International Monetary Fund, the International Finance Corporation, and the US government, especially the US Agency for International Development. (Photo by author)

IESC's Christa

I was fortunate to have great partners at various stages in life. In 1966, Russ White came to work at RSA six months after we opened our doors, and we built a successful business in ten years, a business (and partnership) that I left to work in government. In 1982, Don Regan at the Treasury Department gave me the freedom and support to build a new office in the department. Christa Capazzola was already at the IESC when I arrived there as her boss in 1992. In the next three years, the two of us built the IESC assistance program for the former Soviet republics from zero to $12 million a year. I phoned Christa one Sunday evening and asked if she could fly to Vladivostok the next day, a grueling trip halfway around the world. Christa thrived on such missions. Her bag was always packed, and off she went to face massive challenges throughout the former USSR. She has since held senior positions at USAID and the Office of Management and Budget; as of this writing she is chief financial officer of the US Centers for Disease Control in Atlanta. (Photo by author)

Ruth Lundin

Ruth Lundin speaking at the IESC's February 1993 conference in Volgograd (formerly Stalingrad), Russia. Ruth spoke fluent Russian with an Oklahoma-southern accent. As the IESC's regional director based in Volgograd, she did much to teach and to bring market economics to that region. (Photo by author)

IESC's leaders under Lenin

We often found ourselves preaching the gospel of free markets, democracy, and private enterprise beneath pictures of Lenin or Marx. This image of Lenin is part of the wall, a mosaic of different-colored wood forming Lenin's visage. This meeting took place in Volgograd, formerly Stalingrad, in the dead of winter. From left to right: Bruce Worcester, the IESC's country director for Ukraine; Andrew Wolfe, the IESC's Russian-fluent project leader for Russia, based in the United States; the author, the IESC's vice president for the newly independent states of the former USSR; Larry Michel, a retired investment banker and chief recruiter for the defense conversion effort, based in Stamford, Connecticut; Victor Tchelistchev, the IESC's country director for Russia, based in Moscow, who was of Russian extraction and had been an executive with Kaiser Permanente; and Ruth Lundin, the IESC's country director for southern Russia, based in Volgograd. (Photo by author)

Connecticut governor Lowell Weicker (center) met with Kay Maxwell (far left), the IESC's vice president for public administration, and her two guests from Kyrgyzstan in 1993. Standing behind the governor is the state's attorney general, Eunice Groark. (Photo by author)

14

From a Remote Corner of Turkmenistan

"Gaspadin Shriver, Gaspadin Shriver," said a voice in Russian. It was still dark, and I had been asleep. I dressed quickly and met our host, Mr. Durdaev, who beckoned me outside where the first lamb of the day had just been slaughtered. He picked up what looked like a mason jar, which was filled with the lamb's blood, and headed in my direction. I wondered whether I would be expected to participate in some strange ritual. I had not heard about this cultural practice. Would I be asked to drink the blood?

The previous night we had seen the lights of Iran a few miles to the south as Barb and I headed through the city of Mary past the town of Serahs to the residential compound of our hosts, the Durdaev family. We stopped about fifteen miles short of Afghanistan, possibly as far as we'd ever been from civilization. Though Turkmenistan was poor, we were traveling in the Mercedes limousine belonging to Shiiki Durdaev, the CEO of the Durdaev conglomerate.

Shiiki and his younger brother, Djumamurad, had invited us to Turkmenistan from our home in L'viv, Ukraine, for a week of discussions on how we might work together to attract capital to worthwhile projects in their country—no small task in a nation with four million very poor people and one-fifth of the world's natural gas reserves.

Turkmenistan has twenty-four trillion cubic meters of natural gas reserves, twelve times the reserves of Norway. The two countries have almost exactly the same population, but although all Norwegians share in the natural gas bounty and live in comparative wealth, the 5.2 million Turkmenis, with the exception of a privileged few, live at subsistence levels. This is the result of rule by a dynastic and autocratic family on the one hand and of Russian control over Turkmenistan's exports on the other.

In that regard, Turkmenistan was little different from virtually all the tribal countries among the Soviet Union's former Central Asian republics. When the Soviet Union collapsed, the six republics making up Turkic Soviet-Central Asia (Azerbaijan, Uzbekistan, Tajikistan, Kazakhstan, and Kyrgyzstan in addition to Turkmenistan) found themselves living under tribal leaders self-appointed for life despite a façade of normal elections. In 1991 the Turkmeni leaders understood that although they had riches they were located in the midst of some of the most volatile and hostile nations in the world including Afghanistan, Iran, Iraq, and Russia; someday, one of these neighbors might wish to have Turkmenistan's gas for itself. Consequently, Turkmenistan officially declared itself to be a neutral country along with Switzerland and Sweden.

We pulled into the Durdaev homestead and met father and mother Durdaev, devout Muslims, both of whom had made the hajj from Mecca to Medina. We also met their three daughters, all in their late teens or early twenties. We were led into the great living room. The floor was covered from wall to wall with dozens of overlapping carpets. Visitors dropped by throughout the evening, some with musical instruments, which they played while singing Turkmeni songs.

During the conversation, Barb mentioned how she had hurt her ankle earlier; mother Durdaev massaged Barb's ankle, and the pain (and a headache to boot) soon went away. As a welcoming gift, father Durdaev had given me a small Turkmeni carpet. Workers had spent a week making this in his factory with my name woven into it in Russian. These were a gentle, warm, and generous people who, with some adjustments for cultural differences, were as welcoming as Texans.

We spoke at length with the Durdaev daughters, all three of whom spoke English. On the surface, they had many of the same interests as young women everywhere, such as cosmetics and clothes. They all wore burkas, but a copy of *Vogue* that we had brought for them was like pure gold. After superficial similarities, however, the comparison ended abruptly. We asked one what she thought about her future. She said that her dream had been to study to become a secretary but that her parents would never allow it. She said her other sisters also wanted to go to school as their brothers had done, but it wasn't going to happen.

Barb and I wondered briefly if we could adopt them all (or at least one) and bring them back to the land of opportunity for such people.

Shiiki and Djumamurad told us that they did not believe in the Muslim religion all that much but that they went along with it when in the family compound in Serahs so as not to displease their parents. Shiiki, who lived with his wife and children in Turkmenistan's capital, Ashgabat, was one of the most natural leaders I had ever met. Everything he suggested was possible and exciting—but mainly when he said it.

Shiiki's wife was a Ukrainian Christian from Moldova and was not encumbered by the restrictive traditions of Islam. In our view, their children were destined for a much brighter future than the Durdaev girls in far-off Serahs.

Father had now almost reached me with the jar of sheep's blood. I had decided to drink if asked. Instead, to my relief, he dipped his finger in the blood and placed his finger on my forehead, leaving a red spot. Only men are so honored. Mother was unable to wake Djumamurad, so she placed a fingerprint of blood on his forehead while he slept.

On the business side of our trip, we had made great plans during the week to change the world of the Turkmenis for the better. Then Barb and I returned to Ukraine. One week later, we received a fax from Turkmenistan, saying, "Shiiki and wife, and two of their three children killed in a single vehicle auto crash. Cyril (third child) in a coma." The word *single* was emphasized because a popular form of assassination in that part of the world in those days was a head-on collision between the target's car and a heavy truck. The driver of the truck always survived, though the truck was expendable. The cost of such an assassination: about $5,000.

I phoned Djumamurad immediately. There was no answer and no e-mail contact in the next few months. He disappeared. Perhaps he could not function without his brother. We think often of this family that we came to love, while I continue to wonder if the death was really the result of a single-car accident. In some parts of the world, it's dangerous to try to do something good.

Author with the Durdaev family, Djumamurad, and his mother and father

Djumamurad Durdaev and I with his mother and father. The Durdaev family was among the wealthiest in Turkmenistan, his father having been head of a *kolkhoz*, or Soviet collective farm, which had its own asphalt plant and rug factory and six thousand sheep. After the Soviet Union collapsed, little changed for Mr. Durdaev since he was a net producer of income and did not depend on government subsidies. He simply continued unchallenged as leader of the kolkhoz. This situation appeared to be the case throughout much of Central Asia. In the rural plains of Kazakhstan, a dozen of us foreigners were welcomed into the huge yurt of the head of the kolkhoz where we all slept with our feet pointed toward the center like spokes in a wheel. Our host, Kazak, very publicly offered his wife to me for the evening in exchange for my wife, Barb. My escape route was tricky. (Photo by author)

Author and Susan Johnson, Hon. Rosa Atumbaeva,
and Hon. Wm. Nickerson

Rosa Atumbaeva, third from the right, was minister of foreign affairs in Kyrgyzstan when the IESC conducted a week of public administration seminars and lectures. To her right is Susan Johnson, a US Foreign Service officer on leave of absence while her husband, a Pakistani, served as Pakistan's ambassador to Kazakhstan. Susan was the IESC's principal representative in Central Asia and had developed good relations within Kyrgyzstan. Bill Nickerson, to the right, a Connecticut state senator representing Greenwich, came to Kyrgyzstan's capital, Bishkek, as an IESC volunteer. Rosa Atumbaeva was briefly president of Kyrgyzstan during a period of political instability. She was a good friend of the United States, an anti-Soviet, and possibly helped the United States with logistical support during our war in Afghanistan. She taught me much about Kyrgyzstan's role in training Muslim terrorists during Soviet times. Susan Johnson is today president of the US Foreign Service Association. (Photo by author)

15

Hoshovsky Knew Solsky

Culture matters! If any proof was needed, when Barb and I were in Moscow on business in the midnineties, a Russian American hotel venture there came to an end. The American partner in the Radisson-Slavanskaya Hotel, Paul Tatum, felt he was being cheated by his Russian partners, who included the mayor of Moscow. Tatum did the American thing: he sued the Russians. His Russian partners did the Russian thing: in the center of the city in the late afternoon sun, they shot him dead.

A good deed years ago resulted in my owning a small percentage of a gigantic, decrepit, obsolete, bankrupt Soviet-style nineteenth-century factory in eastern Ukraine that somehow produced marketable (in the USSR) food processing equipment. This included large machines such as shipboard fishmeal processors, food driers, bakery ovens, pancake cooking and filling machines, and an array of stainless-steel vessels for the wine and chemical industries. There was also the never-ending make-work project of machining brake shoes for the Ukrainian railroad. My ownership came about when I helped a US consortium buy the plant.

John, the senior US partner in this venture, had dropped into our office in L'viv in western Ukraine in 1996 where we met for the first time.

He and his two American partners hoped to buy a factory through the Ukrainian government's privatization process. John planned to show that simply by using American ingenuity, experience, know-how, and e-mail, he could turn around one of these monstrous products of communism.

The factory was in Nezhin, Ukraine, a backwater on the northern steppes of eastern Ukraine near Poltava where Sweden's Charles XII met his nemesis, Peter the Great. Nezhin is also close to where World War II turned west toward Berlin following the greatest armored battle in history centered around the Russian city of Kursk. Nezhin itself is famous only for the author Nikolai Gogol, who was educated there and wrote one of literature's best short stories, *The Overcoat*—a classic Russian tale about a poor man who saved up for years to buy a new coat, bought it, instantly had it stolen, got sick, and died.

The Nezhin plant had survived the Soviet style of producing machines in accordance with demand as calculated by Soviet bureaucrats in Moscow. These bureaucrats would then send the necessary funds to buy materials and to pay workers to meet the phony demand. The cost of labor, materials, and utilities was close to zero, so sales revenue meant nothing, and of course neither did profits.

The only skill needed by a Soviet plant manager was the ability to extract the maximum amount of money (revenue) from Moscow.

Following the collapse of the Soviet Union in late 1991, the money from Moscow dried up. Plants suddenly had to seek orders by marketing and sales, and Soviet accounting rules did not allow charts of account for the key expenditures involved in these tasks.

As we American partners in the Nezhin venture grew older and frailer, we sought a buyer for the plant. After rejecting one dubious offer after another (generally involving payment in Ukrainian currency, or hryvnya, a pariah in international monetary affairs rivaling the Brazilian cruzeiro or Thai bhat at their worst), we finally settled on this stipulation: the buyer had to deposit the purchase price, in US dollars, in our Florida bank account.

This was no small matter for potential Ukrainian and Russian buyers. How could they be sure we would sign over to them the ownership once they deposited the money? Escrow accounts and other Western mechanisms for such contracts were unknown to them.

We needed a lawyer who could span the two different legal cultures.

About that time, Barb and I attended a gathering of Ukrainians in New York City and saw some old friends including Serhiy Hoshovsky, a lawyer from L'viv, the city where we had lived for seven years. Since we had last met, Serhiy had emigrated to the United States and, in addition to his Ukrainian law degree, had added a US law degree. Yes, he would be happy to help us sell our plant.

To do the deal-making in Ukraine, we also retained Dmytro Symovonyk, my former partner in the merger-and-acquisition business in L'viv, who had become an expert in helping decent Ukrainian companies go public on the Warsaw (Poland) stock exchange.

The team of Hoshovsky and Symovonyk could do this job, but deals came and went as obstacles arose whenever one of the parties had to trust the other, even if only for a few seconds, waiting for an international payment to clear.

One day Dmytro sent a cheery e-mail to us saying he had found another potential buyer, a Mr. Solsky. Serhiy went ballistic and threatened to quit.

Serhiy had gone to school with Solsky. Solsky was *his* friend. If anyone should get a fee for finding Solsky, it was he, Hoshovsky, not Symovonyk. I went to New York City to calm Hoshovsky with an offer of a generous finder's fee in addition to all the other fees he would be earning.

After Hoshovsky came down from the rafters, we suddenly had trust on both sides of the transaction. What were the odds? We might still own that old rust bucket (the salability of which dropped to zero after Russia invaded Crimea and southeastern Ukraine in 2014) if Hoshovsky had not known Solsky.

16

━━━━◦•◦━━━━

Razz Putin

February 2014

When Bohdan Khmelnitsky, the first leader of an independent Ukraine, took on the Poles after his family had been brutalized and murdered by a rival Polish prince, he signed a mutual defense treaty with Russia in 1654. The treaty was supposed to expire twenty years later, but Khmelnitsky died in the meantime. The Russians overlooked the expiration date, an act of political deception that has characterized Russia's dismissive and condescending attitude toward Ukraine to the present day.

Russia's current president, Vladimir Putin, Russia's state-controlled media, and the undiscerning, condescending, superficial coverage of Ukraine by European and US media all feed off the same false narratives about Ukraine. We are fed mostly modern-day agitprop originating within Russia's Ministry of Foreign Affairs.

As an example, Russia maintains that Ukraine is divided down the middle along the Dnieper River into western Ukraine, which is Ukrainian-speaking and EU/US-leaning, and eastern Ukraine, which is Russian-speaking and Moscow-leaning. Eastern Ukrainians do speak

Russian as their first language, but they were also at the barricades in Kiev in February 2014, loyal to Ukraine. Some of them were wounded demonstrating against the Russian-leaning government of Viktor Yanukovich, who was then Ukraine's president.

Second, Putin and the media have tried to cast the protesters as radicals—that is, a minority. Many of these protesters are our friends from the eight years we lived in Ukraine, first in the capital city of Kiev at Ukraine's center and then in L'viv, the main city of western Ukraine. The Ukrainian protesters are, for the most part, decent, ordinary people who, like Americans of old, may now be ready to confront any danger to attain freedom.

Not all anti-Russian protesters were ordinary Ukrainians, though. Some were prisoners and killers released by the government, which provided them with funds, weapons, and drugs to infiltrate the protesters and to do with them what they pleased. Not all police fighting the protesters were Ukrainian. Some police, captured by the protesters, were wearing Russian badges. President Yanukovich was finished the moment the first Ukrainian protester was killed by the police.

The US ambassador to Ukraine, Geoffrey Pyatt, appears to have done what we could only dream a US ambassador would do in such a situation. In an extraordinary and courageous act, he joined the protesters in the streets, ostensibly directing traffic but clearly interfering in Yanukovich's internal affairs.

Otherwise, US foreign policy has been handicapped by previous displays of weakness and pandering toward Putin. The Russian leader is allied with our enemies, Iran and Syria's president Assad, and is anti-Israel. If this was not enough, at a time when a US-EU coalition for regime change in Ukraine could have been so powerful, we saw Poland, Germany, and France going to Kiev on their own minus the United States. Could it be that the United States was not invited because President Obama, with prodding by Putin, unilaterally decided not to construct the US missile defense complex in Poland? Or that the

Obama government, with scant apology, was caught listening to German chancellor Angela Merkel's private cell phone?

In the middle of the chaos, the Ukrainian parliament voted to release former prime minister Yulia Tymoshenko from prison. This was a transparent case of Yanukovich imprisoning a powerful political opponent. Tymoshenko was imprisoned for doing what government officials do every day all over the world. She signed an international trade deal (in this case, an energy deal with Russia) that was controversial. I met Tymoshenko twice during the late 1990s, once when she was head of Ukraine's parliamentary tax committee and a year later when she was deputy prime minister for fossil fuels. If Tymoshenko, no Joan of Arc, regains her position as one of Ukraine's most popular political figures, she is unlikely to forget how she was treated by her political opponents.

Assuming Ukraine's protest movement results in a renewed effort to establish a fairly elected democratic government, foreign assistance will be required more than ever. But Ukraine will need much more than financial assistance. Ukraine will also need know-how to end the endemic corruption in almost every facet of the public sector, from health and education to laws and the court system. The systemically weak Ukrainian currency (the hryvnya) will need propping up with many billions of dollars from international financial institutions, a tough sell under the best of circumstances. This was true in 2014; it will be the case for at least some years to come.

I was startled during the opening ceremonies of the 2014 Winter Olympics at Sochi: Russia memorialized its great figures from the past such as Dostoyevsky, Pasternak, Nabokov, Solzhenitsyn, and Igor Sikorsky. But Sikorsky was born in Kiev. He was Ukrainian. He despised the Soviet Union, the communists, and communism. He did much early work in Russia during the reign of the last czar, Nicholas II, but he despised the Bolsheviks. His company, Sikorsky Aircraft in Stratford, Connecticut, symbolizes his greatest accomplishments in aviation. He received several invitations from Moscow to receive awards, almost certainly the coveted Order of Lenin among them. Despite the lure of such honors, he never set foot in communist Russia or the Soviet Union. If Sikorsky, who died in Connecticut in 1976, could witness Putin's revanchist attempt to take over Ukraine today, he would counter-rotate in his grave.

17

Hans Jalasto: How to Redistribute Wealth—from the Bottom Up

1991, Just Weeks before the Soviet Union's Collapse

The late Hans Jalasto was one of Estonia's top economists, if not *the* top economist. He was also one of the closer friends in Estonia my CIME partner Russ Deane and I had in 1990–91. Hans was also a world-class sailor and was in charge of the 1980 Olympics sailing regatta that took place in Tallinn, Estonia's capital city. These were the Olympic Games that President Carter had ordered the US team to boycott in response to the Soviet invasion of Afghanistan.

Russ and I were sailors, and Hans had somehow borrowed a nearly new thirty-five-foot fiberglass sloop with sleeping accommodations, a head, and a kitchenette. We had a delightful day sailing out into the waters of the Baltic Sea with a few Soviet PT boats following us out of curiosity.

When we returned to the dock and went to dinner, Russ asked Hans how much one of those boats cost. Hans said the boats were made in Tallinn, he knew the manager of the boat plant well, and he would ask. The next day, Hans reported that after converting rubles into dollars, he had determined that the sale price of the boat was $3,000. This would have been about three years of salary for Hans, providing him and his family just enough to live on.

Russ and I looked at each other and said at almost the same instant, "Hans, how would you like to own a boat?" Russ and I would put up $1,500 each, or three thousand total, and Hans would then buy the boat and maintain it in Tallinn. From time to time, perhaps Russ and I could visit and take a sail into the Baltic. What mattered most, however, was that one of Estonia's great sailors would finally have a boat of his own. By evening, the boat had a name. It was a combination of the names of Hans's two granddaughters, the *Tiki-Marie*. We were all a bit giddy with anticipation.

Hans's salary was probably $1,000 per year, more or less average throughout the Soviet Union. As an official in the Estonian Communist Party, he may have made a bit more, however. Communist leaders in Russia did better than communist leaders from other republics, and communists did better than noncommunists, especially when it came to the perquisites of being a member of the Communist Party. A dacha for noncommunists might be a small garden plot among hundreds of other garden plots, perhaps with a toolshed. A low-level member of the party might get a larger piece of land with a lawn and a weekend cottage. A top party official in Moscow, however, was entitled to a two-story, Western-style brick home, or a duplex, for year-round living in a gated community in a park alongside a river, beyond the view of the proletariat. Their apartments in the city, however, were quite ordinary. In order not to stand out, they were complete with broken toilets.

The next day, Hans went to see the manager of the boat factory and made our offer. The plant manager exclaimed, "Hans, these boats aren't for sale to Estonians! They are all sold to Russians back in St. Petersburg." The manager didn't have to say that many of those boats were then resold throughout Scandinavia for $35,000 or more, with privileged Russian communists pocketing the difference.

At that precise moment, Estonia's top economist suddenly realized how he and his fellow Estonians had been duped by the Russians, how top party officials from Russia made millions from the Soviet Union's 270 million slaves.

Few people realize the extent to which an all-encompassing government, controlling virtually every facet of daily economic life, gravitates inevitably toward endemic official corruption, gathering steam as one nears the top. Twenty million Soviet citizens were members of the Communist Party. Hans was one of those, but he was not Russian. As a member of the Estonian Communist Party, he was slighty privileged, whereas his Russian counterparts who were also members of the Communist Party enjoyed giant perquisites never even seen by those in the lesser republics. Perquisites included exclusive and expensive dachas, air travel, foreign vacations, and profits from international trade deals. While communism preached equality, the only place equality existed was with the 270 million mostly law-abiding, nonparty people at the very bottom of the economic ladder. If they were well educated, they were able to earn $1,000 a year.

Lennart Meri,
President of Estonia, 1992 - 2001

Lennart Meri, president of Estonia from 1992 to 2001, was the most successful leader of any former Soviet republic transitioning from communism. He was also one of the more charismatic. He was educated in France and elsewhere during the thirties and spoke six languages fluently. He was exiled to Siberia in 1941 at age twelve along with many Estonians, Lithuanians, and Latvians. He survived and returned to Estonia after the war; he graduated from Tartu University with a degree in history and languages. A man of the broadest cultural experiences, Meri became an actor, a writer, and a film producer among other occupations. He is credited with the phrase "Traveling is the only passion that doesn't need to feel shy in front of intellect." Recognizing the CIME's work in Estonia, President Meri hosted an official visit to Estonia for Julie Kidd and her family. He also awarded the Order of the White Star to Russ Deane. (Photo courtesy of the Office of the President of Estonia)

18

We Wuz Robbed

On Thanksgiving Day 1999 in L'viv, Ukraine, as one of our Ukrainian friends was stabbing slices of turkey with one hand and holding his side with the other, I asked, "Igor, is something wrong?"

Our mutual friend Roman muttered, "Show him, Igor."

Igor lifted up his shirt so I could see the bullet wound in his stomach. "What happened?" I asked.

Igor explained that three guys had been trying to steal his new Mercedes; he attempted to stop them, so they shot him and fled. We tried to explain to Igor that his life was worth more than his car, but knowing what it took to get the money to buy that car, we were not so sure. Let's say this car cost $60,000. It is next to impossible to save that amount on a $1,000-a-year salary, the norm for honest noncommunists. All the important organizational leaders were communists, and they were the only ones in a position to take bribes or to accept kickbacks. Furthermore, such behavior was expected. The only alternative was to engage in illegal activity or in cross-border trading in the gray market, using small bribes to avoid duties and taxes. Illegal profits were not reported to the tax police (the Soviet IRS). Igor earned his $60,000 through a quasi-legal import-export business, fraught with danger to one's person as well as to one's business.

We were to learn much about crime in that part of the world through personal experience.

In 1995, we were invited by L'viv's governor, Mikola Horyn, to locate the CIME private-sector development office in L'viv in western Ukraine. We felt fortunate to have been permitted to set up our office within the security perimeter of the L'viv Polytechnic Institute, a university of fifteen thousand students. Our office doors had locks, and we had an alarm system connected directly to the nearest police station. The door to the building was locked at night, and there was a fence around the school. There was also a night watchman.

Six months after we had arrived and had hired a staff of four, everything that carried an electron was stolen from our office in the dark of night. The next day we found a hole in the fence. The signal system to the police had been detached by someone with the requisite know-how, the locks on the doors to our building and into our office had been drilled through like hot butter, and the drill was left on the floor. The night watchmen was out cold at his post, a large, empty vodka bottle by his side.

The thieves rang us up, speaking in Russian, not Ukrainian, with our partners. Since the information on our computers was of greater value to us than to anyone else, they reasoned correctly that we would be willing to pay a premium to regain our equipment. There was just one problem: how could we prove to these crooks that they could trust us? They said we could do that by depositing, at precisely three that afternoon, twenty-five dollars in the *R* on the sign for the city's circus (*tsyrk* in Russian). We did as we were told, but they called back and claimed that we had tried to deceive them, that we had brought the police with us. (Fat chance.) We concluded it was impossible to prove to the crooks that they could trust us and declined to play another round.

Barb and I were devastated. We bemoaned our circumstances and cursed the society and the culture into which we had voluntarily inserted ourselves. Our first reaction was "This place is nuts. We could get hurt. We're not smart enough to survive here. Let's quit." Then self-pity shifted to anger toward the government and the thuggery of Ukraine. We lost sight of all the good citizens we had come to know and became surly. No stupid government or gang of thugs was going to push us around. Eventually we calmed down and began anew.

We sought shelter with one of our clients, a building contractor who offered us space in his large house in a dusty suburb near the airport where we joined another tenant.

We were robbed several times in our first eighteen months in Ukraine but not at all during the next five years we lived there. Did Ukraine change, or did we?

The first week we were in L'viv, I bought something at a local flea market and stupidly left my wallet momentarily on the counter. I quickly turned back to retrieve it, but it was gone. The blank stare on the face of the young man at the counter said it all. I asked him for my wallet, but in this case, it was easy for him to play dumb. I was the real dummy.

Another time Barb had just picked up a large sum of cash. Someone was watching, however, and her pocket was easily picked at the first opportunity.

In a third instance, we were on the subway in Kiev, and in the space of one subway stop, Barb's briefcase was slit with a razor-sharp instrument and money lifted from the inside.

On one trip back to the United States, we were advised that the plane from L'viv to Warsaw would not fly because of bad weather and that we should take the night bus to Warsaw. The bus tickets cost just eight dollars apiece. We were the only non-Ukrainians on board. Almost everyone was going to Warsaw to buy things they couldn't get in Ukraine, so they had brought money.

Around two in the morning, in the dead of night, we were well into

Poland when the bus stopped in the middle of nowhere and the driver got out. Three Russian-speaking men in black-leather jackets got in, armed with what looked like wooden-handled Stechkin 9 mm pistols. They noisily cocked and recocked their guns as they walked through the bus saying, "Deklaratzie, deklaratzie"—in other words, "Show us how much money you're bringing in."

This was no official stop. Passengers were paying the bandits a kind of tax, an arbitrary portion of their money. Our driver was clearly in on this heist. As the thugs approached us, pistols snapping into the cocked position and aimed at Barb's side as she tried to shrink into the seat, I hastily stuffed as much US currency into my socks as I could. The thought crossed my mind that once they saw our American passports, they might single us out, march us off the bus, and shoot us. As it happened, they robbed only the poor Ukrainians.

On another occasion, we arrived from L'viv early one morning at the train station in Budapest. We were storing our luggage in the do-it-yourself lockers when a Hungarian man pointed excitedly at the train arrival/departure board. As we looked where he was pointing, from the corner of her eye, Barb spotted our computer case heading out of the large room in the hands of an accomplice. She shouted. Suddenly we were both hollering and running around like crazy, and one of the thieves dropped the computer case as both men fled.[15]

Following the break-in at L'viv Polytechnic, our new landlord sent an unmarked military van to carry our desks and chairs to his building near the airport. Our new office was surrounded by a metal fence, and a trained attack dog inside the compound was on constant alert.

---

[15] Eastern Europe certainly has no monopoly on thievery. During the three years I worked for Chase Manhattan Bank in New York City, traveling downtown by bus in the morning and returning by subway in the evening, I saw many acts of kindness and no hostile act of any kind; on the other hand, almost every woman I knew in my department had been mugged or had had her necklace ripped off. In one case, a woman had been beaten up badly.

During the first few days we worked there, we noticed that the other tenant was often visited during the day by tough-looking, well-built young men carrying thick black-leather purses. They also carried pistols that they laid on the mantel while shooting pool in the basement. I asked our senior Ukrainian partner Lubov if she could find out who our cotenant was. The next day a chill ran down my spine as she said, "The head of the L'viv mafia." But the chill subsided as I thought to myself, *Safe at last.*

19

Irina

Larry emerged from his office and entered mine, closing the door behind him. "This isn't going so well," he said, referring to the fact that he was expelling Irina for plagiarism. She was from Vynnitsya, Ukraine. I had known what was going on and recalled having spoken about our failure as a school to impress upon students, especially those from Eastern Europe and the former Soviet republics, that we had zero tolerance for plagiarism.

There was no doubt that Irina had plagiarized. Whether the faculty and the administration had done enough to define plagiarism to such a diverse group, or to stress the seriousness of plagiarism, was very much in doubt. Larry asked if I could join him in his discussion with Irina.

The school was the European College of Liberal Arts (ECLA) in East Berlin, which offered a summer program and a two-year curriculum of interdisciplinary studies in history, literature, political theory, and philosophy at the college level. Larry had joined the ECLA as head of the college in the fall of 2003. He had had extensive experience in positions of senior academic and administrative leadership, having been acting president of Washington and Lee College. I was provost of the ECLA (now called Bard College Berlin). Once Larry was there full time, I kept my nose out of academic affairs—until he invited me to join him with Irina.

Being from Vinnytsia, Ukraine, was itself an issue.

During Stalin's Great Purge of 1936 to 1938, Ukraine was a special target for assassinations among various ethnic and religious groups but particularly of the communist leaders. About ten thousand residents of Vinnytsia wound up in a mass grave uncovered by the German Wehrmacht in its 1942–43 drive toward the east.

Vinnytsia suffered even more under the Germans. This was the location of Hitler's easternmost bunker, a deep labyrinth of tunnels, offices, and command-and-control centers. The bunker was built by some thirty thousand Ukrainian prisoners of the Germans. Twenty-eight thousand of those Ukrainians were shot and killed to protect the secrets of the bunker. In 1991, I visited what remained of Hitler's bunker and the mass graves and memorials surrounding the town. It was a sad place indeed, and I could not imagine what it must have been like to have been born and raised there.

For Irina, the problem was not her plagiarism but the disgrace of going home after being expelled. Plagiarism was encouraged, if not completely overlooked, in Soviet education. In the early nineties, everything in education was for sale. A friend from Karkhov, Ukraine, once described a conversation in that city between a parent and his child's teacher. The parent had come to see the teacher about his son's bad grades. The father placed a twenty-dollar bill on the teacher's desk. The teacher responded, "That's a very poor grade." The man put down another twenty dollars. (The currency that worked was dollars, not the local currency.) "That's a fair grade." Another twenty. "That's not bad." Another twenty. "That's a good grade." One more twenty. "That's excellent!"

Corruption flourished in the education systems of the former Soviet republics. The head of a large university who officially earned $5,000 a year might take home $1 million, unreported and therefore untaxed. This was the sum of the university rector's share of hundreds of small bribes for admission into popular departments, for good grades, for graduation, and even for acceptance of PhD dissertations forged by other professors for a few thousand dollars. (Rectors were, in effect, college presidents.) Many of these dissertations were direct copies of dissertations residing in Russian universities for which there was no record in Ukraine. Flagrant plagiarism was endemic throughout Ukraine and many of the other former Soviet republics. In the city of L'viv where we lived for seven years, the most corrupt departments at the main university were law (naturally) and medicine (ugh). Larry and I could do nothing to remedy that part of the problem.

For Irina, returning to Vinnytsia after having been expelled—to a culture that looked the other way at parental abuse, to a region (the former Soviet Union) where more than half a million young women had been trafficked into oblivion from 1990 to 1996, to a system that rewarded plagiarism—might well have been terrifying. A US student in the same situation would never experience the same fear.

When Larry and I entered his office, I asked Irina if she would mind leaving us alone for a brief time. After she left, I started to speak but cried for a bit. Once I got myself together, I told Larry that lip service to our students concerning plagiarism was not enough. A paragraph in the student manual was grossly inadequate. A few comments about plagiarism during a meeting with excited students at the beginning of the year didn't even go in one ear, let alone out the other. That was not enough given the cultures from which so many of our students had come.

We needed to hold a special one-hour meeting at the start of the year with plagiarism as the only topic. We had to explain what plagiarism was, how it would be dealt with, and why simply quoting others without attribution wasn't an indication of good research. We had to do our part first, and once we had done that, then we could enforce the rules. In my opinion, we could not expel Irina with a clear conscience.

There was a long pause. Larry then asked, "Should we let Irina stay?"[16]

Note: Fictitious names have been used in various places to protect the innocent.

---

[16] Irina is a fictitious name for the obvious reasons. I see notices about her on social media from time to time. She is a mother and a political activist and appears to be doing extremely well.

Barb Shriver, Elizabeth and Larry Boetsch (President, ECLA), author

Larry Boetsch, former acting president of Washington and Lee University in Lexington, Virginia, was named president of ECLA-Berlin in 2003. He and his wife, Elizabeth, arrived on campus in 1994. (Photo by author)

Florian Hoffmann & Katherin Kirschenmann,
the DO School

Florian Hoffmann (ECLA graduate, Duke University, Oxford) and Katherin Kirschenmann were married on the island of Ibitza. Barb and I attended this once-in-a-lifetime event. The wedding ceremony took place on the edge of a bluff looking straight down hundreds of feet to the Mediterranean. The second-most exciting activity was riding around the island in this Deux Chevaux. (Photo by author)

It's nice to get away from Berlin for a few days after a long, cold winter. Some ECLA students and I organized a one-week bus trip from Berlin to stops in Milan, Pisa, Florence, and Venice. Here some students show their pleasure at arriving at an Italian beach after being cooped up in school in Berlin. The Italy trip became an annual event and part of the college curriculum. (Photo by author)

ECLA students at the Bridge of Sighs, Venice

Six ECLA students at the Bridge of Sighs in Venice on the first Italy trip in March 2003. The tall student in the center is Florian Hoffmann, formerly head of Dekeyser & Friends, who became founder and president of the Do School. This school, which trains social entrepreneurs from around the world, is headquartered in Berlin with campuses in Hamburg and New York City. Eliza Subotowycz, to his left, is a film producer in Poland. Kneeling on the left is Alexandre Nazaru, already a former minister of transportation in Romania. Also kneeling is Dragana Borenovic Djilas, a Serbian student of fine arts, now a wife and a mother, who was moving to Canada. The ECLA arranged an internship for her at the Isabella Stewart Gardner Museum in Boston. (Photo by author)

20

Cable from Kabul

Kabul, 4:00 a.m., August 5, 2002.

It is still night in Kabul with the lights flickering below as I look down on the city from my room at the Intercontinental Hotel. A Turkish quarter-moon hangs over the city, supported, it seems, by Orion reaching up awkwardly from the southeast. As I watch, the mountains of the Hindu Kush are suddenly outlined by the first light of dawn, which has not yet reached down to the city. Three or four mullahs break the silence, rather rudely, it seems to me, with their blatant contradictions: the preachings of feudal fundamentalism promulgated with modern public address systems.

Six of us arrived the day before, on Sunday, as an advance team from a Washington group called the Private Sector Development Task Force for Afghanistan; Ishaq Shahryar, Afghanistan's ambassador to the United States, and I had created this group over lunch months before. As we flew low into the Kabul airport from Dubai aboard a dilapidated Boeing 727 belonging to Afghanistan's Ariana Airlines, we could see mainly brown; we saw the remains of bombed-out buildings, some mud-brick buildings still standing, and then the vast expanse of brown dust covering everything from the plains below up to the mountaintops. Lots of brown. Hundreds of broken airplanes were strewn around the airport from the war of 1996 between Afghanistan's legitimate government and the Taliban.

The plane powered toward the runway at what seemed excessive speed, possibly indicating that the pilot had come in too low. For the first but not the last time that day, I was reminded of a trip I had made to neighboring Iran in 1956 with a group of other newly graduated Cornell students as guests of the shah. We had crash-landed in a DC-3 piloted by an Iranian who overshot the runway at the city of magnificent blue domes, Isfahan.

But I digress. Back to Kabul. The six of us represented several organizations including the Halliburton Division of Kellogg, Brown & Root, the agriculture-focused Citizens Network for Foreign Affairs, the US Geological Survey, and an inveterate Chicago housing developer, Jim Hemphill. Russ Deane and I rounded out the team. Russ, an attorney, had led the CIME's successful legal reform project in Estonia, which started in Tallinn, February 15, 1991, and ran for ten years.

The first four members of our team headed off to meetings at ministries while Russ and I went to meet with Abdul Rahim Karimi, Afghanistan's minister of justice. Two of Afghanistan's ministers had been assassinated earlier in the year, and we noted that the trek up the five flights to the minister's office took us past a guard with a machine gun. As Russ pointed out later, this one was wearing an olive-drab Calvin Klein shirt. We were struck by the dichotomy of the danger and the classiness of the guard's shirt. In an odd way, this scene was reassuring.

The justice minister and his English-speaking deputy minister met us immediately and cordially. We were served multiple cups of hot green tea and large trays of dried fruit and nuts. After a minimum of formalities, we got down to business.

I gave a short preamble on the theme that in order for enough private capital to start coming to Afghanistan to make a noticeable difference in the economy, international investors and business people had to have a favorable perception of the country's legal system—the laws, the courts, and the enforcement mechanisms. If this foundation was built correctly, it would support economic growth in all sectors—and encourage increased delivery and effective use of funding from donor organizations like the United Nations and countries such as the United States. With Ambassador Shahryar, we had also determined that in all areas of our proposed work, which would include commercial law, family law, and so on, the priority would be speed. Afghanistan's government had to show the people as quickly as possible that it was making progress. This was especially important in dealing with the regional leaders, or warlords, who were reluctant to give up their local armies, territories, and taxes to the central government.

Russ then made his proposal. He had read Afghanistan's civil code of 1964, which addressed commercial law, family law, and the court system for enforcement. Few changes had been made due to twenty-three years of war. He had also read the constitution of 1964, which the government was trying to reestablish as the law of the land, with a few provisions tacked on by the postconflict Bonn Accord in December 2001. Russ also referred to other donors, such as Italy, which had committed funds and personnel to help develop a set of world-standard laws for the country. He called this track one, a long effort that would last several years. Russ then recommended track two, to operate in parallel, whereby an interim set of commercial laws could be extracted from the existing civil code, which code he characterized as "not bad." This process would involve perhaps twenty Afghan lawyers working with about ten American and international experts (lawyers, judges, and professors) on matters such as laws of contracts, private property, and obligations. The team would produce a working transitional set of commercial laws within three months. These laws would be consistent with the code to be developed by the track-one team.

After Russ had finished and a new round of tea had been served, the minister spoke. He described the political-religious environment of Afghanistan. He explained how his reform-minded colleagues tried to tell the people how politicians would be elected. The Afghan mullahs had responded by saying God had appointed them as the leaders. Constitutions and laws could change but not the Qur'an— so the mullahs paid no attention to these processes and documents. The minister then went off on what I considered a tangent from our main subject; he said the religious fundamentalists did not believe in human rights laws, the rights of women, or constitutions. I became concerned, especially since we were working through a translator, that Russ's plan had been interpreted to involve far more than commercial law. The translator was also the deputy minister of justice and a British subject and had been careful to make that clear earlier. The minister spent a great deal of time on the difficulties of bringing about constructive change in the feudal environment. "Within Islam," he said, "the people at the top don't want to do anything for their people. We have to move carefully between tradition and reforms." I was seriously discouraged.

Russ had delivered his proposal in fifteen minutes. The minister's response was now approaching forty uninterrupted minutes, and I could feel no convergence with Russ's proposition. When we compared notes later, Russ hadn't either.

We had traveled more than twelve thousand miles, with the rule of law as our number one priority. We had lost four bags in the Paris airport. We had left home in the United States around eight Friday evening and had arrived in Kabul around noon Sunday without sleep or showers. We had been in Afghanistan for only about four hours, and we were plenty tired. Perhaps it would have been better to insist that we rest up and have no meetings before Monday. If this meeting was a failure, there would be little recourse. We might return home with minor gains in the other areas. We knew, however, that the country would inevitably lag behind its potential without the promise of a legal system that met world standards, even to a limited extent. Without a set of simple, clear laws and judicial and enforcement systems that were fair, competent, and swift, the consequences could be disastrous. Without substantial foreign private investment, the resulting slow economic start would lead to civil unrest and possibly the return of the Taliban. We estimated that $25 billion in foreign private capital would be required. This money might never come, but it would absolutely not come without a modern commercial code and independent courts.

The minister's oration was at a very high level from a literary, philosophical, and historical standpoint; we were fortunate in that an Afghan lawyer and British citizen did the translating. The minister wove into his response references to Descartes, Aristotle, Plato, and Khalil Gibran. One of our interlocutors, Hekmat Karzai, a young cousin of the new president, Hamid Karzai, had been educated in the United States and told us later that the minister's monologue had been the most elegant use of Farsi he had ever heard.

We were surprised when the minister wound up his speech by saying, "We wanted all this to fall out of the sky, and now you have given it to us. We give you a green light." He then discussed the nation's problems in the legal sector, noting at one point that "If you could find ten judges out of Afghanistan's four thousand who would not take bribes, it would be a miracle."

The minister closed the meeting by saying that all of us should learn from our mistakes. He added that if Iran were to hold free elections that day (in the fall of 2002), 70 percent of the people would vote for a new shah. In their lifetimes, they had known three systems: totalitarianism, rule by religious fundamentalism, and rule by the shah—and life was best under the shah.

Though plenty of troubles lay ahead for Afghanistan, we signed an agreement with the minister to go to work on legal reforms. Russ and his team were able to put thirteen proposed laws before the parliament, enough to establish a mini-commercial code. The parliament adopted these proposals into law.[17]

---

[17] While we didn't use this terminology, the main thrust of our work in Afghanistan was the much-maligned activity of "nation-building." This label has been earned by the billions of U.S. taxpayer dollars wasted throughout much of the world. If we failed in any of our endeavors, at least the amount of money was small. When we succeeded, on the other hand, the benefits could be huge. The key to success always had, as a common denominator, trust at the level of the individual. Abdullah Abdullah, Afghanistan's minister of foreign affairs, was always our host in Afghanistan, and with him, we had developed that level of mutual trust. His belief in what we were trying to do for his country and what he did behind the scenes to support us, was the key to the modest, perhaps even short-lived, successes we achieved in a country in such a state of chaos and instability.

Abdul Rahim Karimi signing agreement

At no time while we were working in Afghanistan in 2002 did we anticipate another crisis for that country. That was the assumption we needed to make in order to go to work. We heard the occasional bomb going off somewhere, especially at dinner time with Afghan officials. Though everyone heard these explosions, our conversations were never interrupted. If we had anticipated that the United States might allow Afghanistan to become a Muslim country instead of a secular country like Egypt or Turkey, we might not have undertaken the development of a system of laws. In this photo, Afghanistan's minister of justice, Abdul Rahim Karimi, is signing an agreement allowing the Private Sector Development Task Force for Afghanistan to help him and his country develop a modern commercial code and a credible contract enforcement mechanism. The proposal by Russ Deane (who is standing to the minister's right) would encourage badly needed private-sector investment. We estimated Afghanistan would need $20 billion to $30 billion in direct foreign investment. Private investment was essential because Afghanistan did not have the earning power to accept international loans with interest payments, forced payment schedules, and penalties. The country needed to develop an economy capable of defending itself against the Taliban and other regional threats. Unfortunately, Afghanistan fell victim to internal corruption and to strife within the two main American agencies involved in the country's recovery, the State Department and the Defense Department. The task force was a consortium of thirty or so US companies committed to the postwar development of Afghanistan. Ishaq Shahryar, Afghanistan's ambassador to the United States, and I had created it at dinner one evening in April 2002. (Photo by author)

Dick and Abdullah Abdullah and Satellite Radio

Abdullah Abdullah was Afghanistan's minister of foreign affairs from 2001 to 2005 and was our host during our visits to Afghanistan in 2002. He invited our group to his villa high up along the Panjshir River about a two-hour drive from Kabul. I gave him a satellite radio, a gift from the American Satellite Corporation, which agreed to broadcast a message in Farsi on a specified channel every five minutes on the day of our visit. From Abdullah's porch, I aimed the antenna as best I could at the satellite that would be broadcasting, and sure enough, there was the message. Abdullah was amazed that he could receive a signal, let alone a radio broadcast in Farsi, so far up in a mountain retreat surrounded by steep canyon walls. He had never received radio signals other than military messages at his residence before. When I offered to show one of his minions how to use the device, he said, "You can show me." I also gave satellite radios to the minister of communications and to the minister of women. I harbored the thought that we could persuade the Afghan government to establish a satellite radio broadcast center in Kabul and that daily broadcasts would go out at regular published times to the thousands of remote tea shops (the centers of rural social life) in Afghanistan. The broadcasts could cover topics such as education, health, and opportunities for women. The radios and the broadcast center would be paid for by the United States as would training in how to transmit the messages in at least the three main languages of Afghanistan. I understand there are now three private radio stations in Kabul, penetrating that country's deep canyons from satellites high up in equatorial orbit. (Photo by author)

Jim Hemphill, Dick Shriver, President Karzai, Russ Deane

The Private Sector Task Force for Afghanistan met with Afghan president Hamid Karzai on three occasions, once in New York City and twice in Kabul. He was pleasant enough, and we had high hopes that his leadership would be helpful to us and to Afghanistan. There were too many concerns on his mind, however, other than the development of his country. His brother made a fortune in the poppy/ opium/heroin trade. The Afghan tribal leaders distrusted a central government. We may have made one point, however. The international community had offered some $5 billion to Afghanistan, which sounded like a lot of money. We felt that the conditions for taking this money would bankrupt the country and that Afghanistan needed many times that amount to join the modern international economy. Pictured from the left are Jim Hemphill, who helped us in Ukraine, at the ECLA, and with the task force; the author, President Karzai, and Russ Deane. (Photo by author)

Abdullah Abdullah and Russ

Abdullah survived with a single name until he joined President Hamid Karzai's government in 2001 as minister of foreign affairs. Western media, unable to deal with a single name, kept demanding he produce a family name, and so he did: Abdullah. He had been a close adviser to the leader of the anti-Soviet, US-backed mujahideen, Ahmad Shah Massoud. He explained to us how columns of Soviet tanks descended through the narrow Panjshir Valley en route to Kabul where mujahideen, armed with shoulder-fired antitank rockets, took out the first and the last tank, bringing the entire column to a halt. The Afghans then took their time capturing the Soviet troops caught in the middle. On our way to Abdullah's mountain retreat along the Panjshir River, we saw dozens of burnt-out Soviet tanks from the fighting more than ten years earlier. In 2015, Karzai stepped aside, and Abdullah Abdullah and Dr. Ashraf Ghani were in a bitterly disputed runoff for the presidency. Following negotiations between the two Afghan patriots, Abdullah became the chief executive officer of Afghanistan (with focus on national security) and Ghani the president (with focus on the economy). Maybe the arrangement will work. More likely, Afghanistan will once again slip back into failed-state status, revert to rule by tribal chiefs, feed off the sales of heroin in developed countries, and provide a safe haven for the darkest of the dark Muslim extremists. (Photo by author)

21

<hr>

Does Islamic Terror Call for a
Legal or a Military Response?

I n 1985, I was asked to chair the first world conference on counterterrorism, which took place in Washington, DC. I had recently left a position in the US Treasury Department where I had worked on matters related to counterterrorism. Attendees at this conference included more than a hundred counterterrorist experts from a dozen countries, among them Germany, Canada, Italy, England, and Israel. Interpol, the international police organization, was there. Virtually every US agency engaged in counterterrorist activities was represented, including the FBI, the CIA, the Secret Service, the Drug Enforcement Administration, US Customs, and the maverick of law enforcement, the Bureau of Alcohol, Tobacco, and Firearms. The concept of a department of homeland security was not even a gleam in anyone's eye. Retired army general Al Haig, a colleague from my days in the Pentagon, agreed to deliver the keynote address.

The Europeans and the Israelis set the tone for the conference. They had experienced the 1972 Munich Olympics massacre by Palestinians, the Baader-Meinhof Gang in Germany, the hijacking of an El Al flight that resulted in the Entebbe raid by Israel, and the Red Brigades of Italy. Their message to us was "Get ready, America. They are coming to you next."

At that time, the worst act of terrorism inflicted on the United States had been the 1983 suicide bombing of the marine barracks in Lebanon, which killed 243 marines. This attack was deemed a criminal act rather than a terrorist act. However, Hezbollah, a relatively unknown terrorist organization at the time, was the likely instigator of the attack. Germany's Baader-Meinhof Gang and Italy's Red Brigades both received training in terrorist tactics that linked back to Syria. Thus, the developed nations of the West have for decades faced terrorists with roots in fundamentalist Islamic countries.

Our conference and Haig's subsequent publication of an op-ed piece on the topic in the *Washington Post* had zero impact on US policy. In fact, as a group we had little sense ourselves that radical Islamic terrorism would become the threat to the American way of life that it is today. I don't recall that anyone made any serious policy recommendations beyond modest efforts to step up awareness of the matter within the US intelligence and Interpol communities.

It wasn't long before the European predictions became all too real, however. In 1986, Colonel Muammar Gaddafi unleashed Libya's brand of state-sponsored terrorism, mainly against Americans. On April 4, 1986, a bomb went off in the La Belle disco in West Berlin, killing two US soldiers and injuring forty more. US intelligence quickly pinned the responsibility for the bombing on Gaddafi, and President Reagan responded ten days later by ordering US raids on Libya's two capitals, Tripoli and Benghazi. (Libya retaliated two years later by blowing up Pan Am Flight 103 over Lockerbie, Scotland, killing 270.)

State-sponsored terror from Iran, Syria, Palestine, and Libya, among other nations, was becoming well understood as a threat to the United States, albeit a criminal, as opposed to a military, threat. The vastly more insidious threat of a militant ideology, or militant Islam, was less understood until after 9/11. American intelligence agencies and the national security and law enforcement communities are still internalizing the reality of this threat. Islamic fundamentalists capable of doing massive harm to innocent people at any time and in any place are likely to be a threat to Americans and Western Europeans far into the future. The origins of militant Islam go back to the seventh century, and there is likely to be a continuous supply of jihadists (or other unbalanced malcontents) who, armed with modern weaponry and technology, are willing to commit suicide in the name of Allah.

If, in 1985, someone had proposed a consolidation of the multitude of agencies that now make up the Department of Homeland Security, no one would have taken the plan seriously. If anyone had speculated that suicidal Islamic radicals might hijack commercial airliners and use them in an attack, no one would have bothered to take notes.

The fact is, it took vastly more to get the attention of US national security leaders. After the first attack on the World Trade Center in 1993, in which terrorists used a truck loaded with explosives intended to topple the North Tower into the South Tower, our response was a criminal investigation. Six innocent people were killed and more than a thousand injured at what would be the site of the 9/11 attack.

What does it take to get the nation's leaders to deal seriously with such a threat? As long as the threat is deemed a criminal matter, they are not likely to consider major policy change. If the threat is considered a military one, the problem has a better chance of attracting the attention it deserves. If the threat is deemed both a military and a criminal one, maybe we can make some headway.

The professionals in our military intelligence and defense agencies are more likely than our law enforcement community to think in strategic terms about an enemy determined to eliminate us even if it takes centuries. Until we have a better mechanism for categorizing potential major threats to the homeland, we will continue to be vulnerable to attack. President George W. Bush's characterization of our response to

9/11 as a war on terror was correct in the sense that we had to respond with military, as opposed to law enforcement, resources.

Congress does not know how to declare war on a stateless organization. One massive difficulty is that militant Islam is an unseen enemy, and this enemy must be differentiated from ordinary, nonmilitant Muslims.

Congress must consider how to declare war on an ideological movement that may threaten the United States for a long time and require a protracted battle with no measure for success. The US military and intelligence establishments will then have to reevaluate their capabilities and deal with a danger beyond the threats of nuclear and conventional warfare. Defending against Islamic terrorism will require additional materiel resources, personnel, strategies, leaders, and budgets. The FBI will also have to play a role; the FBI is better trained to deal with bad people, acting alone or in small numbers, who don't wear uniforms, let alone the uniform of a specific country.

All military and law enforcement resources must be fused together to combat a menace that can threaten us with weapons that range from box cutters to nuclear bombs. Coordination between military and civilian agencies will be difficult. Such a transition will be neither quick nor easy.

22

War and Morality

E ach fall while working at the European College of Liberal Arts (now Bard College Berlin) in the Pankow district of what used to be East Berlin, I offered new students a short walking tour of the area that we inhabited.

Among the attractions on our walk was the Niederschoenhausen Palace, built in 1701 by King Frederick I. His title was "king in Prussia," not "of Prussia." Leopold I, who ruled Germany and much of Central and Eastern Europe, had insisted on this because there were several other kings whose domains included parts of Prussia. Frederick's grandson, Frederick II, also known as Frederick the Great, inherited the palace but never visited it. Instead, he gave it to his wife, whom he disliked. The palace and the surrounding area became the seat of the German Democratic Republic (East Germany) after World War II. Shortly before the Berlin Wall came down, the palace's guests included the USSR's Mikhail and Raisa Gorbachev.

We also walked to the Soviet War Memorial in Schönholzer Heide, one of three Soviet military cemeteries in Berlin where more than thirteen thousand of the eighty thousand Soviet soldiers killed in the last two months of World War II are buried. It is beautifully designed and is maintained exquisitely by Germany. My sense was that these thirteen thousand men, most seventeen to thirty years old, had little chance and no choice; they were going to be shot either in the front or in the back.

About a mile away, while bicycling in the middle of the woods one day, I had found a small cemetery containing the graves of German males who had died in the final months of World War II. Their ages at death were either under eighteen or over fifty years old. This was a cemetery for the Volkssturm, or People's Army, created by Hitler in late 1944 to prepare for the battle of Berlin. They were a ragtag group wearing old uniforms or civilian clothes, armed with pistols, rifles, and submachine guns but with little training or ammunition. Their mightiest weapon against the overwhelming numbers of Soviet soldiers was the panzerfaust, a bazooka-like tank destroyer that could be (and was) fired from the shoulder by fourteen-year-old boys. Thus, Hitler saw to it that just about everyone under his purview would be killed in carrying out his evil pursuits. This weed-choked cemetery was on my tour.

The next-to-last stop was the square where we lived, Pastor Niemoeller Platz. I had lived there for more than a year before I became curious about Niemoeller. All streets and squares had been renamed by the communists to honor the likes of Karl Marx, Herman Hesse, Rosa Luxembourg, and other socialist or communist heroes. So who was Pastor Niemoeller?

Martin Niemoeller was a naval officer during World War I and commanded a U-boat that sank Allied ships. On one occasion, in accordance with German military doctrine, he ordered his men not to rescue the sailors on a ship his submarine had just sunk, leaving them to drown. Reflecting on that act later, he concluded that letting those people drown was not right. He was ordained as a Lutheran minister and in the early thirties became the minister of St. Ann's Church in the Berlin suburb of Dahlem. Though he had been a strong nationalist and an early supporter of Hitler, he was opposed to the Nazis' attitude toward religion and in particular to their growing anti-Semitism.

His sermons against the Third Reich reached Hitler's desk. I pictured Hitler reading Niemoeller's sermons on Mondays, pounding his fist, and demanding, "Who will silence this man?" In 1937, Niemoeller was arrested and confined to the Sachsenhausen concentration camp near Berlin. He was moved to the Dachau camp and remained there until the end of the war, narrowly escaping death.

Niemoeller returned to his church. At some point in the postwar years, he incorporated several phrases in a sermon that became well known but was often misquoted in the West:

> They came for the communists; I was not a communist, so I did nothing.
> They came for the trade unionists; I was not a trade unionist, so I did nothing.
> They came for the socialists; I was not a socialist, so I did nothing.
> They came for the Jews; I was not a Jew, so I did little.
> They came for me, but there was no one left to help me.

Niemoeller has been immortalized by this excerpt from his sermon, though his precise wording has never been agreed upon. In fact, the sequence of these phrases is often deliberately changed by American politicians to make partisan statements. The above sequence, however, corresponds with the order in which the Nazis attacked classes of people, and according to German scholars, it is the likely sequence in Niemoeller's sermon.

Pastor Martin Niemoeller is one of the world's moral icons. He stood up to a tyrant publicly, paid a not-unexpected price, but was still able to leave a vital legacy. We know too little about the Pastor Niemoellers of the world. After my mini-lecture at Pastor Niemoeller Platz, we all had an ice cream.

23

"What about Humanity?"

Fall of 2006

"What about humanity?" someone shouted over the heads of seven hundred intellectual and generally anti-American Germans packed into Berlin's Adlon Hotel. They had come to hear John Bolton, the US ambassador to the United Nations. At that moment, I feared Bolton might be booed out of the room, one of three possible outcomes I had predicted earlier to my seminar class on world issues at a nearby college. Members of this class, which included students from six countries, were now scattered throughout the audience. Their attendance at the Bolton talk was homework for the week.

Bolton's appearance that evening in 2007 came at a peak of America's unpopularity in Germany especially and in much of the rest of "old Europe." This anti-Americanism was fueled initially by our own anti-Bush media and then dutifully retransmitted by the more prominent political commentators throughout Europe.

The Senate never confirmed Bolton as UN ambassador. Senator Lincoln Chafee saw to that by preventing Bolton's confirmation from coming to a vote during the summer of 2006. This compelled President

Bush to announce his recess appointment of Bolton in August of that year.

Bolton was controversial on at least four counts. First, he spoke out against UN corruption and urged reforms, drawing criticism from many of the UN's 187 members, who always believed the worst of the United States. Bolton gave them an inviting target.

Second, criticizing the UN Human Rights Commission in April 2006, he said, "Membership on the commission by some of the world's most notorious human rights abusers mocks the legitimacy of the commission and the United Nations itself."

Third, Europeans and many American liberals deplored his straight, undiplomatic, tough rhetoric, seeing America's supposed arrogance and desire for world hegemony in his remarks.

Fourth, what made liberals dislike this man most of all was his superb articulation of the issues and the solutions. To them, he was a conservative demagogue who should be stopped in his tracks by any and all means.

A few days before that day in 2007 when Bolton spoke in Berlin, I had asked my students to choose among three possible outcomes for the Bolton speech. Did they think he would be booed out of the hall (two votes, both Germans), receive polite applause (five votes, all students from Eastern Europe), or a standing ovation (zero votes)?

Bolton spoke for twenty minutes and then took questions for an unprecedented hour and forty minutes. Early in the Q and A, on the topic of how UN Human Rights Commission members are chosen from countries with records of gross human rights violations, someone shouted, "What about humanity?" I thought the crowd might erupt and boo Bolton off the stage. He handled that outburst and every question with conviction and without emotion but with knowledge and specifics. He represented America truthfully and well. I don't know if any attendees left with a better impression of the United States and of

Bolton, but he received an ovation that showed appreciation for his tour de force. This was far more than polite applause.

The next time my class met, we discussed Bolton's performance. I noted that he had dealt with a difficult audience well, except possibly for the one tense moment when someone shouted, "What about humanity?" One of my German students raised his hand and said, "That was me, sir."

24

Berlin Diary, 2003

January: Increasingly, we are living proof of the axiom that everybody must be somewhere. I am in East Berlin overseeing a start-up college, the European College of Liberal Arts (ECLA). The school is small with forty-nine students from twenty-two countries studying in English for one year. It is highly interdisciplinary with small classes. The future of the college is uncertain. Barb will join me in May. Meanwhile, I live in what was the Hungarian ambassador's residence in the days of the German Democratic Republic.

Members of churches have a fixed, government-set donation withheld from their paychecks, same as an income tax. One chooses the beneficiary, either Protestant or Catholic. Jews don't pay.

February: Germany's chancellor Schroeder and France's president Chirac abandon the United States on Iraq in a way that will further polarize Europe from the United States. Immanuel Kant might have cautioned Schroeder, citing a moral duty to unite against tyranny. Or Kant might have argued the other way round. I do not profess to understand Kant.

Given our summer program, it occurs to me that I will meet one hundred new young people each year, not one of whom has ever heard any of my stories.

March: Our students live in renovated embassies from the GDR days in the Pankow district of East Berlin. Every day they must take a thirty-minute bus ride to Buch where classes are held in a Harvard-style (ivy-covered brick walls) clinic designed by the famous architect Ludwig Hoffmann and built around 1900. I am told that the place served as a Nazi medical research center. I phone Barb to say I've found a facility where she might get at least the first part of her liver transplant done. She is not amused.

About 90 percent of Germans oppose the Iraq war. Is that because they are antiwar or anti-American or anti-Bush or anti-Semitic? Or are they just smarter than we are?

April: We decide to move the college from Buch to Pankow. The morning I passed four ambulances headed into Buch, and one hearse headed out, was enough for me. Longtime friend Jim Hemphill oversees the renovation of four more GDR structures. Tatayana, one of our students from Belarus, receives a full scholarship to Harvard. We decide to offer a second year, and twenty students are accepted.

I buy a bike.

May: Barb and our Ukraine-born giant schnauzers—Elli and her offspring Shadow—arrive. Students watch a film about Serbia directed by a Serb, Emri Kurusovic. Everything about Serbia, I'm told, is both funny and sad. The students laugh—all but one from Serbia, who cries, her tears glistening in the backlight. Students notice, stop laughing, and continue to watch but from a different perspective. We may offer the richest multicultural experience of any institution in the world. Barb and I go to Cologne where I have been invited to speak on "Tactics of American Elections." Young people from all over Europe are there to plan the politics of an expanded European Union. The East Europeans are relatively informed and sophisticated. The West Europeans have a scary, twisted view of the United States.

We should move our troops from Germany—maybe to Romania or Poland—before the Germans get testy.

June: A German friend, Immo Stabreit, a contemporary and a graduate of Princeton, who served as German ambassador to the United States, feels Germany is suffering a host of self-inflicted problems in foreign and domestic policy. Another German friend, Jens Reich, worked as a top biological scientist for East Germany and then ran for president of Germany as head of the Green Party. He perceives the United States as having been misguided or the victim of shallow analysis with regard to prewar negotiations and postwar Iraq. Our German students, who represent a small plurality of the school, are rather aggressive on the topic. The famous Humboldt University hosts seven hundred people at a conference, the theme of which is that the CIA sent two planes into the World Trade Center by remote control on 9/11. The speakers say there was no crash at the Pentagon, just an explosion triggered by US agents. Where is the Voice of America? Bruce Macdonald, an old friend now with the Washington and Lee University Business School, brings his wife, Sunny, to Berlin as he and I run our first two-week program for students interested in becoming entrepreneurs.

I feel like I am the only Nixon-Ford-Reagan person in the world engaged in liberal arts administration.

July: Our six-week summer program kicks off with sixty students from twenty-two countries, including China. One of the Chinese students tells me there are more Chinese studying English than there are native English speakers in the world! Meanwhile, the thinly varnished veneer of pan-European civility comes unlacquered when Italian premier Silvio Berlusconi, on the second day of his six-month EU presidency, fires back at a German member of parliament who had taunted him with insinuations about Mafia connections. Berlusconi says that the Italians are making a film about German concentration camps and that he, the member of parliament, could probably get a part as a kapo. (Kapos were prison guards selected by the Nazis from the Jewish inmates.) Berlusconi's remark causes Chancellor Schroeder to cancel his vacation trip to Italy. The Italian minister of tourism, in a dazzling career finale, refers to German tourists as "fat, blond, beer-guzzling annoyances," thereby causing $1 billion in tourism to vanish. Jim and Peggy Hemphill's granddaughter, Anjali, attends the ECLA for the summer.

I would like to find the thief who stole my bike—and thank this person. My new bike is much better, with vertical and horizontal shocks for the cobblestone roads here.

August: I am asked to play the part of Dr. Pangloss in a college performance of *Candide*. I am to sing "Best of All Possible Worlds." I get some back-channel feedback that I must have orchestrated the whole thing since one verse goes, "War? Though war may seem a bloody curse, it is a blessing in reverse … thus war improves relations." Egads! Barb and I visit southern Germany where son Andrew's wife, Claudia, and our granddaughters Emma and Juliane are spending the summer. Juliane, five years old, elects to go with us on a trip to Meersburg on Lake Constance where she does the translating. With German-American relations at the lowest point in recent memory, it is ironic when a local band ends a concert with "Stars and Stripes Forever." Barb gets another award from Ukraine for the design of her book of illustrations of village life by Ukrainian artist Volodymyr Shagala. Son Rich startles me by strolling into my office on my seventieth birthday after a spontaneous five-thousand-mile trip.

I paid more for my new bike than the down payment on our first home.

September: Fourteen Romanians took part in our six-week summer program. They quickly perceived an age gap between me and the rest of the faculty and administration. Apparently, a nineteenth-century Romanian prime minister had a young cabinet. They called the old prime minister *closhka cupuy*, or "mother hen." Our professor from Romania told me the Romanians were referring to me as *closhka cupuy*. I received a message from one of our German girls, who began with a loose translation of the Romanian nickname, "Dear father of all ECLA chicks." This destroyed my fifty-year façade of scientific objectivity. John Costello, visiting from Washington, DC, finds the Berlin Wall and the local markets vastly more interesting than dissonant modern German music, the superb execution of which (or so I'm told) notwithstanding.

I order new glasses.

October: The school year begins with forty-four students in the first year. We don't call it freshman year since some students already have their BAs. We have twenty students in the second year, which we call academy year. Faculty members are from the United States, Italy, Germany, Denmark, Romania, and Hungary.

The new glasses cost more than my bike. Carl Zeiss himself must have ground the lenses.

November: We hold the first-ever State of the World Week at the ECLA with the theme "Political Developments in the Middle East and Central Asia." Dan Coats, the US ambassador to Germany, gives a superb lecture. Political experts from Germany, Israel, Romania, Afghanistan, and Palestine also speak. There are three films. I am criticized for lack of balance in our program. Barb and I return to L'viv, Ukraine, for the first time in nearly two years. Business there is good despite a lousy government. The thugs at the top tilt toward Russia, while the people of western Ukraine lean toward the European Union, NATO, and the West. Our Georgian students go through an agonizing week as there is turbulence in their capital city, Tbilisi.

I order a pfannkuche—a kind of cold pancake—also known in Berlin as a Berliner. My German colleague refers to John F. Kennedy's immortal pronouncement, "Ich bin ein Berliner." He says Kennedy should have declared, "Ich bin Berliner." Because of shoddy staff work, Kennedy told the people of Berlin, "I am a pancake."

December: Berlusconi says he is astonished at the talk of American imperialism from the European left, adding, "The only territory occupied by the United States is that in which their soldiers, who died for our freedom, lie." Though he's not popular at home, it seems a friend of America is running Italy. Saddam Hussein is captured. And so to bed.

Pat Horner at the Glienecke Bridge, Potsdam

Pat and Melinda Horner joined us in Berlin in 2001. Pat, retired president of Perot Systems, is standing at the Berlin entrance to the Glienecke Bridge, which crosses over into Potsdam. This bridge is a focal point of *Bridge of Spies*, a 2015 movie. The plot of the movie runs close to what happened: KGB spy Rudolf Abel was exchanged on the bridge for downed U-2 pilot Francis Gary Powers plus an American student, Frederic Pryor, who had been captured by the East German police. Berlin and Potsdam are well worth a visit by Americans. There is much history, spanning the age of Queen Nefertiti to the Wild West movies of Karl Mai (who never visited America) and his Indian hero Winitou to the Holocaust, World War II, the Cold War, and the Berlin Wall. (Photo by author)

25

"Iran Has a Right to Develop the Bomb!"

2011

A female cadet made this comment during a seminar I was leading at the Coast Guard Academy on the proliferation of weapons of mass destruction, and she stopped me in my tracks. I offered a prosaic reply about the consequences, especially for ordinary Iranians, should that country's theocratic leaders elect to bomb Israel with nuclear weapons. I also said developing a bomb wasn't logical, and virtually all the other students agreed.

The cadet was technically correct. A sovereign nation has the right to build nuclear weapons if that is what it wants to do.

But a second sovereign nation can bomb the first nation beforehand if that is what it wants to do and doesn't need the permission of any institution or other nation. A just war may involve a preemptive strike. Israel, for instance, might knock out Iran's nuclear-weapons development capacity if it feared Iran would carry out its oft-repeated threat to destroy the Jewish state. Israel has shown great restraint during this tense period.

The vast majority of the 187 countries that have signed the Nuclear Non-Proliferation Treaty believe it is wrong for Iran to build the bomb. In 2010, the UN Security Council voted twelve to two, with one abstention, for new sanctions against Iran, the fourth round of sanctions. This action was intended mainly to prevent the importation of weaponry. Unless some country or entity launches a preemptive strike against Iran's nuclear capability, Iran will not be stopped in its quest for nuclear weaponry or be deterred from threatening other nations with such weapons.

In maintaining that it wasn't logical for Iran to build nuclear weapons, I was absolutely wrong. A decision to build the bomb may be completely logical from Iran's standpoint.

The problem is that few can or will understand Iran's logic. First, to whom are we referring when we say, "Iran"? Not all Iranians believe their country should develop the bomb. Some do, but this view is likely held by only a tiny fraction of Iran's sixty million citizens. The country is ruled by a small number of all-powerful mullahs who do not speak for all Iranians. We are talking about the logic of a handful of Islamic-extremist theologians turned politicians who believe they are entitled to eternal control over Iran and its people.

Their logic might be as follows: "We will destroy Israel with a preemptive nuclear attack. If the Israelis retaliate, this may result in the annihilation of Iran and ourselves, but we will be immortalized in Islamic history for ridding the world of Israel and for helping bring the return of the twelfth caliphate."

All this is quite logical—or, more aptly, theo-logical—though only to the mullahs in charge. The suicidal decision to bomb Israel would be made by the fewest possible leaders. What may be perfectly logical to a small number of leaders in a theocratic tyranny, looking toward their place in immortality, may defy the logic and the wishes of the vast majority of citizens. Most Iranians have no interest in risking the annihilation of their country to satisfy the delusions of their undemocratic and unwanted leadership. One of the hopes for Iran is that its citizenry, sensing that the worst could happen under the current leadership, will one day rise up and overthrow the mullahs.

That a decision to begin the destruction of civilization might be made by only a handful of mullahs in far-off Qom demonstrates the superiority of a democracy, no matter how bad, over an autocracy, no matter how good.

As for the ability of sanctions to influence autocratic leaders who care nothing about ordinary citizens, Iran's former president Mahmoud Ahmadinejad once said sanctions are "annoying flies, like a used tissue."

The United States has removed ten-year-old sanctions against Iran, which now enjoys renewed membership in the international community. Tensions in the Middle East are on the rise again, however, and Sunni and Shiite Muslims, enemies for centuries, are battling each other. Finally, lifting the sanctions resulted in the release of more than $150 billion to Iran. Nuclear weapons and their delivery systems are expensive. Let's see how the mullahs spend that money.

26

Oh, Pshah

1956

The three-day train trip from Istanbul to Erzurum in the shadow of Mount Ararat in eastern Turkey had taken its toll on the group of newly minted Cornell graduates traveling to Iran as guests of the shah. Each of us from the classes of 1955 and '56 had some manner of digestive malfunction, which did not make travel into this part of the world, difficult at best, any easier. Nonetheless, we made it to Tehran, where we began a tour of Iran with all arrangements and costs within that country handled by the Iranian government.

This included the flight into the magnificent city of blue mosques, Isfahan, where our Iranian pilot crash-landed our DC-3 onto the tarmac, scattering our welcoming committee, which included the mayor. We never did meet him.

The plane had landed without flaps, a pilot error that meant the landing speed was much too fast for the short strip at Isfahan. The runway was short because the Iranian air force had constructed a hangar precisely at the end so that fighter planes could scramble straight out of the facility for takeoff to engage an enemy. We were approaching from the opposite direction, so the end of the runway and the front door of the hangar were synonymous.

Inside the DC-3, we could not see in front of the plane, so our guide unstrapped his seat belt and stood up in the aisle in order to be first out the door as a matter of protocol. We were still moving down the runway at nearly one hundred miles per hour when the pilot veered sharply to the right to avoid the hangar. The plane hurtled toward the mayor and his party as the left wing and the landing gear sheared off. The resulting centrifugal force sent our guide down the aisle toward the rear of the plane at high speed. He flew squarely, spread eagle, into a bunch of large mail bags, unhurt except for his Persian pride. For the rest of the trip, we traveled by first-class railcar.

Among other sites, we visited Persepolis, the ruins of the ancient palace established by Persia's great kings Cyrus and Darius the Great in 500 BC. The last few miles before we arrived at Persepolis took us through villages where small children sat on the sidewalks brushing flies away from their diseased eyes. Abject poverty abounded, just as it must have years later, in 1967, when the shah threw a hundred-million-dollar party for his coronation. His party for VIPs from around the world was held at Persepolis to celebrate 2,500 years of the Persian dynasty. The excruciating contrast with the poor people along the streets on the way to Persepolis could not have been lost on the thousands of foreign dignitaries.

Our Cornell group witnessed an ancient Shiite tradition of one hundred bare-chested men, in military formation in a gymnasium, slapping their backs with chains, first across one shoulder and then over the other, until blood flowed from the self-inflicted wounds. This ancient ritual was conducted to the intense, rapid beat of tambours, goat-skinned drums on tapered clay bases. These instruments dated from the Dark Ages.

Finally, our sightseeing came to an end, and we had to make good on our share of the bargain by visiting the shah's camp at Ramsar on the Caspian Sea for ten days.

We spent much time getting to know our camp mates, about one hundred in all, mostly students from Iran. There were also a half dozen from each of the other Middle Eastern states except for Israel. The shah was building relationships with the offspring of those in power throughout the region. It appeared that he harbored visions of becoming the de facto leader of the Middle East. There was a leadership void.

Shah Reza Pahlevi, heir to the peacock throne of ancient Persia, was thirty-seven years old when we met. He had inherited the throne at twenty-two when his father was forced to abdicate following the swift Soviet and British military takeover of Iran in 1941. Iran then became an important part of a route for delivering military equipment from the United States to the Soviet Union during World War II.

The young shah was shot by a dissident at the University of Tehran in 1949 and spent some years in Europe recovering and plotting his return. During the shah's absence, the nationalist mullah and Swiss-educated lawyer Mohammed Mosaddegh ruled Iran as prime minister. Mosaddegh objected to British control and to the fact that the lion's share (84 percent or possibly more since the British did the accounting) of the profits from Iran's massive oil refinery at Abadan on the Persian Gulf went to Britain. Mosaddegh forced out the British with a promise that Iranians would get 100 percent of the oil profits. The British, however, took with them all the blueprints and the tools and much of the know-how to operate the refinery. Soon, 100 percent of the profits turned into 100 percent of the losses. The public's confidence in the previously popular Mosaddegh waned, opening the door for the United States and Britain to neutralize him and for the shah to return.

The CIA and the British Secret Intelligence Service conspired to arrange Mosaddegh's arrest and to bring back the shah. Mosaddegh was imprisoned and then placed under house arrest until his death in 1967. Fearing repercussions after his death, Iranian officials had him buried in his house. Mosaddegh was popular and had risen to power democratically. After the US role in the coup was exposed years later, many in America questioned the wisdom of this act of US foreign policy. In 2000, Secretary of State Madeleine Albright said, "The Eisenhower administration believed its actions were justified for strategic reasons. But the coup was clearly a setback for Iran's political development, and it is easy to see now why many Iranians continue to resent this intervention by America."

The Cornell students who made this 1956 visit had spent the previous school year writing a small book on Iran. We had written chapters on its history, culture, economy, politics, and religion, among other relevant topics. When the shah flew into Ramsar in one of two (for security) twin Beech aircraft and then arrived at our camp in one of three (also for security) lapis-lazuli-blue Chrysler Imperials, we were fairly well informed about him, his country, and the problems he faced. When several of us interviewed the shah at length on his last day at the camp, it was our first experience speaking frankly and openly with a head of state.

My notes from this interview foretold his problems in the late seventies. The shah, who named Walter Cronkite among his friends, spoke colloquial American English. "Those crazy mullahs," he said. "I'm going to drag this country kicking and screaming into the twentieth century."

Those crazy mullahs took over in 1979 and are still dragging their country kicking and screaming back toward the seventh century.

Shah and students, 1956

This photo was taken when the shah of Iran met with our group from Cornell at his camp at Ramsar on the Caspian Sea in August 1956. At the time, he seemed like the best kind of benevolent dictator. In the late fifties, however, he took the first of several steps away from a form of democratic leadership by creating his secret police, Savak, which became accomplished at spreading terror among political and other domestic adversaries. In 1967, the shah had himself coronated in an extravagant international spectacle amid his country's grueling poverty. Though his plans for Iran's economy in 1956 sounded good, he never executed these plans. By 1979 the shah was in failing health and was forced out in the fundamentalist revolution. Even if he had had a succession plan, it would have lacked the support of the country's citizens. As late as the 1970s, the shah might have gained insights into a proper form of government by studying the success of a peer, King Juan Carlos of Spain. Carlos took that country, successfully by most measures, from a constitutional dictatorship to a constitutional monarchy with democratic safeguards and separation of powers. The shah's utter failure in all such matters was a shock to his friends, including David Rockefeller, who went to great lengths to see that, toward the end of his life, the shah was allowed into the United States to receive this country's best medical care. (Photo by author)

27

One Terrorist Group Disbands—in Spain

"We don't come from anywhere," said our Basque friend and host Jose in the five-star (my rating) Urepel restaurant in the old part of Spain's Basque enclave, San Sebastian. Jose and his colleague Niati[18] then gave us a lesson in Basque history, explaining that there were many theories about where the Basques came from but no proof that they came from anyplace else but where they are today. There are two million Basques in the northwest corner of Spain at the westernmost junction of France and Spain. There are several million other people of Basque ancestry, mainly in Latin America and especially in Chile, where Basques at one point constituted nearly half the population.

Traces of civilization dating back 150,000 years can be found in the Basque country. Cave drawings created twelve thousand years ago have been discovered. The Basque language has no obvious connection with any other, certainly not Spanish. Ethnic homogeneity has doubtless played a role in the Basques' insularity and desire for independence. While dictator Francisco Franco favored the Nazis over the Allies,

---

[18] My spelling since my computer has no Basque letters; the name is derived from Ignatius.

Basques helped Allied aviators who had been shot down escape over the Pyrenees.

Mention the word *Basque* in the United States, and many people think of ETA, which in the Basque language stands for Basque Fatherland and Liberty. ETA conjures up an image of an ethereal group of scheming terrorists eager to topple the Spanish government and killing others indiscriminately. This was an apt description of the outfit during the mid-twentieth century. ETA's initial and primary goal had always been greater autonomy for the Basques living mainly in northwestern Spain, with violence as an accepted tool. Members assassinated Generalissimo Franco's chosen successor, Admiral Luis Carrera Blanco, shortly before Franco's own death in 1975. This assassination may have aided Spain's multiyear emergence from a dictatorship to a democracy under Franco's second choice, King Juan Carlos I.

Our two Basque hosts described how ETA had all but disappeared. This was accomplished through a combination of amnesties, international police actions, and laws passed by the Spanish government aimed specifically at ETA that prohibited violence to achieve political ends.

ETA, infamous for its terrorist tactics from the late 1950s into the 1990s, had originally been blamed for the Madrid train bombing in 2004. Subsequent investigations, however, led to the indictment and conviction of a single Moroccan nationalist with no known ties to ETA or to any Muslim extremist group. In 2011, ETA signed a permanent peace treaty with Spain ending its sixty years of assassinations, kidnappings, and bombings.

ETA was not an international terrorist organization. It was established to achieve Basque political autonomy from Spain. Religion was not a factor (as in Ireland, say), since the Basques, like the Spanish, are largely Catholic. A minority of people were determined to break away from Spain. For a time, they attracted a measure of sympathy from other Basques and from socialist and communist groups around the world.

The Spanish government held the line and played an effective game of carrot and stick, using spies and remaining patient until the dissidents were worn down. The ETA ranks dwindled after 2000. Terrorist acts and deaths caused by the ETA all but ended. Members began to fight among themselves. Their funds dried up, in large part as a result of international police cooperation and of confiscation. Finally, by early 2011, only a handful of ETA leaders were left to surrender and to receive amnesty, to be released from prison with full rights restored, and to sign the peace treaty.

In the Hotel Mont Igueldo, on a five-hundred-foot promontory looking almost straight down into the Atlantic and with a view of the entire city of San Sebastian and its harbor, we could see a small country within a country that is at peace with itself today. Unemployment is half that of the rest of Spain, and Basques enjoy a prosperous regional economy. It is questionable whether ETA served any useful purpose, and it certainly caused much harm. At a minimum, it gave the region a bad name for decades. But ETA may also have given Spain its king, Juan Carlos, who converted a dictatorship into a democracy. The heads of state in Morocco, Egypt, and Jordan might well wish to study this amazing story.[19]

---

[19] Jordan may actually be an exception. King Abdullah graduated from a US prep school and has exhibited extraordinarily modern, civilized leadership in the face of threats from ISIS and neighboring Syria.

Chillida sculpture on the Atlantic Ocean in Basque country

Eduardo Chillida is one among many famous Basque sculptors. He may be the best and the most famous, however. I took this photo along a walkway near San Sebastian. I believe this work of forged iron and steel is part of his montage known as "Comb of the Wind." This work is remarkable artistically and from an engineering standpoint, given its weight and the ceaseless pounding of waves from the Atlantic Ocean. Chillida's works are displayed all over the world including outside the German chancellor's office in Berlin and inside the World Bank headquarters in Washington. He died in 2002 at seventy-eight. (Photo by author)

28

Crimea River

2000

As John leaned over the velvet-covered chain intended to prevent him from doing what he was doing, the ancient docents stationed at each door gasped audibly. The large round table he was reaching for was covered with a white tablecloth. John had just asked our tour guide, Andre, if that was the real table underneath—the one at which Stalin, Churchill, and Roosevelt had sat with their aides during the Yalta Conference of February 4–11, 1945, just three months before World War II ended. The conference took place at the Livadia Palace in the city of Yalta in the Ukrainian region of Crimea. We were there in the summer of 2000.

Andre was a tenured guide from the Intourist era of Soviet times, an era that had ended ten years earlier for every Soviet citizen except him. He had forgotten nothing from his early training. In the first hour of an all-day tour, we were already growing tired of his propagandizing for communism and of his flexibility with the truth. Andre confirmed that the real table was underneath the tablecloth.

As the tablecloth rose with John's help, Andre's assurances notwithstanding, underneath was a plywood fake. As soon as we found a comfortable place to do so, we paid Andre for the full day and sent him on his way.

Barb and I had organized this week's vacation in Crimea with our friend the Washington political commentator John McLaughlin and his wife, Christina. In addition, we asked Natalie, a bright, cheerful, and fearless Ukrainian, to join us. Natalie was fluent in all the languages needed for this trip and could help with what we knew would be McLaughlin's relentless demands for information about Ukraine and Crimea. As it happened, McLaughlin gave Natalie a nearly impossible task on the first day: could she arrange an interview with Ukrainian president Leonid Kuchma in Kiev? With countless phone calls over the next three days, Natalie secured the longest interview ever granted by Kuchma to a foreign correspondent for the forthcoming Saturday when we were scheduled to be in Kiev.

We spent the next few days as sightseers. Crimea in 2000 was an amazing tourist spot despite a lack of funds and the interest to convert it into an international attraction. Crimea's geology and topography offer world-class opportunities for hiking and sightseeing. There are few places on earth where one can see the architecture and the cultural remains of the Greeks, the Romans, the Mongols, the Genoese, the Venetians, the Ottomans, and the Slavs all in one spot. In 1783, Russia annexed Crimea, which in Soviet times became the Crimean Autonomous Soviet Socialist Republic. The fortress at Sudak was built by the Romans in the sixth century AD and still looks formidable. Palaces and churches like the Swallow's Nest or the Church of Christ's Resurrection, perched on spine-chilling promontories, are extraordinary examples of nineteenth- and early twentieth-century Russian architecture (and likely examples of forced labor).[20]

---

[20] Today Crimea is closed to foreign tourists.

We visited Balaclava. Natalie showed us where the Crimean War was fought in the 1850s and where the infamous Charge of the Light Brigade took place. (The war pitted the British and the Turks against the Russians for control of the port of Sevastopol.)

We had a guide take us through the decaying underground Soviet submarine base at Balaclava. Stalin had ordered that this massive labyrinth of harbors be built beneath a mountain in the early fifties, and this supposedly secret base was considered invulnerable to nuclear attack. It occurred to me that the electromagnetic pulse from a single nuclear blast anywhere in the vicinity of this mountain fortress would blow out every radio and other electronic device, rendering the dozens of submarines based there useless. Today, the Balaclava sub base is a modern tourist site, well lit and beautifully presented for visitors. At the time of our visit, however, it was simply the wreck of a once highly technical submarine base that had been stripped of anything that could be sold as scrap. Lighting was poor, flashlights were all but useless, and dangerous holes were unmarked. At one point, Barb dropped out of sight in such a hole—up to her armpits. Twenty feet below her was twisted metal and water, a mess she might not have survived.

Our final stop on this journey was the port of Sevastopol, former home of the Soviet Black Sea Fleet and the Soviet Union's Annapolis-like naval training center. After the breakup of the Soviet Union, Ukraine and Russia divided the materiel and the personnel of the Black Sea Fleet into two fleets, one Russian and the other Ukrainian. Russia continued to lease much of the port and the naval training center there. Over time, the relationship between Ukraine and Russia deteriorated over Sevastopol and the Black Sea Fleet. In 2009, Ukrainian president Victor Yushchenko decreed that Russia's lease agreements in Sevastopol would end in 2017.[21]

---

[21] When Russia seized Crimea and Sevastopol in 2014, many Ukrainian seamen, including Ukraine's chief of naval operations, defected to Russia, and in a hastily

Following our visit to the naval training center, we boarded the US Sixth Fleet flagship, the USS *La Salle*, at Sevastopol. Vice Admiral Gregory "Grog" Johnson, who commanded the Sixth Fleet, was our host. He explained that by virtue of an old treaty, the United States was permitted to visit Sevastopol but that if a country failed to exercise such rights, they had a way of vanishing.

Our invitations had come from Carlos Pascual, the US ambassador to Ukraine. After our lengthy stay in Ukraine, it was a breath of fresh air for Barb and me to be with so many enthusiastic and patriotic young American naval personnel.[22]

Finally, the time came for John's interview with Ukraine's president. The preparations were time-consuming, the tension palpable. I was permitted to sit in during the interview while our wives were excluded. During the preceding few days in Crimea, John had prepared extensively for the interview, which became obvious as he peppered Kuchma with questions about the decline in Ukraine's economy and the apparent escalation of official corruption under his ten-year administration. As the interview neared its end, John asked about the possible connection between Kuchma's administration and the assassination of Georgi Gongadze, a relatively minor reporter who had written opinion pieces critical of the Kuchma regime. Kuchma became angry, complaining that this was the only thing of interest to Western reporters. The interview came to a tense and hurried finish.

At this writing, Kuchma is Ukraine's representative in the peace talks with Russia about the conflict in southeastern Ukraine, a region where he grew up to became head of one of the world's largest rocket plants. He had been Ukraine's president for a year before he dared to speak Ukrainian in public, having grown up with Russian as his first

---

arranged communist-style plebiscite ("Vote for me or I'll kill you"), Russia was chosen as the rightful sovereign by more than 90 percent of Crimean voters.

[22] In 2006, the *La Salle* was sunk as part of US Navy target practice off of Pensacola, Florida.

language. His ten-year presidency is the longest tenure for any president of an independent Ukraine.

When Kuchma has visitors for dinner these days, perhaps they are seated at a round table large enough to accommodate fifteen guests, the same number who occupied the table at the Livadia Palace during the Yalta Conference.

Ukraine's Chief of Naval Operations; Commander of the U.S. Sixth Fleet, Vice Admiral Gregory Johnson; author; Dr. John McLaughlin

Crimea was an exciting place to visit before Vladimir Putin's 2014 takeover. Today, it is closed to foreigners. John McLaughlin and I were aboard the USS *La Salle* as guests of Carlos Pascual, the US ambassador to Ukraine, and of Vice Admiral Gregory "Grog" Johnson, commander of the US Sixth Fleet. Admiral Mikhael, on the left, was the chief of naval operations for Ukraine. We were in the port of Sevastopol, one of the world's more complex pieces of real estate at the time. Under a Russia-Ukraine treaty, Russia's only sovereign rights in Crimea were in Sevastopol. Russia's naval academy at Sevastopol continued under Russian leadership and ownership. Also, after the USSR's Black Sea fleet was divided unequally (with Russia getting the more important assets) between Russia and Ukraine in 1993, Russia had the right to base and to maintain its share of the fleet in Sevastopol. This was probably one of the last visits by a US warship to the Black Sea. (Photo by author)

29

Amman, a Man, a Plan, Japan—Kaboom!

"Hi, Dick. Jerry Jones here. Can you come to Jordan week after next?"

Jerry was the Pentagon's liaison to the White House and asked if I could participate in a meeting in Amman, Jordan, starting August 6, 2005. He said I would be one of eight Americans at this meeting with a group of Iraqi business leaders. Jerry was the senior American official in attendance. Two other officials were from the US Overseas Private Investment Corporation, and four Texas businessmen with much commercial experience in Iraq were also on hand. The only other non-Iraqis at the meeting besides me were two investment experts from Japan's development bank.

When Jerry's call came, I was in my office in Berlin, Germany, where I was provost of the European College of Liberal Arts. Jerry explained that I was to address issues of economic and legal development in Iraq and that my experience in national security would also be helpful. He had expected someone from the State Department to fill that role, but he alluded to serious dysfunction in the government between State (Condoleezza Rice) and Defense (Donald Rumsfeld). It seemed the two cabinet officials did not agree on US policy toward Iraq and were barely on speaking terms. (I saw evidence of this rift later on. The problem is said to have resulted in a delay of about a year in the construction of a militarily critical highway in Afghanistan between the key cities of Kabul and Kandahar. This delay aided the resurgence of the Taliban in Afghanistan.)

Our hosts in Amman from the Iraqi side numbered about eighty. When we entered the meeting room on the first day, we found twenty Iraqis in Western business suits and sixty in Arab robes and headdresses. One chieftain, dressed totally in black with a gold aqal, or rope headpiece, was the tribal leader of eight million people, not all of whom lived in Iraq. We understood this group was representative of Iraq's economic leadership. The group included a few Kurds and Shiites, but most members were Sunnis. In fact, these Sunnis were the Baathists who had ruled the Iraqi economy under Saddam Hussein and who had been largely disenfranchised following the US invasion three years earlier.

Only years later did I realize that this meeting in Amman was likely the last attempt by Iraqi Sunni business leaders to communicate to the United States what a mess it had made in Iraq and to seek some mechanism for recovery. In point of fact, the US delegation of which I was a part was largely powerless to speak on behalf of the US government. The meeting seemed to be a unilateral effort by Jerry Jones as the principal liaison between Rumsfeld at Defense and the Bush-Cheney national security apparatus at the White House. Lacking support from the State Department, Jerry had few tools at his disposal to deal with this opportunity to engage with a room full of important Iraqi leaders. He had deemed it advisable that the United States should at least commit a small team of experienced Americans to attend this meeting. The main function of this team would be to listen.

The meeting had been concocted in some haste with little in the way of briefing papers or coordination among interested and knowledgeable US officials. Jerry had apparently considered all this and done everything he could do within a reasonable time and with limited cooperation from within the US government. He presumed that if I agreed to go I could, on cue, say something passably sensible about the matters of legal and economic development in troubled countries.

In retrospect, I understand why I was asked to attend and am glad I went, but having an explanation of the context would have been helpful. For that, and in hindsight, I defer to James P. Pfiffner, professor of public policy at George Mason University. In the article "U.S. Blunders in Iraq: De-Baathification and Disbanding the Army," appearing in the January 2010 issue of the publication *Intelligence and National Security*, he wrote:

> Early in the occupation of Iraq two key decisions were made that gravely jeopardized U.S. chances for success in Iraq: (1) the decision to bar from government work Iraqis who ranked in the top four levels of Saddam's Baath Party or who held positions in the top three levels of each ministry; (2) the decision to disband the Iraqi Army and replace it with a new army built from scratch.
>
> These two fateful decisions were made against the advice of military and CIA professionals and without consulting important members of the president's staff and cabinet. This article will first examine the de-Baathification order and then take up the even more far reaching decision to disband the Iraqi Army. Both of these decisions fueled the insurgency by: (1) alienating hundreds of thousands of Iraqis who could not support themselves or their families; (2) by undermining the normal infrastructure necessary for social and economic activity; (3) by ensuring that there was not sufficient security to carry on normal life; and (4) by creating insurgents who were angry at the U.S., many of whom had weapons and were trained to use them.
>
> These two key decisions, however, were presaged by President Bush's decision in late April 2003 to remove Jay Garner and put Paul Bremer in complete charge of Iraq. Garner had experience in Iraq in the 1991 Gulf War and

had been a career Army officer. In his preparations, he had worked closely with military planners. Bremer, who had no experience in Iraq or in intelligence and national security, worked in the Pentagon for the first nine days of May, and he arrived in Iraq on 12 May 2003.

In early May the plan had been to send to Baghdad both Paul Bremer and Zalmay Khalilzad, who was a Sunni Muslim, grew up in Afghanistan, and went to the University of Chicago; Bremer would be in charge of U.S. reconstruction efforts, and Khalilzad was to help put a Muslim face on the occupation and facilitate the convening of an Iraqi assembly. This was consistent with making a quick turnover of control of Iraq to the Iraqis. But the Bush administration decided that the U.S. would not turn over Iraq until they found Iraqi leaders who were acceptable.

On May 6 the announcements for both appointments were ready for release, but at a lunch with President Bush, Bremer made the argument that the plan would violate the principle of unity of command and lead to confusion. Bush concurred and decided to send Bremer alone to lead the Coalition Provisional Authority (CPA) and to give him supreme authority over all U.S. actions in Iraq; Bremer was, in effect, the U.S. viceroy in Iraq. President Bush's important decision was made without consulting his secretary of state or national security adviser (Stephen Hadley). According to Colin Powell, "The plan was for Zal to go back. He was the one guy who knew this place better than anyone. I thought this was part of the deal with Bremer. But with no discussion, no debate, things changed. I was stunned." Powell observed that President Bush's decision was "typical." There were "no full deliberations. And you suddenly discover, gee, maybe that wasn't so great, we should have thought about it a little longer."

Further, these decisions were made in the face of CIA intelligence judgments that, in the aftermath of an initial

U.S. military victory, significant ethnic political conflict was likely to occur. The former chief of the CIA Directorate of Intelligence, Richard Kerr, headed a team to analyze the CIA's intelligence performance before the war in Iraq. Kerr concluded that the CIA "accurately forecast the reactions of the ethnic and tribal factions in Iraq. Indeed, intelligence assessments on post-Saddam issues were particularly insightful. These and many other topics were thoroughly examined in a variety of intelligence products that have proven to be largely accurate." Kerr concluded that policy makers, though relying heavily on the inaccurate judgments about WMD, largely ignored the accurate CIA reports. Had the accurate CIA intelligence judgments about the effects of Saddam's fall been heeded by policy makers, they might have been more hesitant to de-Baathify the government and disband the Army. In May 2003, Paul Bremer issued CPA orders to exclude from the new Iraq government members of the Baath Party (CPA Order 1) and to disband the Iraqi Army (CPA Order 2). These two orders severely undermined the capacity of the occupying forces to maintain security and continue the ordinary functioning of the Iraq government. The decisions reversed previous National Security Council judgments and were made over the objections of high-ranking military and intelligence officers.[23]

The abstract of this article concludes with the telling statement that the person who had the most influence on the president's decisions about Iraq was his vice president, Dick Cheney.

As for our meeting in Amman, like a very light brigade, on the morning of August 6, 2005, our band of ten plunged into the valley of death on a raised stage before the eighty Iraqi leaders. We felt like we were on the wrong side of a firing squad. One by one, the Iraqis stood

---

[23] This excerpt is reproduced with full permission of the author.

up, took the microphone, and lambasted the United States. This went on all day. We sat and listened. I had never experienced anything like this. By the end of the day, our hosts had had their say, and I was exhausted and depressed, having contributed nothing and having absorbed the animosity of these people for the entire day.

The Iraqis wound up the first day of their diatribe about American mistakes and stupidity. Searching for appropriate words to close the meeting on the lightest possible note, Jerry Jones noted, "Winston Churchill once said that Americans always do the right thing—after they have tried everything else."

People started shuffling their papers and stirring in their seats, assuming the day was at an end, when the senior official from the Japanese development bank raised his hand. The room settled down with a hush. He said something like this: "You know, it was exactly fifty years ago today that the Americans bombed Hiroshima. Thousands of my countrymen were killed. We later surrendered to the United States unconditionally. We then started to rebuild our country with American help. Meanwhile, the United States had total control of our laws, our constitution, and the functioning of our newborn democracy. Today, we have a working economy and a stable society. We are no longer subordinate to the United States in any way. We are no longer junior partners on the world stage. We are full partners with the United States. I hope you will pay attention to and work with the Americans tomorrow."

You could have heard an agal drop.

Postscript: Our hotel for that meeting was one of three blown up by Al Qaeda terrorists fifteen months later. Furthermore, I have little doubt that these eighty Iraqi leaders never lost control over Iraq's oil profits and that these people are now a primary source of ISIS's estimated income of $2 billion a year, many times that of Al Qaeda or Hezbollah.

30

George Odora: Making His Dream Sustainable

Father Heinz Kuleuke, a Catholic priest from Germany, found his calling among the millions of impoverished people living on the Philippine island of Cebu. In 2010, he began to see the fulfillment of at least one of his goals when he met with German philanthropist Bobby Dekeyser and his friend (and mine) Florian Hoffmann, cofounder of a German charity, Dekeyser & Friends (D&F). Kuleuke believed the residents of the tin huts on Cebu's garbage dumps were the poorest of the poor, the world's most destitute people. If these people could show the way and, with help, dramatically raise their standard of living, all good things might be possible on Cebu. The three men agreed to give the four hundred scavenger families living on the garbage dumps opportunities for a new life with decent housing plus the resources and the know-how to make a better living by growing crops in the communal soil surrounding the housing development the three would create.

D&F initially committed to building a community center in the middle of a verdant jungle some forty miles from the garbage dumps. The labor for this project was supplied by seventeen aspiring social entrepreneurs from around the world who volunteered six months of their time. In exchange, D&F promised to help these young entrepreneurs achieve their own dreams in their home countries, which included Austria, Uganda, Namibia, and the United States. I was invited to Cebu by D&F to critique their business plans during their last week on the island. The best plans could expect to receive up to $15,000 in seed funding in the form of loans or grants from D&F.

During my week on Cebu, I met Kuleuke, visited some of the tin-scrap shacks that served as homes for the four hundred families, and met representatives of those families, mostly young mothers ages thirteen to twenty-five who hoped to move to the new site and to take up farming. I also listened to the seventeen presentations by the volunteer workers.

George Odora of Uganda had come eight thousand miles to Cebu at D&F expense to take a shot at having his project chosen for a ten-thousand-euro grant (about $15,000 at the time, enough to build thirty decent homes in Uganda). George's plan was to help some of the thousands of displaced persons in refugee camps return to their property and to new homes that he would build.

I liked George and thought his project not only was a commendable idea but also might be practical. I told George that if he won the grant, he should save enough money to come to the United States where I would help him raise additional funds for his project. That's what happened. George spent three weeks in the United States after traveling another twelve thousand miles in the fall of 2011.

Barb and I organized three events for him—in Old Lyme, Connecticut, New York City, and Washington, DC. People heard his story and donated a total of $15,000 net after expenses (about equal to another grant of ten thousand euros). Our friends also gave George useful advice. Most important, they said, "Make sure you offer to build homes for families that are strong and healthy enough to farm so they can pay you back through the farm profits." In this way, they said, George's dream could become sustainable.

George made connections with major US agricultural assistance agencies that had programs in Uganda. Back in Uganda (another twelve thousand miles), he brought the pieces of the puzzle together and began building homes for people who, after twenty-two years, returned to their farms, planted crops recommended by US advisers, and began to repay George with interest. Not bad for George Odora, boy soldier (retired).

George Odora, boy soldier

George Odora, shown here with a Kalashnykov rifle, was forcibly conscripted by the insurgents in Uganda's civil war to fight against his own government.

George Odora was born in northeastern Uganda in the middle of the twenty-two-year civil war. George not only survived, but he applied for and received a grant to travel to Cebu, Philippines, to work as a volunteer with the German foundation Dekeyser & Friends; in exchange, George was eligible to apply for a grant to do good work in his own country, Uganda.

"Northern Uganda is the worst place on earth to be a child today," says a former United Nations undersecretary-general for children in armed conflicts. According to the British human rights group Oxfam, the rate of violent death in northern Uganda is three times worse than Iraq's. Since 1996, the government has herded more than 1.6 million people in northern Uganda into displaced persons camps. The World Health Organization reports that in northern Uganda more than one thousand people die each week of starvation and preventable diseases. The group Doctors Without Borders describes the level of suffering in northern Uganda as "an emergency out of control."

"Since 1986, the Ugandan civil war has claimed hundreds of thousands of innocent lives. Over twenty-five thousand children have been abducted by the Lord's Resistance Army (LRA) and forced to kill their friends and relatives. Each night a terrible saga is played out when approximately forty thousand children flee their homes in the rural areas to escape abduction, torture, or murder by the LRA. These are northern Uganda's 'night commuters' or 'invisible children'" (Daniella Boston, "The Blog," *Huffington Post*, May 17, 2006).

George at Cosmos Club

George Odora was an effective speaker about his homeland and his mission. He is shown here at the Cosmos Club in Washington at a fundraiser for his project. (Photo by author)

Author with leader of 400 families living
on the garbage dumps of Cebu, Philippines

Florian Hoffmann, the former ECLA student turned social entrepreneur, invited
me to Cebu in the Philippines to help with the business plans of George Odora
and his colleagues on the Cebu assignment. The task was to construct a community
building for a future village that would be populated by some of the four hundred
families currently living in shacks on the Cebu dumps. One of the two leaders of
these families was the fifteen-year-old mother walking with me and describing life
on the dumps. She told me the women were enthusiastic about moving to a new
agrarian community in the jungle. (Photo by author)

Life on the dumps of Cebu. (Photo by author)

The new community center built in the jungle
for refugees from the Cebu garbage dumps

Katherin Kirschenmann is in the foreground, with the new community center built by the Dekeyser & Friends volunteer group over a six-month period in the background. Within the next year or so, Father Kuleuke and Dekeyser & Friends would have the resources to begin homes for the first group of families to leave the Cebu dumps some fifty miles away. They would move to their new agrarian community and be taught how to make ends meet, or even to prosper relatively speaking, in their new environment. (Photo by author)

31

—————✦◦◦◦=———

How the United States Pays China to Help Africa and China Gets the Credit

2009

Before heading out to the village of Chambasho in Tanzania where I would be working for the following ten days as part of a US assistance program, we had to check in at the county headquarters in Kongwa. After doing some necessary paperwork there, we headed back to our SUV. Since this was the county seat of a fairly large piece of Tanzania, all foreign business was handled through this office. Along one side of the parking lot, I spotted about twenty brand-new walk-behind garden tractors, each with several attachments, and even a cart for hauling things.

I recognized the tractors instantly as Gravelys. My father had once owned a tractor of that type, and I thought, *That's exactly the kind of aid we Americans should be giving to Africa.* When I came closer, however, I discovered that the tractors were Gravely knockoffs from China, products of intellectual property theft by that country. The next day in the village where I was to work, I saw one Chinese tractor being shared by the villagers, and two sunflower-seed-oil presses, also from China.

In other words, the main technology supporting the economy of the village was from China. Nowhere was there any sign of US machinery or technology; the only indicator of American aid was an adviser who would be gone like a puff of smoke in a matter of days.

Here's the way I think it works.

USAID allocated $464 million, or roughly a half-billion dollars, for Tanzania for fiscal year 2010. These funds were distributed among twenty-four categories or line items of assistance. One of those line items was HIV/AIDS to which $336 million, or 72 percent of the total, was dedicated. This was a legacy of George W. Bush, who set out to eliminate HIV/AIDS in Africa and who greatly increased US public and private support in this area.

What follows is mainly speculation.

Ten percent of US assistance ($46 million) is siphoned off for other purposes; let's say half ($23 million) of the 10 percent is lost to bribes, kickbacks, and other forms of corruption. The other half (another $23 million) is redirected to the Tanzanians' legitimate needs, such as tractors from China. (A popular scheme in Russia was for officials to charge Russian farms and companies a fee for the otherwise free services of American volunteers provided by the US government. Nothing kick-starts underground economic activity like a kickback.)

The Chengdu is a Gravely look-alike for which no royalty is paid to Gravely, so all that is necessary, in addition to the reverse-engineered blueprints of a Gravely, are labor, materials, and transportation costs for the Chengdus to make it to Tanzania. Labor in China is paid for in the tongue-and-lip twisting Chinese currency, the renminbi, a phony currency in terms of international trade that gives workers a subsistence wage and renders a hard-currency profit for the Chinese government. This tractor probably needed no imported materials or parts; under communism, all domestic raw materials and even energy are essentially free, allocated on the basis of the government's estimated need (in this case, China's needs for hard currency and political sway in Africa).

So the cost for the Chinese to make the Chengdu tractor is close to zero. Transportation is another expense, but it is via Chinese ships, and the cost to build and staff them is also close to zero, though fuel must increasingly be imported at world prices. Still, transportation would be a minor cost of a market-priced Gravely tractor, so the Chinese will have a huge cost/price advantage for a long time.

The bottom line is that the United States provides "soft" aid in the form of, say, advisers and volunteers for large sums of US taxpayer funds that pay for travel plus local and US-based staff and about 30 percent in overhead. US assistance (of all kinds, not just technical assistance) is then monetized by any number of possible shenanigans, and the money is used to line pockets and to pay for a multitude of Chinese tractors and sunflower-seed presses and the like—things the Tanzanians badly need. Thus these people are given the false impression that the Chinese are outdoing we Americans in generosity.

Technical assistance or consulting is basically invisible to the beneficiary country. At least that is the case the minute the adviser or consultant leaves. Therefore the United States offers no visible evidence of its support as powerful as shiny new Chengdu tractors. China looks good, gets free advertising from the new equipment, earns prelaundered US dollars, makes a dollar profit, pays off its workers and manufacturers in Chinese checkers, and Tanzania is forever grateful.

Meanwhile, the US presence is best seen in the form of used American-provided condoms hanging in the trees along the roadside.

Dick in Tanzania

I was told I was the first white person to set foot in the village of Chambasho (four hundred families) in the Kongwa district of central Tanzania. I was there on a micro-credit assessment since the local credit union, funded by several international financial institutions, was always losing money. Once we had devoted the three days necessary to translate the profit-and-loss and balance sheets from Swahili into English, I asked why the balance sheet showed no liabilities for shareholder deposits. "Oh," they said, "we thought those were assets." I doubt the international lenders had ever seen a true translation of the financial statements. After figuring out how to manage the credit union with this accounting change, I was rewarded with the official village robe and permitted to hold the official village rooster. Tanzania was lucky to have the British appoint Julius Nyrere as the liberated country's first leader. He wanted every village to have a road, a clinic, and a school. Chambasho has these three things, as does almost every village in Tanzania today. (Photo by author)

These tractors are not Gravelys. They just look like Gravelys. They were made in China and given or sold to Tanzania. (Photo by author)

32

Truman's Fifth Point

After a few decades of foreign development experience late in the last century, I became increasingly convinced that it was foolish for the United States to provide foreign assistance without understanding beforehand substantially more than it did about local cultures and histories. Language and religion are basic to a nation's culture, but sometimes the more critical considerations are attitudes toward law and order, the quality and the fairness of local laws, the degree to which courts are independent, attitudes toward paying taxes, honesty in contracts, and attitudes toward Americans, toward criminal behavior, and toward women.

Unless we understand such matters, foreign assistance may accomplish precisely the opposite of what we intend. The good people for whom assistance is intended may never receive it or may receive no more than what is needed to provide evidence that our wishes were observed. When all is said and done, we may succeed mainly in lining the pockets of local potentates and, in various ways, the pockets of our own potentates.

Further, and most important, if we do not understand other cultures, threats to the United States and its main allies can fester and build for decades without catching our attention.

The importance of culture was driven home to some of us in 2007 during a seminar at a small college in Berlin where I was provost. This optional seminar was held in the evening. Twelve students from ten countries attended, as did I. The seminar was led by Dr. Jens Reich, a colleague and a friend who had been a biological scientist for East Germany and the Soviet Union but who by the late 1980s had become a dissident and a thorn in the side of the German Democratic Republic.

In September 1989, Reich coauthored the paper "Fresh Start 89— New Forum." A few months later this paper went viral (before the expression had been invented) throughout communist East Germany. This caused much confusion and hesitation among the GDR authorities, who had lost control of the situation and who were no longer allowed to use violence against protesters. On November 9, 1989, East Berliners were told that they could thenceforth move freely throughout the city, and this led later that day to the fall of the Berlin Wall.

Reich's seminar at our college focused on a single poem, "Wanderer's Nightsong," written in 1780 by Johann Wolfgang Goethe.

The professor never stated a purpose for his seminar. He simply handed out copies of this immortal poem (in thirty-two languages), which consisted of a mere twenty-four words in German. In the English translation by Henry Wadsworth Longfellow, the poem grew to thirty words:

> Over all of the hills
> Peace comes anew,
> The woodland stills
> All through;
> The birds make no sound on the bough.
> Wait a while,
> Soon now
> Peace comes to you.

Reich, the Green Party's candidate for president of Germany in 1992, described the poem's free rhythm and its perfect rounds. He read it in the original German. In German, the poem is suspenseful, and there is tension as the birds "hold back" their song, an active verb in German for which there is no single-word counterpart in English.

Students were invited to read the poem in their own languages. (Ten were represented at the seminar.) Then the students described what the poem said. The rhythm, the sound, and the feeling were different in each case. The meaning also changed. Sabina Amanbaeva from Kazakhstan read slowly in the Kazakh language the 1892 translation by her country's poet laureate, Abai Kunanbai-uli, as tears rolled down her cheeks. "Wanderer's Nightsong" was apparently a moving poem in Kazakh, but when she described the poem's story in English to the class, it differed significantly from Goethe's original. Someone asked if the Kazakh poet had translated the work from the German. "Oh, no," she said. He had translated it from Russian into Kazakh from the earlier translation, German into Russian, by the famous Russian poet Mikhail Lermontov.

Reich had made his unstated point: culture matters.

President Harry Truman did not mention culture in his 1949 inaugural address, though he might have. His address was one of the most amazing speeches in modern history. In it, he laid out the substance of the next fifty years of world affairs with just four points. He said, in short, that we must repair a broken Europe (the Marshall Plan), that we must protect Europe from the East (NATO), that we must support the United Nations (we have been its biggest supporter), and that we must help less fortunate countries. We have the technology, Truman said, and it is in our best interests to do so.

Truman's fourth point became known during the fifties as America's Point Four Program, and today, after some organizational iterations, is called the US Agency for International Development.

I met point-four workers building schools in Iran in 1956. They were using local materials (mud bricks, for example) and did not stand out in any way. These Americans were civil engineers working for a pittance who did a great deal of good for the poor people in countries the United States assisted. They expected nothing by way of thanks and shunned the limelight. They had no political agenda and represented the best of American ideals.

Had Truman made a fifth point, he might have said,

"Point number five: the vastly different cultures in our world today will make it difficult for Americans, who are so isolated from the rest of the world, to participate in the new and complex environment of the future. We must be prepared to communicate our principles, ideals, and policies in such a way so as not to offend foreign cultures but nonetheless to get our points across with the utmost effectiveness. Furthermore, we should understand foreign cultures at least enough to engage with them in productive activities in our mutual interests such as trade, treaties, and cultural exchanges. We should especially understand their attitudes toward us. We should therefore encourage our colleges and universities to offer courses in major cultures throughout the world."

Thirteen years after Truman's speech, as if in response to this imaginary point five, the Peace Corps was founded, and its first director was Sargent Shriver, my late cousin. Thousands of young Americans engaged with cultures throughout the world, countries in need, but for the most part, countries friendly toward the United States. Many were predominantly Muslim.

More than a hundred years ago, Winston Churchill had developed a sense of radical Muslim extremism based on his service in Sudan among other experiences.[24]

---

[24] What follows is from Churchill's book *The River War*, first edition, volume 2, pages 248–50, published by Longmans, Green & Company in 1899.

How dreadful are the curses which Mohammedanism lays on its votaries! Besides the fanatical frenzy, which is as dangerous in a man as hydrophobia in a dog, there is this fearful fatalistic apathy. The effects are

Churchill and Truman were together only once as national leaders, and for just a few days at the Potsdam Conference in the summer of 1945 after the war in Europe had ended. At the time, they had more important issues to deal with than the possible rise of Islamic fundamentalism. But what if Churchill had given Truman his views on radical Islam and Truman had added my imaginary fifth point?

We might have found a means, without war, to liberate the good people of Iran from the mullahs of Qom, if not to rescue the shah. Our national security experts would almost certainly have seen radical Islamic terrorism as a high priority well before 9/11.

Cultural ignorance results in much clumsiness in our foreign affairs, with at least two questionable wars in my lifetime and thousands of dead and wounded American soldiers as well as Iraqis and Vietnamese. We have rarely been pressured into war and have had time to reflect on intelligence and on whether to choose diplomatic, economic, or military measures. Our presidents have had time to confer and to debate with their top national security advisers.

The main problem I have observed, mostly as an outsider, is the disconnection within our national security team. For example, when

---

apparent in many countries, improvident habits, slovenly systems of agriculture, sluggish methods of commerce and insecurity of property exist wherever the followers of the Prophet rule or live. A degraded sensualism deprives this life of its grace and refinement, the next of its dignity and sanctity. The fact that in Mohammedan law every woman must belong to some man as his absolute property, either as a child, a wife, or a concubine, must delay the final extinction of slavery until the faith of Islam has ceased to be a great power among men.

Individual Moslems may show splendid qualities, but the influence of the religion paralyzes the social development of those who follow it. No stronger retrograde force exists in the world. Far from being moribund, Mohammedanism is a militant and proselytizing faith. It has already spread throughout Central Africa, raising fearless warriors at every step, and were it not that Christianity is sheltered in the strong arms of science, the science against which it (Islam) has vainly struggled, the civilization of modern Europe might fall, as fell the civilization of ancient Rome.

our State Department goes in one direction, the Defense Department may lean in another.

In a frivolous response to serious matters, we send reset buttons to Russia. This is our culture talking, not theirs. Europe views our culture as a shallow pop culture. Russian culture must be viewed in the context of centuries of imperial history, the abuse of human rights by the czars, and the deaths of more than forty million Soviet citizens under Stalin (half in wars and half through mass killings of his own people).

We might have avoided trouble if our translation of *reset* had been accurate. Russia's foreign minister, Sergei Lavrov, was sufficiently fluent in English that he was able to chide Secretary of State Hillary Clinton by noting that her translation meant "to overcharge." She intended to say, "Now that we Democrats are in charge, we will work toward better relations with Russia."

Truman might have foreseen all this and even considered a fifth point. His other four points were timelier, but a fifth point on culture would have further immortalized his speech. On the other hand, he gave the American people enough to digest with his four points. Indeed, we did not begin to understand the importance of cultural matters in world affairs until Samuel F. P. Huntington published his 1993 classic *Clash of Civilizations*, with its prescient allusion to forthcoming troubles with Islamist fundamentalism. Even so, it took more than a decade for Huntington's wisdom to become clear.

33

Muddy Sunshine:
Overture to a Musical Tour

Repeating myself, I stressed, "It won't sound right. Furthermore, Bill Monroe (the father of American bluegrass) would turn over in his grave."

Ben had been pestering me for some time to invite his friend Alex to join our Sunday night bluegrass sessions at our house in Berlin during the spring of 2005. But Alex didn't play the mandolin or fiddle or banjo—instruments basic to the style of bluegrass of which Bill Monroe would approve. Alex played the soprano saxophone, an instrument I considered alien to bluegrass music.

Ben, a German, had been a student at the ECLA and had learned bluegrass songs and played the guitar when he was a high school transfer in Vermont some years earlier.

Despite my protestations, Alex showed up one evening with his soprano sax. To make a tediously long story short, it worked. This was in part because the soprano sax is nothing like its cousins, the alto and tenor saxes. Mainly, however, the experiment succeeded because of Alex, his personality, and his formidable improvisational skills. He played with us from that moment on. I would later introduce our sax player by saying, "Alex always wanted to study law, but his father insisted he take up music." There was apparently some truth to that. A few months later, I was listening to a 1950 recording of Hank Williams's songs when I discovered that taking a break in "Hey, Good Lookin'" was a soprano saxophone.

From 2002 until 2007, ECLA students who wanted to try bluegrass, as players or singers or both, came to our house on Sunday evenings. I grew up with old-time American music, and Barb had sung harmony with a classical jazz group for a decade. We often played as a family. In a weak moment when I was fifty, I took up the banjo. It was always just for fun. At the ECLA, however, talented European students began to provide serious leadership for a possible US tour.

Not everyone who played with us in Berlin made the tour. Julian Triandifyllou, a self-declared Byzantine, had brought his grandfather's one-hundred-year-old Italian mandolin to Berlin. He played with us in our first official gig at the Lyrik Café in Berlin's Prenz-Lauerberg district. Liv, a German, also joined us at the Lyrik, playing a violin she had made herself. Firat, from Turkey, played the bass. After we had practiced the gospel hymn "Driftin' Too Far from the Shore," he told me he couldn't play the song because it had the word *Jesus* in it.

Dan, a German-Czech, and Maria, a German, brought their tenor and alto saxes, and I was right. They didn't work.

Paula, another German, an accomplished violinist in the classical mode, decided that our style of music was not for her. Dasha, from Moldova, could do a reasonably stirring rendition of "Bobby Magee." With the exception of Ben and Alex, none of the others mentioned above came on our 2007 tour.

The US tour became a possibility during the spring of 2006. One of our singers, Sofiya Skatchko, a Ukrainian, had been our star performer. She would borrow a CD of the Country Music Hall of Famer Patsy Cline and return the following week with a song memorized and perform flawlessly, with no accent except maybe a touch of a southern drawl, just like Patsy. On the strength of Sofiya's abilities and her expressed interest in the tour, I began to lean on friends throughout the United States for the summer of 2007. Dates started to gel. We had more than a dozen commitments by August 2006. That was when Sofiya told me she would be unable to join us. I was devastated. I planned the cancellation of the tour.

(When Sofiya arrived at the school, I asked her where she was from. She said Ukraine, not knowing I had lived there for eight years, seven in L'viv in western Ukraine.

I asked, "Where in Ukraine?"

She said western Ukraine. I then asked her the name of the main city in her oblast (Ukrainian for "region"). When she heard the word *oblast*, she knew something was up.

She said, "L'viv."

"And what was the name of your village?" I asked.

"Borislav," she answered.

Having been there on business several times, I asked, "Do you know the Borislav paint factory?"

Obviously taken aback, Sofiya said, "The paint factory? That's where both my mother and father work.")

I also had to break the news to those who were planning to go on the tour. Ben and Alex were committed. Friederike, also German and a graduate of our college, had expressed an interest. I had sent a message to Laszlo, one of our graduates in Budapest, who played the viol, er, fiddle, but who was already playing bluegrass with a band in Hungary. Dirk, the German teacher at our college and one of the last escapees from East Berlin before the wall came down, wanted to sing about a rose in a city he'd never seen, San Antone. Barb and our son Rich were also prepared to participate. Charles Lang, a Californian employed by the ECLA, was on board to join us. Dan Whitener, son of our friends Mark and Sarah, had signed on as musical director for our group, a kind of internship consistent with his curriculum at Bard College. Without Sofiya, however, I couldn't see how we could pull it off.

Before scrubbing the tour, I cornered Natalia Kowalcziek and asked if by any chance she could sing some of Sofiya's songs. Natalia, who was from Wroclaw, Poland, had participated in our group, but I could not conceive of her singing songs like "Lovesick Blues," yodel and all. Natalia looked me square in the eye and replied, "I can sing them all." And sing them she did, plus some others. While on the tour, Dan, Alex, Laszlo, and Natalia merged two songs, "Muddy Water's Takin' Back My Home" and "Ain't No Sunshine When He's Gone." This medley morphed into "Muddy Sunshine," the title of our priceless (so far) CD.

Whenever I introduced Natalia Kowalcziek to our US audiences, I mentioned her eye problems when she first arrived. I said we took her to see our friend Bob Klimek, a noted eye doctor. Bob asked Natalia if she could read the fourth line on his eye chart.

"Read it?" she replied, "I know the guy."

By the time the tour ended in August, we had given sixteen performances in Virginia, Connecticut, Maryland, New York, Texas, California, Massachusetts, and New Hampshire. During those fifty-six days we ate, drank, and slept bluegrass, or more appropriately, given our style and our mix of bluegrass, jazz, and blues, bluegrazz Berlin.

American music is an important part of our culture. It exports easily and comfortably. Jazz, blues, mountain music, and country and western are uniquely American. On this tour, young Europeans enjoyed performing our music and did it beautifully.

If Bill Monroe could have heard us, he would have approved.

BlueGrazz Berlin warming up in Berlin for U.S. tour

One day I popped into the Lyrik Café in the Prens Lauerberg district of Berlin and offered the owner a bluegrass band. She immediately answered, "Sure, bring me a CD." We scurried about for a week and finally had a CD, though it was flawed at points. When I brought it to the Lyrik, I took two members of the band with me, Sophia Skatchko from Ukraine and Lucian Cosinschi from Romania. They took our CD into the Lyrik while I parked the car. When I entered the café, our hastily crafted CD was being played for a live audience. Each time the CD neared a bad spot, I said something to the owner to drown out the sour notes. We had two gigs at the Lyrik. This photo includes, from left to right, Sophia Skatchko (Ukraine), Alex Tischbirek (Germany), Natalia Kowalczek (Poland), Barb, Charles Lang (California), and me. When it came time to get visas for the Bluegrazz Berlin tour to the United States, Lucian was denied one. I offered to intervene, but Lucian demurred. (Photo by author)

34

The CIA and I

My adventures in the Soviet Union and in the post-Soviet states led some to conclude that since I had no affiliation with a known entity during most of those years, I must have been associated with the CIA. Many Soviet officials I encountered thought the same and were especially attentive whenever I was invited into classified defense plants or research facilities. The fact is, no CIA spy could possibly have been as free to roam the Soviet Union as I had been. As far as Soviet border and other officials were concerned, I was a harmless teacher, which was pretty much the truth. I may be, however, the only American who has been inside both a US and Soviet ICBM silo facility. At one point, I knew much more about the Soviet KGB than I ever knew about the CIA.

Whenever I entered the Soviet Union, I had an official invitation from someone trusted by the KGB. American-citizen agents of the CIA who are stationed overseas are, to my knowledge, embedded with innocuous titles in our embassies and consulates.

Soviet citizens who were spies for our side were native personnel and were few and far between. Indigenous spies in countries with aims inimical to our own operate under deep cover and are extremely valuable.

In the future, we will need more who speak Arabic, Farsi, Dari, Pashtun, or Swahili.

While with the Defense Department, I received a briefing a day from the CIA. I could ask for specific briefings, or the CIA would call when it had something it thought was important for me to know. I never set foot in the CIA building at Langley. I held a "top secret" clearance during all my travels in the Evil Empire. The reason for my clearance had nothing to do with my work in the USSR and its successor states. The clearance simply allowed me to be a board member of a small foreign company engaged in classified US defense contracting.

In 1999, I received a phone call from the Pentagon's Defense Legal Services Agency. The agency wanted to know a lot about me, and a year or so later, I received notice that my security clearance would be revoked. I no longer needed the clearance, but I appealed because the arguments were false. The agency said I would not need a lawyer. I should have known this was bad information coming, as it did, from the plaintiffs against me, the defendant. To my surprise, I wound up being Perry Mason at my own trial, calling witnesses to testify on my behalf. The three witnesses who kindly and generously offered to testify on my behalf were Bob Marik, Pat Horner, and Marty Hoffmann.

Judge Burt Smith of the Defense Office of Hearings and Appeals wrote this in an April 7, 2003, synopsis of his decision: "Applicant's [mine] business activities in a foreign country are arms-length transactions with minimal financial investment, and applicant is not subject to coercion or duress by foreign interests. Applicant's family relationship to a foreign citizen is not the subject of potential exploitation by a foreign power. Clearance is granted."

Six months later, my clearance expired of its own accord.

Part 2

Domestic Affairs

———————

Has the art of politics no apparent utility? Does it appear to be unqualifiedly ratty, raffish, sordid, obscene, and low down, and its salient virtuosi a gang of unmitigated scoundrels? Then let us not forget its high capacity to soothe and tickle the midriff, its incomparable services as a maker of entertainment.

—H. L. Mencken, *On Politics*, 1956

35

No More Pasta for Walt

When I opened the door of my conference room in the Pentagon one day in February 1977, I was stunned to see Dr. Eugene Fubini addressing my entire staff (about twenty of the nation's top technologists and communications experts), having called them together without my knowledge. I was a Republican appointee from the outgoing Ford administration and had been asked by the new secretary of defense, Harold Brown, if I would remain in my position until he found a replacement, a request to which I had agreed. Fubini was a Democratic apparatchik who had worked in the Defense Department during the Johnson administration. Reappearing as soon as the Democrats were back in power, he was throwing his weight around like the weasel he was. In the few remaining contacts I had with Fubini, I do not recall any redeeming features in the man. I'm sure both parties had their Fubinis— people who thought the other political party, and not, for example, the Soviet Union, was the real enemy—but the experience was a shock and an eye-opener.

Fubini's needless, rather public violation of the statutory authority and responsibility that still rested with me for a few more months not only rankled; I thought it was dangerous. The position I held was director of telecommunications and command-and-control systems in the Office of the Secretary of Defense. I was the third and last person to hold this office since it was reorganized by the Carter administration soon after I left. During my tenure, 1976–77, the mission was to ensure proper strategic and tactical communications in peace and war. The budget for this office covered all military services and included $2.5 billion for routine operations (basically, a secure, reliable telecommunications company connecting all US military establishments throughout the world), $1.5 billion for procurement (radios, satellites, encryption capability among many other items), and $.5 billion for research and development. The total of $4.5 billion was almost exactly 4.5 percent of the defense budget that year.

The office had been created in 1972 to bring all communications planning and capabilities under one roof so that the different services had compatible communications systems that could operate effectively with one another. One of the programs managed by this office was the Advanced Airborne Command Post, a modified Boeing 747 shielded from radiation in the event of nuclear attack, inside of which a large battle staff could manage two conventional wars or one all-out nuclear war. Much of the technology that became known as Star Wars under President Reagan had its origins in this office. The office was honored on official visits to military bases by three ruffles and flourishes and a seventeen-gun salute. I presented two consecutive budgets for this office in congressional testimony and led one US delegation to a NATO conference on command, control, and telecommunications. (If we had trouble rationalizing the communications technology between our four services, one can imagine the complexity of rationalizing the communications of fifteen allied countries then and twenty-eight countries in 2016.)

Five years later, in 1982, I returned to Washington in an appointed position in the US Treasury Department as assistant secretary for electronic systems and information technology, a new office I was asked to establish by Treasury Secretary Donald Regan, former CEO of Merrill-Lynch.

At my first meeting with Regan, he told me to take two months, to visit every part of the Treasury Department organization, such as the IRS and the US Customs Service, and then to tell him what I thought our new office should do. When I returned with the requested presentation, Regan endorsed every proposal and we were in business.

I had said it was worth looking into securing (i.e., encrypting) the telecommunications system of the Secret Service. Since its creation in 1865 after the assassination of President Lincoln, the Secret Service had been part of the Treasury Department. Its initial responsibility was dealing with financial crimes, especially counterfeiting of bills immediately following the Civil War, which explains its location in the Treasury Department.

In 1901, when President William McKinley became the third president to be assassinated, the agency began its protective mission for top US government officials and for foreign heads of state visiting the United States. In this dual role, agents shifted between these two missions—protection and anticounterfeiting—as circumstances dictated. The Secret Service developed its own mystique, a unique sense of pride that was envied among law enforcement groups.[25]

I became interested in the Secret Service in connection with the shooting of President Reagan by John Hinckley at the Hilton Hotel in Washington, DC, on March 30, 1981. Gerry Parr, at that time the person in charge of protection at the Secret Service, was also the leader of the Secret Service detail that day. I joined Treasury in the summer of 1982, and some months later, I met with Parr to discuss the incident. (He passed away in 2015.)

---

[25] In 2003, the Secret Service was transferred to the Department of Homeland Security. The argument was that it made sense to place the responsibility for protecting the homeland, including presidents, under one person. I'm not so sure. Much was lost in terms of focus and pride.

Parr said that since he had become the head of protection, he did not have to go out on assignments but that he elected to go on two or three a year to maintain his proficiency. By sheer chance, he had chosen that day in March 1981 to be in charge of the president's safety. After the first shots, he pushed Reagan into the presidential limousine ahead of him, keeping his own body large and in the way of further shots. (You can see this in videos of the incident.) Secret Service agents are trained to get in the way of bullets, and all did so heroically on that day, with two agents left injured.

Once inside the car, Parr said, "Mr. President, were you hit?" Reagan replied he didn't think so, whereupon Parr told the driver in Secret Service lingo, "Rawhide [Reagan] okay. We're going to Crown [White House]." Then Reagan coughed up blood. Parr reached under Reagan's armpits and found blood. He then told the driver to head for George Washington University Hospital. Now Parr was in a quandary. Should he phone ahead to the hospital so doctors could be better prepared to keep the president alive, or were there multiple assassins along the way, some listening in on his phone calls at that moment? If other assassins heard Parr call the hospital, they would be there in advance, ready to finish the job. Parr processed a lot of information quickly, banked on much training and history, weighed the probabilities, and phoned ahead to get the hospital staff ready.

As we now know, there was only one assassin. Parr had made the right decision. At one point, as Reagan looked up at the medical faces staring down at him, he made his now-famous statement, "I hope you're all Republicans." Later, in his first words to his wife, he said, "Sorry, honey. I forgot to duck."

Parr and I discussed the pros and cons of Secret Service vehicles and personnel being equipped with secure telephones. He thought that encryption would be expensive but that it was also fast becoming a necessity. To get started, I paid a visit to the National Security Agency where I met with Walter Deeley, head of the encryption division in the

NSA's Department of Communications Security. Dr. Bob Conley, the navy's former chief scientist, had come to work for me at Treasury and accompanied me on the visit. Bob and Walt knew each other well, which was a big help.

Under Walt's leadership, more than ten thousand technologists designed and fabricated the US government's own computer chips at the NSA to protect the chips from compromise by spies and enemies. Our highest grade of encryption was reserved for our highest security needs, mostly at the Defense Department and the CIA. We had lower grades of encryption for allies, with protocols to protect us should the chips fall into enemy hands. No civilian agency used encryption at the time.

Walt, Bob Conley, Gerry Parr, and I designed a project to allow encryption of all Secret Service communications. This protection included Secret Service vehicles operating in teams anywhere in the world. The result was that Treasury and the Secret Service became the first civilian agencies to procure, install, and operate secure telecommunications technology from the NSA.

In the process, Walt Deeley and I became great friends. He lived with his wife, Pat, and their eight children in a simple two-story frame house along the Baltimore Beltway. After I had left Washington and started working in New York City, I stopped to visit Walt whenever I was passing by. (He had retired from the NSA by that time.) We enjoyed reminiscing and drinking good beer, and Walt always had an ample supply of Irish jokes.

Suddenly, in May 1989, Walter died of cancer at age fifty-nine. I was shocked and attended his funeral. After the religious part of the service, friends of Walter rose and told stories about him. Most were insider accounts that meant little to me.

As the service came to an end, however, one man stood up and said he wanted to tell a story about Walt and Dr. Eugene Fubini. I was floored. As close as Walter and I had been, we never discovered that we had both known Fubini. I wondered if Walt's experience with him had been more positive than my own. The storyteller proceeded.

"It was 1967, and Dr. Fubini, a political appointee to the Pentagon during the Johnson administration, had requested that Walter, who was working at NSA at the time, come to his office in the Pentagon. Walt was asked to present an overview of the plans for his department. He gathered up flip charts and headed for Fubini's office. As Walter later described the meeting, Fubini interrupted Walt at the very outset and began to quibble over minutiae. When Walter finally made it to page two, Fubini started in all over again, not listening to, and showing little interest in, the substance of what Walt had to say. By the fourth chart, as Fubini continued his harassment, Walt said, 'Dr. Fubini, this presentation is over. If you ever want to hear it, you can come to NSA ... And I'll tell you one more thing: for the rest of my life, I'm never having another plate of spaghetti.'"[26]

---

[26] "The Eugene G. Fubini Award, established in 1995 by then secretary of defense William Perry, is an award by the Defense Science Board, named after Eugene G. Fubini, on an annual basis to recognize an individual from the private sector who has made highly significant contributions to the Department of Defense in an advisory capacity over a sustained period of time." Eugene Fubini was the first recipient of this award; he passed away shortly thereafter. Source: Wikipedia

36

Civilian Control of the Military

In 1976, when President Ford was commander in chief of the US armed forces, he appointed his friend and former colleague in Congress, Donald Rumsfeld, as secretary of defense. The deputy secretary of defense, and the day-to-day manager of the department, was William P. Clements, a highly successful businessman from Texas, who had been appointed to his position by President Nixon. Reporting to Clements and Rumsfeld were fourteen additional civilian appointees, for a total of sixteen. As director of telecommunications and command-and-control systems, a position at the level of assistant secretary, my position was the sixteenth.

On my second day on the job I received a routine message from Air Force General George Brown, chairman of the Joint Chiefs of Staff. In addition to its chairman, Brown, the Office of the Joint Chiefs included a vice chief of staff (also four stars), the three chiefs of the army, navy, and air force plus the commandant of the US Marine Corps. The chairman had direct access to the president (and vice versa) if such communication was desired, though for the most part, he served as adviser to the secretary of defense. (Today, the Joint Chiefs also include the chief of the National Guard Bureau; in the event of war, the chain of command would bypass these top military leaders, going from the president through the secretary of defense and thence directly to the ten unified combatant commanders, four-star military leaders, of whom six cover the geography of the world and four represent key functions including strategy, special operations, space, and transportation.) Some positions, such as the head of the National Security Agency, were "purple suited," so the person filling the position could be from any of the services; such was the case with the US command-and-control position at NATO.

Brown wanted to seek my concurrence by signature in the appointment of Army Major General Thomas Rienzi to the top US communicator position at NATO headquarters in Brussels. If I signed this document, Rienzi would move to Brussels for his final three years of military service. He would be honored and rewarded by receiving his third star and would retire more comfortably with the increased income of a three-star general, a fitting end to a distinguished career; he would finish having reached the highest attainable rank in his field. I had met Rienzi a few days earlier on a brief courtesy call and thought him to be a friendly, outgoing gentleman.

I asked my principal deputy, John Stenbit, who knew the Pentagon's people and procedures, if I should approve this nomination. John, also a civilian appointee and a brilliant integrator of technology, was headed for greater things. He nearly shouted, "No! You can't sign that! Tom Rienzi, as good a man as he is, he is no diplomat and will fail at NATO." John went on to back up his statement.

Since I had only a few days to respond, I met with Bill Clements and sought his advice. His response: "Dick, you can do whatever you want—as long as you're right." I asked around about Rienzi. It seemed that many shared Stenbit's views. I called high-ranking military communicators at NATO and explained the situation to them. A British air vice marshal (a two-star equivalent to a US rear admiral or major general) was especially candid: "Tom Rienzi would be a poor choice for the United States."

Meanwhile, Rienzi had asked to see me. In our private meeting, Tom, a man of deep faith, got on his knees and beseeched me, with tears in his eyes, to approve his nomination to NATO.

I wrote "Request denied" on Brown's memo and sent it back to him.

Within hours, my secretary said, "General Brown on the phone."

I picked up.

"Shriver, George Brown here. Regarding the NATO communicator position, what the hell do you know about our people?"

"Not much," I admitted, "but I did a lot of asking around, including at NATO itself."

"Okay," he said, modulating his initial gruffness. "So who do *you* want for the job?"

I said, "Well, Jon Boyes (a rear admiral and the top navy communicator) seems like a good candidate."

"You've got him," said Brown, and hung up. The general knew me only as a new political appointee inexperienced in the ways of the Pentagon. He did, however, appear to respect the office I held and the principle of civilian control of the military, an example of which he had just seen.

Another possible explanation, however, is that this decision was not that important to the Joint Chiefs relative to other decisions on their plate. Such appointments were often rotated on the basis of which service was in line for the next general officer promotion. (My recollection is that at the time, the Joint Chiefs sent recommendations for four-star promotions directly to the Senate and to the president's national security adviser through the secretary of defense. The secretary could comment on but not stop this communication directly from our top military to Congress.) Tom Rienzi had been nominated not necessarily based on ability, qualifications, performance, or any assessment that he was the absolute best choice for the position. It was simply the army's turn. Next up would be a naval officer, then an air force officer, and every so often the Joint Chiefs would nominate a marine.

In a 2001 article in the *American Forces Press Service*, Jim Garamone wrote, "Civilian control of the military is so ingrained in America that we hardly give it a second thought. Most Americans don't realize how special this relationship is and how it has contributed to the country. The framers of the Constitution worked to ensure the military would be under civilian control ... The colonies had just fought a war for freedom from Britain. The king (effectively a military dictator) controlled the British military, and the framers had no interest in duplicating that system." They accomplished civilian control by giving Congress the power "to raise and support armies." They made the president commander in chief, but they gave enough power to Congress to require that the two institutions work together before going to war.

I once took part in a war game at Site R, a quasi-secret alternate Pentagon built into the Blue Ridge Mountains near Camp David. All participants were at the three- or four-star level. We were divided into three teams dealing with a series of scenarios in which both sides had to make decisions independent of the other.

The blue team was always the United States, red was the opposing force, and a neutral team planned the next scenario based on the decisions by the two teams in the preceding scenario.

At the outset of a war game, each side is given the conditions at that moment, always with a realistic but hypothetical threat situation to the United States. The situation could take a turn for the better or for the worse, presumably as a result of the decisions of the blue and red teams. In this game, the top military participants were generally less likely to support a declaration of war than were the civilians. The military officers were reluctant, above all else, to make any decision that might increase the probability of a fighting war. The civilians (also all at the three- or four-star level), on the other hand, were more likely to declare war to demonstrate intent in order to avoid a shooting war. Civilian leadership was more likely to make a largely political decision to alert and to prepare the American public for a threat of dramatic proportions and to warn the potential enemy in an effort to forestall fighting. In other words, the civilian leadership in our group was more likely to take an aggressive stand at the outset in a last-ditch effort to cause the enemy to back down. At least that's what happened in the war game in which I was involved. This conflict between military and civilian colleagues, working together on the same team, was exactly what the war-game designers wanted us to experience.

The fact is, civilian political leadership may often make very different decisions than military leadership. Truman's firing of General McArthur is a prominent example. We have also seen examples of such conflict between military and civilian leadership in the debate over a strategy to end the growth of ISIS and the possible creation of Islam's twelfth caliphate.

As for NATO's command-and-control appointment, six months after newly promoted Vice Admiral Jon Boyes had reported for duty at NATO headquarters in Brussels, he was mustered out of the navy prematurely due to a case of asthma that was exacerbated by the damp Belgian air. He had two and a half years to go in his position. He retired to his home in the Southwest with his three-star title and his retirement package. Meanwhile, Jimmy Carter had been inaugurated as president, and by late spring, I, too, had been mustered out to make way for a Carter appointee. Rienzi's name was submitted once again by the chairman of the Joint Chiefs, and this time the nomination was approved. Six months later, I understand that NATO's top leadership asked the US military to retire Rienzi (at the new level of lieutenant general) since things "just weren't working out."

Civilian control of the military is a useful ideal. For one thing, civilian control can head off a military coup. Such a coup is more likely in South America or Africa where, more often than not, military establishments are run by military, not civilian, leaders. In a democratic republic like the United States, civilian leadership is essential for the big things, like providing political leadership as chosen by the electorate. Civilian leadership of the military is no assurance of better national security decisions, but it links such matters to the American people, who are also fallible.

Tom Rienzi died in 2010 and was rightly buried with a hero's honors. He had earned the retirement pay of a three-star general, having fought with distinction in three wars.

37

Soros Makes Sure No One Follows in His Footsteps

2010

Even when we're down, there's not much to complain about. Official unemployment (for which people receive unemployment checks) is stuck around 9 percent. Real unemployment (the sum of all those looking for jobs) is stuck around 18 percent, affecting mostly young people and minorities. Nonetheless, thousands from these ranks have the time (and the money) to congregate around Wall Street and half a dozen other locations in the country for days at a time to protest against ... well ... to protest against something.

The still-nameless group has chosen Wall Street, not Washington, as the villain. That's great. Apparently these people are not looking for Washington to spend more money on something. That must be, in part, because Washington has already spent money on just about everything, including projects that might really help.

No, members of this group, which shows evidence of funding from Moveon.org (i.e., capitalist turned rabble-rouser George Soros), seem to agree on "greed" as the target for their protests. They have a left-leaning bias and would like to eliminate the greedy rich from our land, for which Wall Street is their symbol.

Now isn't that something! The icon of the greedy rich is none other than George Soros himself. No one has said he isn't smart. No one has said he made his money illegally. But he emerged from Hungary as a young man with nothing and used every trick Wall Street and the US securities and tax rules allowed to become one of the world's richest men.

When people make money on Wall Street, it's not because they gave the world lots of useful things like Steve Jobs gave us Apple; it's because they took the money out of someone else's hide. They knew something others didn't. They took risks, certainly, but if they got rich enough, they could hedge those risks against big losses unlike the poorer clients of Wall Street with just a few thousand dollars to invest. If you have enough money, like Soros, you can make even more money by being a bully.

Soros made a killing in the early nineties by betting against the Thai baht. The Bank of Thailand was pouring precious hard currency into the market. It was buying its own currency to maintain that currency's value in world markets. When Thailand's economy was strong, Thai business leaders invested hard currency in high-rise apartments, which were to be rented out to local people for rents paid, not in hard currency, but in Thai baht.

Meanwhile, Soros was selling the baht. The Thai government offered to make him very rich if he would stop doing this. Soros said he'd think about the deal. Meanwhile, he kept right on selling until the baht was nearly worthless. A recession followed in much of the Thai economy and in the economies of several surrounding countries. Could this have been an example of greed? The same greed the Wall Street protesters are complaining about?

I later learned that the fallout from the collapse of the Asian Tigers led to Russia's bond default in the late nineties. This default, in turn, may have caused the math/computer models of Long Term Capital Investment to turn on the firm's inventors, resulting in another financial collapse far removed from Thailand. Soros, having cut his teeth on Thailand's Central Bank, later famously took on the British pound in a similar challenge, and again he won.

Soros is shielded from much criticism because he has joined the far left. He is now against all those institutions that made him wealthy and is on the side of the have-nots, the wannabes, and other malcontents. He finds them easier to work with, perhaps. Or maybe they are the only ones who will work with him today.

No one has accused Soros of being overly virtuous. He will not, to my knowledge, leave behind a legacy of green parks, economic improvement programs around the globe, and other good works as did the Rockefellers, the Fords, and the Mellons (all people who made things, by the way). His endgame is difficult to discern, though control of international education is among his goals. He has been generous to Bard College, which is run by a fellow Hungarian, Leon Bottstein. One thing is clear: he will have done what he could to ensure that others will not have the same opportunities to amass excessive wealth that he did.

By the way, he owes me $6,000. In the spring of 1991, months before the USSR collapsed, he learned that two top-level Baltic government executives were staying at our house in Connecticut, one a vice president of Lithuania and the other Jaak Leimann, Estonia's minister of economy. Soros and I had met before, in Kiev in 1990, when he donated $1 million to establish his Open Society office in Ukraine.

Anthony Richter, his top aide for Soviet matters at the time, called and asked if my two guests from the Baltics and I could join Soros for dinner at his Washington, Connecticut, mansion. We accepted. I believe the servants were Korean, and there were plenty of them. His wife (who appeared to be in her early twenties) joined us briefly with two young children in tow. After dinner, Soros asked me if my company, the CIME, could put together an eighteen-week course in international accounting standards to be offered in St. Petersburg.

I accepted the challenge. We scouted around for the right professors.

The United Nations proved to be a good source for people to teach the standards. This path took us to the University of Texas, which had such a team. After negotiating an agreement with the professors, I sent a proposal to Soros under which the professors would travel to Russia to give the course. The cost to the CIME would be $60,000. I added $6,000 for the CIME's work in developing the program and for a midcourse visit I would make to Russia to see how the course was going.

My follow-up efforts suggested that the matter was no longer important to Soros. Months later, however, I read a quarterly report for the Soros Foundation, and there was a photo of the professors from Texas in St. Petersburg conducting the course on international accounting standards. Today I would scrub the trip to St. Petersburg, but the remainder of the $6,000, compounded over the past twenty-four years at the growth rate of Soros's Quantum fund, might be interesting.

38

After the Muslim Extremist Attacks,
Americans Ask, "Will They Come Here?"

Well, yes. They have already come here—in fact, long before
9/11—and they will be coming again. The attacks of 9/11 were
not a one-off event. They were the product of a movement that has
existed since AD 659. Figuratively, Muslim extremists have been out
to behead us since Islam was established more than thirteen hundred
years ago, more than a thousand years before America was born. One
interpretation of their religion, held by a minority but an undeniable
reality, demands obeisance to sharia law and the Qur'an and the
annihilation of nonbelievers in non-Muslim countries. That is to say us.

They hate Americans so much and place us at the top of their
hit list first because we are the most successful country in the world.
We are also free to do as we wish within the bounds of our own
comparatively modern, civilized, and reasonable laws. But worst of all
from the extremists' standpoint, women in America have rights beyond
comprehension in the more regressive Muslim regions of the world. In
the United States and throughout the free world, women can dress as
they wish, they can work, they can receive education to any level, they

can hold public office, and there are laws to protect them from abusive spouses.

At this writing, Defense Secretary Ashton Carter has just announced that women can apply for any combat post in the US military. I have met many outstanding women in the military, from navy helicopter pilots to air force bomber pilots to coast guard ship commanders. I applaud women who may elect to join those men in our military who face the gravest dangers. Our volunteer military and our ability to outsmart and to outshoot an enemy will be greatly enhanced, the logistical and temporary morale nuisances of this change notwithstanding.

Some opinion leaders have wished out loud for the good Muslims, the vast majority, to clean up their religion. At least one problem is the disincentives for decent Muslims to denounce their extremist coreligionists. They wonder if the radical extremists might not prevail and establish a caliphate like the Ottoman Empire, only this time a well-armed, well-funded, modern caliphate with a global focus or more likely, a focus on the United States and Europe.

The good Muslins see the extremists, who represent many sects, gaining ground in terms of territory, sources of financing, and advanced weaponry. They have much to lose if they renounce their radical brethren. If the good Muslims side with the civilized world, they are much more likely to face torture and death than if they muddle on and mind their own business.

Muslim extremists have a long history of terrifying their enemies with torture. Immolation in a cage and beheading are vastly better ways to go than being impaled, the practice in the Ottoman Empire. An accomplished impaler could inflict unimaginable pain on a victim, sometimes for days, before inevitable death. I am surprised we have not yet seen such a video aired by Al Jazeera.

A good Muslim is unlikely to risk the animus of his extremist brethren unless he happens to be the US-educated king of a Muslim country. Following the ghastly incineration by ISIS of a captured

Jordanian pilot in early 2015, King Abdullah of Jordan acted within twenty-four hours, summarily executing two ISIS prisoners. As a result, Jordan became the leading country in the world in terms of respecting individual life, an honor that had belonged almost exclusively to the United States. Life is cheap in much of the world today but not in Jordan.

Radical Muslim terrorists come in many forms: Al Qaeda and Taliban, of course, but also Hezbollah, Hamas, Boko Haram, ISIS, and many others. Some of these Muslim extremists come from the Sunni sect (the Baathists of Saddam Hussein, the Wahhabis of Saudi Arabia whence came most of the 9/11 attackers). Others come from the Shiite sect emanating from and controlled by the unseen mullahs in Qom, Iran. Equally important, the Sunni business leaders of Saddam Hussein's Iraq, among others, provide ISIS with $1 billion to $2 billion a year for weapons and other military needs and $300 million to $400 million each for the Taliban and Al Qaeda.

We Americans tend to think of national leaders such as Iran's president as representing and speaking for the people of their countries. That is a reasonable assumption only with democracies. From 1953 to 1979, the shah was Iran's leader. Though his intentions were probably good, he failed to move Iran toward a more democratic system, did too little to eliminate poverty and disease in his country, imprisoned his political enemies, annoyed the increasingly powerful mullahs, alienated much of the civilian population, and failed to plan adequately for his succession. The mullahs seized their opportunity in 1979 and have remained in power ever since. They have a stranglehold over the Iranian population, maintaining a police state designed to remain in power in perpetuity through force, with presidents coming and going at the pleasure of the invisible mullahs of Qom. Those presidents are puppets of the Shiite religious leadership.

In 1985, I was asked to chair the first world conference on counterterrorism in Washington, DC. Top counterterrorist leaders from

Israel, Germany, Italy, and the UK, among other nations, attended as did about fifty people from the FBI, the Secret Service, US Customs, the Bureau of Alcohol, Tobacco, and Firearms, and the CIA. The message from Israel and Europe was "Get ready, America. They are coming for you next." General Alexander Haig was our keynote speaker. His remarks were dutifully published in the *Washington Post* the next day. Other than that, there was not a ripple of interest in the subject from anywhere in the Reagan administration or in Congress and effectively not until 9/11, sixteen years later.

Muslim extremist groups do not like one another all that much. During the Iraq-Iran war, pitting mostly Baathist Sunnis against Iranian Shiites, more than a million soldiers and citizens died. The only people the Muslim terrorist groups hate more than each other are us.

39

Judith

Jim and Judith Connors worked in Washington, as did Barb and I, and we both had farms in southern Pennsylvania. The Connorses lived near Mercersburg among rolling green hills dotted with their prize Black Angus cattle; we lived on 176 acres on the Pennsylvania-Maryland border not far away in Waynesboro where we and our two sons had a small mixed-breed cow-calf operation.

We had a one-ton Simmental bull, thirty-odd brown-eyed Herefords, and two Charolaise. Our bull, Elliot Toro, produced more than thirty calves a year from that motley crew.

Years later, those cows provided conversational fodder (pun intended) for Barb and David Rockefeller's wife, Peggy, when they were attending official functions at Chase Manhattan Bank. Mrs. Rockefeller maintained a herd of purebred Simmental at her upstate New York farm.

Judith Connor and I had gotten to know one another when we were filling political positions in President Reagan's first administration. Judith was an assistant secretary of transportation. When she was in her late twenties and looking even younger, she had been with Pan Am where she attracted notice as an expert on the pricing of airline fares among other talents concerning airline industry matters.

Jim was very good with the gin and tonics, and one pastoral summer day while we were all sipping his libations, watching over the fields, and telling stories, Judith told of a plane trip she had taken that week from Washington, DC, to Chicago. She was seated next to a man who sold innocuous items, the incredible intricacies of which the verbose and chauvinistic gentleman spent the duration of the trip explaining to Judith.

Judith was caught. The salesman was rude enough, but to escape the conversation would have caused her to be, in her mind, equally rude. She elected to soldier on and listened patiently for more than an hour as this boorish man recounted, detail by excruciating detail, his life of widget selling. (Disclaimer: I have nothing against widgets; indeed, I've sold a few myself, but I never found anyone else particularly interested in hearing about this work.) Finally, the captain announced they were about to land in Chicago and said it was time to buckle up.

As the wheels skidded on the tarmac, the salesman turned to Judith and asked, "By the way, what do you do?" Judith replied, "I work at the Department of Transportation."

"Ah," said the boor, "are you a secretary?"

"Oh, no," said Judith, ensuring she got in the last word. "I'm just an assistant secretary."

40

A Trillion in, a Trillion Out

1983

D on Regan was a better treasury secretary than history will ever credit him with being. For the son of a railroad conductor to make it through Harvard Business School and rise to the top position in Merrill Lynch, one of the world's largest financial institutions, was accomplishment enough. Unfortunately, he rose to the top by getting close to the person who had preceded him to the top; this may work in business, but it doesn't work in government. Regan missed having a closer relationship with his boss, the president of the United States. When I resigned from my position as assistant treasury secretary in 1984, I gave a brief talk on the difficulties of reaching people in high places. Regan muttered under his breath, "Yeah, tell me about it."

Two years earlier, he had asked me to prepare a presentation for President Reagan seeking his support for a plan to have the Treasury Department lead an effort to improve cash management throughout the government. Peter Grace, CEO of W. R. Grace Chemical Company, had done a pro bono survey of the US government, looking for areas where private-sector management techniques could help. The Grace

Commission report identified one such project as managing the government's annual expenses and income of $1 trillion each. This report had little impact on government operations outside of the Treasury Department. I witnessed Grace's irritation over this during our one meeting at the department.

The Grace report had identified more than two hundred government programs in which better management of cash would produce billions in one-time savings. One example was farm loans offered through US Stabilization and Conservation Service (SCS) offices nationwide. Farmers had been loaned $80 billion to build silos and barns and to purchase equipment. This money was repaid mostly through monthly checks. The checks went to the more than two thousand SCS offices across the country.

Barb and I owned and operated a small farm at the time. We had purchased a grain silo with a $10,000 loan from this program. I noted that the check was not debited to my account for six weeks or more. Since the loans were repaid over a period of, say, five years, this meant that about $16 billion in small checks was being sent each year to the two thousand SCS offices. This $16 billion sat for an average of about four weeks in each office before the checks were sent to a central processing bureau in St. Louis. The people in St. Louis then took about two weeks before recording the payments and sending the canceled checks back through the Federal Reserve System to local banks. If the checks could be processed in one week (it takes even less time today), the government would save five weeks of principal and interest. Five weeks equals 5/52 of a year, or about 10 percent, and 10 percent of $16 billion is $1.6 billion. The second type of savings was the interest on the one-time savings—at the time, 5 percent of $1.6 billion, or $80 million a year. There were more than two hundred programs similar to this one, according to the Grace report. The total one-time savings possible was enormous, in the tens of billions, and the interest savings possible year after year was in the low billions. This was worth a visit to the White House.

Regan wanted to take this message to Reagan. Would I be good enough to prepare his presentation to seek the president's support to have the Treasury Department work on these problems government-wide? Regan liked to use charts in his presentations. Three weeks later, Regan approved our charts, and he scheduled a presentation for the president and his Cabinet Council on Management. This committee included Vice President George H. W. Bush and the secretaries of defense, agriculture, state, and health and human services.

As the meeting got under way, I was quite relaxed, having only to manage the charts. Regan, on the other hand, showed a trace of nervousness. (This was the only formal presentation he ever made to the president.) Characteristically, Reagan instantly put Regan at ease with a few jocular comments. As Regan made the presentation, it wasn't certain to either of us that the president had all that much interest in what was being said. However, when Regan used the word *inflation*, Reagan shot up in his chair and said, "Inflation! Boy, when we came into office, inflation was so bad that when you went to the grocery store, it was cheaper to eat the money."

Reagan ended the meeting by asking his Cabinet Council on Management to support Secretary Regan's cash management initiative in every way.

President Reagan was very different from President Carter when it came to hiring and getting the most from his cabinet. Carter was perceived as selecting people whose personalities he could dominate; Reagan, on the other hand, was more consistent in trying to get the best person for the job, not worried in the least that a member of his cabinet might upstage him or even disagree with him in front of others. According to members of the Secret Service, when Carter first observed that members of his cabinet seemed to be nervous in his presence, he presumed the cause to be the majesty of the Oval Office. Thereafter, whenever he met with a member of his cabinet individually, they convened in a small side office.

Don Regan at Shriver farewell event

Treasury Secretary Donald Regan is shown here at my farewell event in 1984. Regan had just given me the department's highest award, the Alexander Hamilton Medal. He was a formidable treasury secretary, though he will not be remembered as such. The son of a railroad conductor, Regan was a Harvard Business School graduate and a retired Marine colonel. He rose to the top of Merrill Lynch, one of the world's largest financial institutions at the time. Instead of business lunches, he preferred a sandwich at his desk where he used a computer terminal to gain access to the world's financial system. His ability to integrate changes in bond prices in the Far East with political, economic, or other pending disasters around the world was second to none. He had three staff meetings each week, Monday, Wednesday, and Friday at eight in the morning. Those attending had to be prepared to respond to any articles in their sphere of responsibility that had appeared that morning in the *Washington Post*, the *New York Times*, or the *Wall Street Journal*. Unfortunately, Regan will be remembered for his role as chief of staff to the president after he and James Baker agreed to swap positions in late 1984. Regan, self-assured and often perceived as imperious, was a bad choice for the role of the president's gatekeeper. Never one to suffer fools, he made the mistake of offending senators and representatives, endangering President Reagan's relationship and reputation with Congress. Nancy Reagan was quick to pick up on this matter and engineered Regan's ignominious ouster from the White House in January of 1986. (Photo courtesy of the US Treasury Department)

Dick, Pam, and Bush

When Don Regan moved to the White House as chief of staff, he retained me as a consultant to work on communications and information security matters, especially those associated with the president being outside of the White House—say, in a hospital. In one case, when President Reagan was recovering from a minor operation, his national security adviser had to borrow a quarter to use a pay phone to make a sensitive call from the Bethesda Naval Hospital. In those days, such a consultancy came with a pass to the White House that included permission to bring in total strangers without passes as long as I was responsible for them. I gave tours of the place to many people, including my niece Pam. During our tour, we met the vice president, George H. W. Bush, coming up the narrow stairs in the West Wing. I introduced Pam to him. He already knew her by name. Bush invited her to Camp David as a doubles partner with him against his sons. Pam played there many times, enjoying the company and a peek into American politics. Pam and her partner from Czechoslavakia, Martina Navratilova, won 109 tennis doubles matches in a row, a world record that no pair of women players is likely to approach. Pam won 133 top-level titles, including 111 women's doubles titles, most with Navratilova and Natalia Zvereva from Belarus. She was proud to play for the United States at the 1988 Seoul Olympics where she and Zina Garrison partnered to win gold medals. Pam announces the major tennis matches for ESPN today and was inducted into the International Tennis Hall of Fame in 2002. (Official White House Photograph)

41

Where to Cut Defense Spending? Health Care?

2011

Whenever the defense budget is under attack, most people picture eliminating battalions of troops or expensive advanced weapons systems such as F-35s, stealth bombers, and submarines. In the August 15, 2010, issue of *The Weekly Standard*, Gary Schmitt and Tom Donnelly mention the possibility of saving a "few billion" dollars annually by better management of the military's health care plan, TRI-CARE for LIFE, but they underestimate the magnitude of what is possible.

The US defense budget of nearly $700 billion in fiscal year 2011 does not include the roughly $35 billion to support the wars in Iraq and Afghanistan but does include $25 billion for the F-35 Strike fighter plane, ballistic missile defense, and the Virginia-class submarine, the three largest US weapons programs today. These are juicy targets for determined defense belt-tighteners. There is also a movement to reduce overseas troops and the number of troops on active duty in each of the services, especially in the largest service in terms of manpower, the army.

The trouble is, we may actually need these capabilities, and by the time we find out for certain, it may be too late to recover such massive programs in any reasonable time. That's not to say that the strategies used to justify these assets are without fault. These are deservedly contentious areas worthy of debate. Furthermore, almost all major weapons systems experience huge cost overruns, diluting the original returns expected. And finally, any important new weapons system may take ten to fifteen years from concept to deployment, a span of three to four presidential terms.

In 2009 the current administration cut $400 billion from defense over the ensuing ten years. Now it's looking for another $500 billion to $600 billion in cuts over the next ten years.

The administration seems intent on reducing our war-making capability. There is other low-hanging fruit to be examined, however.

The TRI-CARE for LIFE program is $50 billion of the defense budget, about 12 percent of the total, and applies to military personnel only in their peacetime capacity. (Medical care of wounded soldiers is not in this budget, and the cost is quite small by comparison.) It has been demonstrated that with proper incentives for patients and doctors, the claims paid by an insurer like TRI-CARE for LIFE could be cut dramatically, almost in half, according to some studies. In other words, the key to maintaining our military readiness might be to incentivize military families to take better care of themselves. If this were done, and it has been demonstrated to work in test sites around the country, the cost of medical insurance for the military could decrease from $50 billion to, say, $35 billion, a savings of $15 billion a year, or $150 billion over ten years. Is it not worth a modicum of effort to determine the feasibility of such an idea?

Given the choice of maintaining a flat budget for the Defense Department, I would rather see the relatively disciplined members of our armed services and their families keep themselves in better shape. They should eat better, take their meds, feel better, and visit fewer emergency rooms and surgeons. At the same time, they could see improvements in our nation's security with, say, more F-35 fighter planes and no increase in the defense budget.

This could happen—but it won't. (Since I wrote this piece, Ashton Carter has been named secretary of defense. In an op-ed piece in the *Wall Street Journal* on October 21, 2015, he said he was looking for savings in the Defense Department's huge health care budget.) Instead, we have sequestration, mandatory cuts in years when Congress fails to approve a budget. President Obama has referred to sequestration as a "meat cleaver" approach with little regard for comparative values.

The Defense Department should periodically reexamine all potential threats to the nation, work out the corresponding military scenarios, and determine the resources needed to deal with those threats. This periodic analysis should assess the probabilities that each threat will occur and that threats might occur simultaneously. Next, the Pentagon should calculate the resources needed to deal with each threat or combination of threats. It should also estimate the cost of failing to prepare for each threat. In this way, the US military could be designed to be prepared for the worst, most likely threats. By preparing in such a way, the United States is more likely to fend off such threats and to avoid violence.

For example, the likelihood of cyberattacks might be high today and for the next few years, whereas the likelihood of nuclear attack may be low for the foreseeable future. We should not abandon a nuclear force; the cost and the time to rebuild are unacceptable. The level of effort could be reduced, however, with enormous savings in order to fund an increase in preparedness against current threats such as cyberwars. Scrapping the incremental resources needed for low-probability, low-risk events could lead to savings of tens of billions of defense dollars, perhaps a savings of 10 percent or more.

Of course, as President Dwight Eisenhower warned us, these studies would have to be made independent of the military-industrial complex.

42

End of the US Hegemon

2010

Each Thanksgiving I try to recite my own version of the first Thanksgiving—that is, if my family lets me get away with it. It goes something like this: "Over the first winter of their existence in America, many of the original one hundred Pilgrims were half starved, sick, or had died. Then, after the remarkable harvest in the summer of 1623, due in large measure to technical assistance provided by the Native American tribes, they had the celebratory feast we now know as Thanksgiving. Governor William Bradford made a speech at the feast. At the end of his address, after giving thanks to God and the Indians, he told the remaining fifty-three souls, many barely able to stand, 'Now, let us all go forth and create the world's greatest hegemon!'"

One hundred fifty-three years later, in 1776, the United States was set up specifically to prevent it from becoming a hegemon, nor has our nation ever expressed any official desire to become a hegemon in the sense of controlling other nations. (The Spanish-American War stands as a possible exception, although how much the public supported the war is a question.) Serious hegemaniacs require a great deal of government control over citizens' lives along with an overbearing influence on foreign nations, especially those poor and relatively defenseless countries with resources that the hegemons desperately seek.

Our founders fought for guarantees that America would not become a hegemon. Federal control was carefully circumscribed by the Constitution. These principles were gradually eroded by the cuts (though not in spending) of a thousand congressional knives over the past two centuries, especially since the Great Depression of the thirties and even more especially since the start of the present century.

Russia has sought to become a hegemon since the fourteenth century when the Mongols, weary of slaughtering and plundering and lacking a long-range plan, assimilated with and largely subordinated themselves to those they had conquered. Russia under the czars was every bit as aggressive territorially as Europe's colonial nations. In August 1991, one of the world's true hegemons, the USSR, came apart at the seams, yielding up fifteen new independent states as well as freeing up some dozen countries in Eastern Europe.

There was no cheering from Europe and the United States when the Soviet Union collapsed. The Cold War ended without a peep. There were no parades with Russian and American troops marching together in front of the Kremlin or down Wall Street. President George H. W. Bush had no desire to gloat or to take military or diplomatic advantage of the fallen giant. The Cold War, which had dominated world affairs for half a century, just went away, exposing a whole different world that had been neglected for decades, a world of famine, civil wars, atrocities, disease, and abject poverty.

The Cold War, during which the two principle combatants never fired at each other, was perhaps the greatest military victory in US history. Here was an example that gave credence to those who maintained that a strong US military is the best way to avoid a shooting war. The end of the Cold War led to the bankruptcy of the USSR, a nation that had been perhaps the greatest threat to world peace.

At the end of the Russian hegemon there remained a disciplined, well-paid military-industrial complex. When the source of sustenance for this huge complex collapsed, however, and Moscow no longer sent money to support its defense industry, the husk of a country that emerged served mainly basic consumer needs. Those who controlled the consumer sectors, largely women, began to prosper. Food service, private transportation, and agriculture, all sectors of the economy weakened by the Soviet system, began to prosper. The Soviet Union had funneled 40 percent of its gross domestic product into its military budget. (Experts argue over this percentage, but the 40 percent estimate squares with what we observed empirically inside the beast.) The Soviet military, its research laboratories, and manufacturing facilities were alive and well, even prospering, right up until President Boris Yeltsin climbed atop one of his tanks and declared the hegemon at an end.

The economic and social shock to the system was palpable. Men who no longer had status, or who continued to preside over shells of companies that had to pay their workers in groats, vodka, and cheap wine, drank themselves into oblivion by lunchtime. Many died early, reducing the average lifespan of Russians from sixty-three to fifty-eight in only five years, from 1989 to 1994. The statistics are probably questionable, but the trend was undeniable.

Now we have the decline of the American superpower, a giant that seeks no foreign territory. Interestingly, one major sector of the economy that is operating effectively is the US military and, to a decreasing extent, the industrial complex that supplies it.

The US consumer sector, however, is on life support. Politicians decided we should no longer include food or gasoline when calculating inflation as if these were no longer important factors for American families. This sleight of hand hides warning signs of economic decline. The major engines of America's economy—finance, housing, health, and energy—are sputtering because of the intervention of big government.

And so much for self-regulation, especially of the financial industry, where true grit was replaced by true greed.

Careers in public service are amply rewarded by early retirements and lifelong health care and pensions. Such expenses are increasingly funded with the taxes paid by companies that employ a declining segment of the population. Forty million people are on food stamps. The poverty line in the United States is drawn at twenty to fifty times the average income of most people in the rest of the world. Fifty million wage earners pay no taxes.

We are not sustainable.

We have brought it on ourselves. The ideals of Horatio Alger are long gone from memory. (We all remember that Horatio Alger succeeded by hard work, pluck, and—most important—by marrying the boss's daughter.) Keynes's "animal spirits" of investor optimism are about to sink beneath the waterline for the third and final time. Adam Smith's "unseen hand" has been lopped off.

The hubris of today's presidents and their cabinets, all too eager to write their legacies while still in office, has replaced the humility, brilliance, critical thinking, and patriotism of a Harry Truman.

So what will be the result? We will see a long-term decline of the US private sector, perhaps haltingly at first, with an occasional victory by a pseudo-conservative president. There will be an occasional uptick in the financial markets supported mainly by memories of a glorious past but with a largely invisible but steady downward trend. Eventually bloated government, obsolete entitlement programs, and a currency of declining value and importance will bring us to a place much like where the Soviet Union found itself in 1990.

The final sector to expire before the rise of an agrarian subsistence economy will be the world's finest-ever military force. Yes, even the US military will be eclipsed. China, the world's next aspiring hegemon, will miss us as supplicant borrowers and as customers, while its armed forces will dominate the globe.

I wrote the above in 2010. My editors asked me to bring this chapter up to date for 2016. I reviewed what I had written one more time and made no changes. I think that the problem lies with an entrenched short-range mentality in business and government and that voters and candidates will have to get on board for a long, difficult overhaul aimed at bringing economic opportunities, entitlements, and taxes into balance. The task will not be easy.

Let's hope there is enough left of capitalism and of individual ingenuity so that our economy can right itself despite the US government and despite fiscal nihilism in states like mine, Connecticut.

If so, Americans will continue to give thanks on the last Thursday of each November for millennia to come.

THE WHITE HOUSE

WASHINGTON

April 22, 1983

Dear Dick:

I want to take this opportunity to extend my
personal thanks for your fine efforts as a vital
member of this Administration.

I can assure you that your personal contribution
to our common goal of a leaner and more efficient
Federal government will not be forgotten. You can
be very proud of the service you are rendering to
your Nation.

At this midterm period, it is time to rededicate
ourselves to those fundamental principles that the
American people entrusted us to carry out. Now,
more than ever, I need your continued commitment
to provide the leadership this Nation demands and
deserves. There is much left to do.

The challenges of the 80's are great. Yet
together, with God's help, we will meet them.

With best wishes,

Sincerely,

Ronald Reagan

Mr. Richard H. Shriver
Department of the Treasury
Washington, D.C. 20220

Letter from President Reagan

One reason to work for the government is that someone will think that you
did a decent job or that you at least did not do a bad job. A thank-you letter
from the president of the United States, however perfunctory, can go far toward
compensating for the inevitable agonies experienced along the way. (Photo by
author)

43

Connecticut Serves a Great Sub,
but We Need Sandwiches

This piece was published May 14, 2011, in the *Day of New London* and is reprinted with permission of *The Day*. While this piece is now five years old, the situation in Connecticut and many other states has worsened in the interim. We are now hearing about a new tax to be levied on private automobile mileage. How invasive to our personal lives will that be? The issue is not how to find more ways to tax but how to condition ourselves to seek less support from the government, to live on less of it, and to see that government reduces its burden on the taxpayers accordingly. Avowed socialist countries do a better job than we do.

Connecticut's new governor, Daniel P. Malloy, has proposed a tax plan under which everything that moves or doesn't move will be taxed or retaxed, causing New Jersey's governor, Chris Christie, to suggest he would be waiting at the "border" (between Connecticut and New Jersey) to welcome the migration from Malloy's state.

I can't speak to how many people will move from Connecticut to New Jersey, but Malloy has fired back, saying something to this effect:

"Who says Connecticut is not business-friendly? If you want a sub, come to Connecticut; if you want an aircraft engine, come to Connecticut."

When I heard the phrase "If you want a sub," I immediately thought of the sandwich and said to myself, *Finally, here's a politician who really gets it.* The sub sandwich evolved into Subway, which was founded in Connecticut with $1,000 in capital. How clever of Malloy to invoke this jewel of American ingenuity and entrepreneurship! Today, the company has more than thirty thousand outlets in ninety-five countries and annual revenues in excess of $15 billion. This is one of America's great success stories, and now a politician was going to try to restore the conditions that were so favorable to business start-ups in the 1960s.

Alas, Malloy was not referring to the "five-dollar foot-long" for millions but to the $2 billion 375-foot-long for a single customer, the US Defense Department.

Giants take priority in Connecticut.

Surely Malloy doesn't think a lot of Americans would like to have their own submarine or their own forty-thousand-pound-thrust aircraft engine? No. But the only businesses Malloy cares about are those that had their infancies a long time ago. His world is one of giant companies that sell to giant companies or to one mammoth government.

Rare is the politician who has any knowledge or recollection of what it takes to start and to manage a real business. This is what made Connecticut and the rest of America great—a phenomenon that no one with a career in government can understand or explain, let alone export to others less well off than we.

Connecticut has three hundred thousand small and medium-size businesses. These are the seedlings of tomorrow's growth, jobs, and economic strength. Embedded somewhere among these seedlings are the Electric Boats and Pratt & Whitneys of tomorrow. Malloy could not care less about them except that in aggregate they will be a source of tax revenue—if they remain in Connecticut and if they succeed in fighting their way through Connecticut's ever-increasing regulatory barriers.

General Dynamics, parent of Electric Boat, maker of the 375-foot-longs, employs more than eighty thousand people around the world but laid off more than five hundred people in Connecticut last year. United Technologies, parent of Pratt & Whitney, employs 215,000 people worldwide and has laid off eighteen thousand employees in the past two years, and its Pratt & Whitney forty-thousand-pounds-of-thrust-aircraft-engine-maker is trying to move one thousand jobs out of Connecticut.

Great. Please pass the mustard.

44

Penny Foolish in Connecticut

2011

This story is about my home state, Connnecticut. As I read about other states, I see the same kind of problem.

The new governor of Connecticut, Daniel P. Malloy, is raising taxes, cutting costs, eliminating government jobs, and increasing budgets, all with such breathless abandon that no one quite knows in which direction the state is headed. One can hazard a guess, however, that the direction is down. He also plans to eliminate 6,500 state jobs.

The governor started the year with a plan to raise existing taxes and to impose new taxes on more than sixty goods and services; Connecticut residents already pay state and local taxes of 12 percent, more than double the 5 percent–plus of twenty years ago, and Connecticut has one of the highest state income tax rates in the nation.

Malloy forecasts an increase in spending at the same time that he proposes to close the $1.6 billion budget gap. In other words, he's going to try to close the gap while increasing expenditures. Revenues (i.e., taxes) will therefore have to increase even faster than rising expenditures to catch up, a bit like trying to pass Secretariat in the stretch. This will not be fun for the people of Connecticut.

As part of his $1.6 billion gap-filler, Malloy proposes to scuttle the historic and picturesque Rocky Hill-Glastonbury and Chester-Hadlyme ferries. This will save the state $1 million (I rounded $700,000 up to that number) out of an annual budget of $20 billion. Could this be a case of being penny wise and pound foolish? Or is it a case of being penny foolish as well as pound foolish?

Considering that Connecticut collected no state income taxes until 1989, total income taxes collected went from zero to 40 percent of the $20 billion state budget in a little more than twenty years. The governor's efforts to balance the budget are laudable, but $1 million is one half of one thousandth of 1 percent of the budgeted $20 billion. This action will eliminate eight of the 6,500 state jobs targeted by the governor.

Concerned citizens are fighting to keep the ferries afloat. After all, there is something to be said for tradition. The Chester-Hadlyme ferry has been operating since 1769, or 242 years; the Rocky Hill-Glastonbury ferry, however, has been working since 1655, or 356 years—the oldest ferry service in continuous operation in the United States. There are bridges close by, but plenty of people, especially tourists on a holiday, prefer the leisurely break on the ferry.

Tourism, in fact, is one of Connecticut's remaining healthy business sectors, and the ferry operations contribute to it. Since no one can calculate the additional revenue brought to the state because of the ferries, they have become a political football to be kicked around to raise attention, which Malloy may have had in mind all along. The controversy focuses the public's attention on minutiae (one half of one thousandth of 1 percent qualifies as minutiae) while the good governor sets a horse race in motion with his expanding $20 billion budget. In the end, he may grant the ferries a pardon, thus appearing to be the good guy with his right hand while the left is fleecing the public out of $1 billion that we simply don't have and don't need to spend.

Finally, we have to wonder when enough is enough. Malloy's plan involves raising an additional $2 billion in taxes in 2012. Eighty percent is to come from individuals, the wealthiest of whom have already calculated how much they can save by changing their official residences to Florida. That $2 billion is a whopping 10 percent of the $20 billion budget, vastly more than one half of one thousandth of 1 percent. The $2 billion increase should be the focus of the news, and the need for such spending should be debated.

What are the chances that Malloy's plan will work? Will he be able to increase taxes fast enough to meet the expenses of his growing budget (albeit with fewer employees) without further hurting the state's already deteriorating economy? What are the chances of another Secretariat?

45

━━━━━◆◦◆◦◆◦◆━━━━━

The Lady Doth Protest Too Much, Methinks

The late Martin R. Hoffmann (secretary of the army from 1975 to 1977) was intellectually honest—perhaps even to a fault, if that is possible. Following the post-9/11 wars in Afghanistan and Iraq, Hoffmann led the Pentagon's Afghanistan Reachback Office. This was a small office established to link US civilians and nongovernment organizations on the ground in Afghanistan with the full range of US government interests back in Washington. In that capacity, Hoffmann detected what he believed to be a singular lack of effective effort by the US Army and the Department of Veterans Affairs (VA) to help American veterans suffering from traumatic brain injury (TBI) and post-traumatic stress disorder (PTSD).

TBI and PTSD are hard to distinguish from one another without thorough diagnostic testing, because many of the same symptoms may be involved. TBI is a physical wound inside the brain, undetectable from outside the body but detectable inside the brain with modern imaging and other technology, which can show the location and even the level of severity. PTSD is defined by Medicine.com as a "common anxiety disorder that develops after exposure to a terrifying event or ordeal in which grave physical harm occurred or was threatened." On the battlefield the US military faces a major problem in determining the existence of either and in distinguishing one from the other; the difference can be important. How can the army and the VA be certain they have done the right thing by those with one or the other or even with both of these combat-derived diseases? Even more troubling, how can the army know that a soldier is underperforming his or her duties in combat or stateside while suffering from a TBI?

Hoffmann decided to do something about the TBI situation and devoted the last seven years of his life to lobbying the army and the VA to do right by these wounded veterans. Well into 2015, however, the army and the VA maintained that there was no treatment for TBI. Hoffmann had reason to believe otherwise.

As head of the Afghanistan Reachback Office in 2007–08, Hoffmann witnessed civilian and military personnel suffer from improvised explosive devices, or IEDs, and the aftereffects, TBI and PTSD. He observed how soldiers with no known wounds could return from ground combat and be unable to perform their stateside duties satisfactorily. He then saw those same soldiers mustered out of the service with "less than honorable" discharges. Hoffmann felt that any soldier who had been in ground combat and had later been classified as unable to perform his or her duties should have been examined for the presence of TBI or PTSD before discharge. This implied a moral obligation toward those who had previously been treated badly by the army and the VA. The situation began to smack of cover-ups and worse.

Hoffmann had learned of some success in treating TBI with what is known as hyperbaric oxygen therapy. HBOT involves two prescriptive ingredients. First, the patient is placed in a chamber, which is then pressurized to a prescribed number of feet below sea level, forcing more blood to flow to the extremities of the vascular system, including injured parts of the brain that need more oxygen to survive or to heal. Second, the doctor may prescribe up to 100 percent pure oxygen. The combination of the two effects gives cells in the damaged region of the brain the fuel needed to help heal a wound. The Food and Drug Administration (FDA) controls the use of both the chamber and the dosage of oxygen since both are considered prescriptive medicine.

Hoffmann personally observed how HBOT could be effective in healing brains, returning veterans to productive occupations, and restoring healthy family relationships. He had sent a friend and sitting judge, T. Patt Maney, to Afghanistan as part of a civilian team to help improve the rule of law in Afghanistan. (Russ Deane and I had been in Kabul in 2002 to help kick-start a modern system of laws and courts in Afghanistan.) Maney was also a brigadier general in the US Army Reserve. On August 20, 2005, he was injured by an IED in Afghanistan. He hoped to hang on to his reserve status but knew the army could kick him out after a year of hospitalization. Maney spent twenty months recovering at Walter Reed Army Hospital. Then, to paraphrase his words, "HBOT totally turned that around for me. After I had made eight 'dives,' my wife thought I was better but was afraid to say anything. After twelve dives, I thought I was better but didn't say anything. After twenty dives, other people started remarking, 'You are doing better.' HBOT made my wife's life better."

Barb and I had the pleasure of sharing a bed-and-breakfast in Virginia with Patt and Caroline Maney in the spring of 2008, though TBI and HBOT were not topics we knew enough about to discuss at the time. Today, Maney says he feels good; he has retained his reserve status and is again a judge in Florida.

Of course, one positive experience means nothing in the world of science, medicine, and proposed new healing treatments. Scientists conduct double-blind, randomly sampled tests of thousands to produce the statistically significant evidence for FDA approval of a new medicine or treatment. However, such tests can cost tens of millions and require many years to complete.

Still, the number of successful applications of HBOT for TBI grew, with little or no downside risk observed. At first, there were a handful of success stories, then a hundred, and by 2015, several hundred and not a single reversal. Wounded soldiers were showing up for HBOT treatment at the few US clinics willing and able to provide it and were paying for the service out of their own pockets or with private help. Several clinics have performed the treatment free for wounded vets. Joe Namath, the Hall of Fame quarterback, publicly credits his recovery from TBI to hyperbaric oxygen therapy and has loaned his name and has provided capital to a Florida-based neurological clinic for brain injuries.

In early 2014, I met a doctor of optometry who had left the VA to start a private clinic. One of the clinic goals was to diagnose TBI among wounded veterans based on low-performing eye functions. I phoned Hoffmann to get his opinion on the matter. He confirmed that the doctor was on the right track. He then brought me into the debate he was having with the army and the VA, among others.

I asked friends if they would join me in a volunteer effort to understand the TBI problem better and to determine if there was anything we could do to assist Hoffmann in his efforts. At the time, we viewed our mission as trying to determine the effectiveness of HBOT therapy and, if successful, persuade the Defense Department, the VA, and the FDA to approve HBOT as an on-label treatment for TBI; this, of course, meant accepting Hoffmann's conclusions despite strong disagreement at the VA.

John Forbis, a former McKinsey partner, joined me in this effort. It took time to gather and to absorb the abundance of information about the subject, much of it technical. Just as we were beginning to get our arms around the subject and had outlined a plan of action, Hoffmann passed away suddenly on July 14, 2014.

Hoffmann was buried with full honors in Arlington Cemetery on a hilltop from which one could look down upon the US Capitol and the Pentagon, two buildings that best symbolized his life's most important work. It was some weeks before our Connecticut team got back to the matter of wounded vets with TBI.

In the meantime, Forbis had put us in touch with Hamilton Moses III, who had been a senior neurologist at Johns Hopkins Hospital where he also became chief operating officer. Moses advised us against aligning ourselves with a specific treatment, including HBOT. Instead, he told us to find out what top neurologists and others thought about possible treatments for brain injury and the direction in which related research was headed.

We shifted gears as he suggested, but now we needed someone on our team who was a peer of the nation's top neurologists and who could communicate with scientists engaged in this matter. As it happened, such a person resided less than a mile away from me in Old Lyme, Connecticut. Dr. Ted VanItallie, professor emeritus of medicine at Columbia University, joined our group, and we began learning a great deal about how the brain functions and how it can be repaired if injured.

I have since reviewed the abstracts of more than two hundred scientific studies funded from 2010 to 2014 by the National Institutes of Health, on TBI and brain injuries in general. Abstract after abstract said, "There is no treatment for TBI." This line was repeated with such lock-step regularity as to raise a question about how interested the army and the VA were in confronting this problem.

Such information may exist, but we found little in the scientific literature on the impact of a blast on the human brain. A blast injury can be very different from a concussion, for example. Such information, even from tests on animals, could be helpful in understanding approaches to treat TBI.

There are many TBI-related questions, and the army and the VA should address them publicly. They should be out in front on such scientific matters, but we have seen no evidence that that is the case.

For example, how many of our wounded veterans are suffering from PTSD and TBI, the invisible wounds of warfare? The Rand Corporation estimates the number at between three hundred thousand and one million. How many of our soldiers returned from combat wounded but didn't know it and were pushed out with the shame and life burden of "less than honorable" discharges because of such wounds?

Veterans are committing suicide at the rate of twenty-two per day, or about eight thousand a year. This is the US government's official statistic, which it claims is twice the national average of forty thousand per year, or one civilian suicide per year out of every eight thousand citizens.

There are twenty-three million American veterans. Suicides at the rate of twenty-two per day from this population equals one suicide per year per three thousand veterans, or almost three suicides per eight thousand veterans, or nearly three times the average for nonveteran citizens. This is not a useful number, however. The most important question is how many veterans who are taking their lives are among the small minority of veterans who are also suffering with PTSD or TBI? No one knows, or no one will say. Congress should ask for this number. It could provide just the shock necessary for Congress and the executive branch to take proper action. A proper accounting for these suicides might (I believe it would, absolutely) reveal an epidemic and a disgrace, with a staggering social cost for the United States passed along by DoD and the VA to society at large.

The Defense Department and the VA owe it to the American public to gather, to validate, and to share statistics of such importance to our country.

To what extent could those conditions that were called shellshock in World War I and battle fatigue or combat fatigue in World War II have been invisible wounds? Based on what is known today, is it possible that in slapping two soldiers he thought were cowards seeking refuge in the hospital, General George S. Patton actually struck two American heroes whose brains had been wounded in combat? Would we, today, be able to see those wounds? Such an image over the bed of those two humiliated soldiers would have gotten an entirely different reaction from General Patton.

TBIs can be detected in increasing detail with the help of modern imaging technology. The cognitive abilities of such wounded veterans can also be measured. More important, these abilities can be measured before and after combat and before and after treatments. This is significant because TBI, untreated, can progress to chronic traumatic encephalopathy (CTE), leading to dementia and death or to depression and suicide. A treatment for TBI might at least arrest, if not reverse, the disease. But according to the VA authorities, "There is no treatment for TBI."

A Defense Department policy established in 2011 says that every soldier with a suspected TBI or PTSD should be measured as soon as possible for cognitive powers to establish a baseline for further care and treatment. Of course, not every case of TBI is recognized or reported by the soldiers affected. Soldiers with TBI may now be awarded Purple Hearts, but not every eligible soldier has elected to claim this medal.

In early 2015, thirteen members of Congress sent a letter to the VA's new secretary, Robert A. McDonald, former CEO of Procter & Gamble, urging him to consider HBOT as a therapy for wounded veterans.

McDonald had been asked to become VA secretary because he had been a successful manager and problem solver in a large organization and presumably had the ear of the president of the United States. I envision him seated at a conference table with his medical staff, including Dr. Carolyn M. Clancy, the VA's interim undersecretary for health. Earlier, of course, McDonald's office would have forwarded to Clancy the letter from the members of Congress so that she might report on it at the next VA staff meeting.

She says (in my mind, remember), "Mr. Secretary, this letter addresses the use of hyperbaric oxygen therapy for treating traumatic brain injuries in our wounded veterans. This is contentious, but it is strictly a medical and scientific matter. The risks of using this therapy are significant, including damage to the ears, lungs, and so on. I suggest you let me reply to the letter." McDonald, unable to see any policy implications in Clancy's carefully worded explanation and knowing that he was appointed to focus on the VA's more visible problems, such as the large number of veterans who die while waiting for appointments with a VA hospital, nods in agreement. Clancy relaxes. Mission accomplished.

I obtained a copy of Clancy's one-page response to the members of Congress, and have seen several C-SPAN videos of Clancy testifying before Congress. She is an accomplished professional bureaucrat who has set goals and knows how to achieve them.

Clancy responded to each member of Congress individually. She explained (with some condescension) what HBOT is, saying that it "*attempts* to provide oxygen into injured or diseased tissue" (italics mine). She said she recognized that oxygen and a pressure chamber are different from addictive pills, but "there are still associated risks when using the therapy at higher pressures, including middle and inner ear injury, lung injury, and central nervous system toxicity (confusion, seizures, brain damage)."

In fact, a wounded veteran—tearing up his or her life and family because of TBI, unable to get or to hold a job, and taking the VA's prescribed medicines, many of which are known to be addictive, and antidepressants with stated risks of suicide—faces much greater risks. Why would such a person care about the remote possibility of an injured eardrum? An experienced physician would not send a patient with a punctured lung to a simulated seventeen feet below sea level. The risks of HBOT are nothing compared with the risks of adhering to the VA regime and suffering degeneration, depression, and death by suicide or advanced brain disease.

I visited an HBOT clinic in Bethesda, Maryland, where I met Dr. Bob Moyzeyani, who has prescribed HBOT as at least a partial treatment for his patients with TBI. His clinic has two single-patient chambers. Patients are subjected to different pressures, and they will be denied HBOT treatment until they are physically able to handle it. The risks of HBOT that Clancy listed can be virtually eliminated when the treatment is prescribed and administered by skilled professionals.

HBOT is clearly just one source of hope, and hope can be an important ingredient in the recovery of the wounded, the depressed, and the socially isolated. The VA diktat denies that hope to far too many people.

Clancy soldiers on in her one-page letter by touting the Defense Department's own "first ever placebo-controlled studies … to provide objective scientific data that is missing from earlier studies and anecdotal reports. This rigorous line of DoD research … included three randomized, blinded, placebo-controlled trials that examined the effect of HBOT on service members with symptomatic mild TBI … None of these investigations were able to demonstrate any positive effects attributable to the HBOT therapy … There is currently no objective empirical evidence indicating that HBOT is effective or of benefit to veterans with TBI or PTSD. Given the current lack of medical evidence, HBOT is considered a treatment where the risks of the procedure outweigh possible benefits."

Does the doctor know best? Or is it the case that "The lady doth protest too much, methinks," as Shakespeare put it in *Hamlet*?

Clancy has enormous influence over VA policy toward wounded veterans. When and if something eventually causes her to support a treatment for TBI, and if she hasn't retired by then, she will be a hero in the eyes of hundreds of thousands of wounded soldiers with TBI.

Sadly, costs could be a factor clouding bureaucratic objectivity and scientific detachment regarding HBOT as a treatment for TBI. If three hundred thousand veterans suddenly appeared for HBOT therapy in private clinics, with the treatment funded by the Defense Department, forty dives at $200 each would add up to $8,000 per veteran. To treat all three hundred thousand would cost $2.4 billion. If, as some believe, there are actually a million veterans suffering from TBI, and they all sought treatment, the cost would approach $8 billion. In an era of sequestration of defense funds, such money can only be appropriated by the Congress.

Veterans with TBI and with access to enough money for private treatment, and with family members or friends able to examine carefully all the options for treating TBI, are less and less likely to choose the care offered by the VA. Instead, they will increasingly seek help in private medicine or even alternative medicine. They will arrange to see the top neurologists at Johns Hopkins Hospital in Baltimore, Maryland. They will visit the Cerebrum Health Centers. They will visit Brain Advantage in Georgia. They will visit one of the clinical members of the International Hyperbaric Medicine Foundation.

Dr. Paul Harch is the founder and the head of one of the first such clinics, Harch Hyperbaric Oxygen Therapy in New Orleans. Along with Hoffmann and others, he founded the International Hyperbaric Medicine Foundation (IHMF). Its member clinics offer HBOT treatments for TBI off-label. (Since TBI is not one of the thirteen FDA-approved uses of HBOT, the use of such treatment in this instance is referred to as off-label.) Doctors therefore prescribe HBOT at some risk to their professional standing, so like Harch, they have to know what they are doing. (For more on Harch and his seminal work in the face of detractors within the hierarchy of neurological medicine, go to HBOT.com.)

The combined successes of IHMF's member-clinics are formidable. The Harch clinic reports, for example, "Each veteran we have served achieved clinically significant recovery after completing forty treatments (dives) of HBOT. Despite persistent misunderstandings in general medical training today, it is possible to rebuild a brain in one hundred fifty days with eighty hyperbaric oxygen treatments." In addition,

1. Eight IHMF clinics in the United States are willing to treat brain-injured veterans, soldiers on active duty or with the national guard, reserves, or others; more clinics are opening and treating TBI off-label.

2. There are nearly one thousand success stories of brain-injured veterans helped by HBOT, with 5 or 10 percent showing no improvement but zero setbacks.

3. More state governments and members of Congress are warming up to the idea that HBOT has a role to play in stemming the epidemic of suicides by veterans and in healing brain-injured veterans.

4. Oklahoma has passed legislation creating a state fund to which charitable donations can be made solely to help pay for HBOT for wounded veterans with TBI; a dozen or more states are considering similar legislation. Many special operations soldiers have been able to remain on active duty because of HBOT treatments.

5. Some VA hospitals and TRICARE (the Defense Department's health insurance carrier) apparently have paid for a few TBI treatments using HBOT.

Our team in Connecticut met in the fall of 2015 to discuss what we should do. Should the army and VA be permitted to conduct another multiyear study, with all the conditions of such a study, while thousands more wounded veterans committed suicide or deteriorated into dementia and death, and Defense Department surgeons general and top VA bureaucrats moved on or retired?

Dr. VanItallie recommended a one- or two-day conference, convened by an objective, independent institution and attended by invited qualified experts, representing all important sides of the significant issues. We felt we should ask the secretary of defense to sponsor the conference so that the discussion could rise above the parochial views of the army and the VA, among others.

With VanItallie taking the lead, we prepared one request for Columbia University to provide the venue and a second request for the secretary of defense to sponsor the conference. We cited four goals for the conference:

1. To understand the physiological mechanisms that give rise to TBI. To do this, it is necessary to review and to integrate all the scientifically sound information from published findings of animal models of TBI, and with this information, to construct the best possible prototype of the brain's response to TBI.

2. To study the effects on wounded veterans of carrying the Apoe4 gene. Do carriers of this mysterious gene progress more quickly from TBI to CTE? VanIttalie maintains that too little is known about this potentially troublesome gene.

3. To develop a set of biomarkers (a blood test can be one) to enable an attending physician to predict if a patient is headed for an uncomplicated recovery or for a chronic state of brain deterioration.

4. To resolve the conflicting reports in scientific literature about the effectiveness of HBOT in treating TBI or concussions.

On the theory that our letter would not make it to the new (at the time) Defense Secretary Ashton Carter the normal way, I sent it by way of William Perry. As secretary of defense under President Clinton, Perry had been a mentor to Ash Carter. I had worked with both during the International Executive Service Corps' defense conversion efforts in the four nuclear states of the former USSR—Russia, Ukraine, Kazakhstan, and Belarus.

The little-known gene variant called Apoe4 deserves more explanation. Dr. VanItallie had quietly slipped this into an earlier conversation about the proposed conference. He explained that if one carried the ApoE4 gene, the body's mechanisms for repairing a wounded brain after an injury were impaired. For us lay people, he explained that the body has a kind of vacuum cleaner to clean up the mess after a brain injury. Carriers of the Apoe4 gene do not have the same capability. According to VanIttalie, 23 percent of Americans carry this gene, and testing for it is easy. If people have this gene, should they avoid ground combat? Football? Do the military services and the National Footbal League have a moral obligation to inform potential recruits of this risk?

Well, that's where we stand in the final days of 2015. We have been working on this matter for two years. If the VA bureaucracy can brush aside thirteen members of the United States Congress, our small team far from the action will not easily get such an important set of considerations into the hands of the people who can do something about them.

Are we Americans doing our best for our wounded veterans? Not even close. Is anyone at the Defense Department concerned that service members who carry the ApoE4 gene may have a much tougher time dealing with TBI, the signature wound of warfare today, than those who don't? We see no evidence to that effect. Does the US Army plan to determine which GIs were pushed out of the service with "less than honorable" discharges when they should have been treated like General Patt Maney and to make redress? A small effort to accomplish this is underway.

Referring to the use of hyperbaric oxygen for those with TBI, Martin Hoffmann's plea before he died was "Treat now!"

Part 3

Tapering Off

Age is an issue of mind over matter. If you don't mind, it doesn't matter.

—Mark Twain

This last section of the book is a reflection on what it's like to work steadily for more than fifty years and have all that come to a sudden halt. I neither planned on it nor saw it coming. I have to say it was a shock. Perhaps others in similar situations will at least derive some amusement, or glimmers of *schadenfreude*, from my experiences at this stage in life. I flailed away at different activities, mostly volunteer in nature, but found my unique retirement its own kind of hell. Barb and I are so fortunate to have lived long enough, and to have remained in good enough health, to see grandchildren graduating into this and that circumstance and our two sons carrying on productive lives. Both of them are already better prepared for retirement than I.

46

———— ◦◦◦◦◦◦ ————

I'll Be a Home for Christmas

2006

We had planned the builders party on Labor Day, believing this to be both a fitting holiday on which to celebrate the completion of renovations to our "new" 1740-vintage one-bedroom colonial and a date that allowed for plenty of time, or so we thought, to complete the renovations. As it happened, the Labor Day time frame would also have been convenient for everyone because all the workmen were still busy on the place anyway.

By then I had learned what a renovator of an old house means when he says, "Uh-oh." He means that on average the cost of the project just went up another $5,000. For example, one of the carpenters had removed a 266-year-old floorboard or the like and discovered rotten beams, joists, and risers about to collapse, corroded pipes ready to burst, electric wires bared by varmints that thrive on insulation, and a twelve-division army of flying ants. "Uh-oh" also means that the building codes have changed somewhat since 1740. To improve certain items like a staircase, for example, the outer walls of the house should be moved apart ever so slightly to make room for wider (according to code) stairs;

or, in order to move a door on the first floor, the roof should be raised ever so slightly to allow for enough headroom (according to code) in the new doorway.

I also understood what "uh-oh" does not mean. It does not mean, for example, "Dick, I'm happy to tell you we're bringing this project in on time and under budget." How many times was I reminded, "Remember, this estimate was based on the assumption that we wouldn't find any unusual problems"?

Unusual problems? None of our problems is unusual any longer. When a plumber removes an old sink, we expect the pipes to instantly vaporize into a pile of toxic waste. When a carpenter touches an old plank, we expect the other side to be eaten to the point that it is only a matter of days, or even hours, before someone falls through the floor. When an electrician replaces a wire, we expect him to say, "They stopped approving this type of wiring around the time of Edison." When the inspector comes, we expect him to say, "That's funny. My chart don't show no septic system over here."

We have often thought these past few months of our many friends who retired to their lock-and-leave condos. Not for us. We just had to buy this cute little fixer-upper.

The good news? The price of copper is up—and we were able to collect $154.67 from the old copper pipes removed from the house.

47

Pergolatory

October 2012

We were pleased that our purchase of a farm in southern Pennsylvania in the late seventies had provided a great education for our sons, Rich and Andrew. They learned how to work with all kinds of machinery, animals, and crops and to observe common courtesies in hospital emergency rooms; for example, we always waved the chain-saw injuries in ahead of us to see the doctor.

It was therefore with trepidation that I embraced Andrew's idea that we construct a pergola for our front patio from scratch. To what extent was this from scratch? Andrew's recipe called for a hurricane to knock down large trees to provide the raw material. Hurricane Irene soon obliged, and neighbors allowed us to take timber from their woods. Barb sensed Andrew and I had bitten off more than she could chew when we declared we were going to build not just any old pergola but a post-and-beam pergola.

Andrew had an impressive array of gear for climbing trees, pulling megatons of large trees in the direction we wanted them to fall, and positioning heavy logs. This project called for so many different devices, in fact, that we found ourselves raiding both Rich's and Andrew's tool shops in addition to mine, discovering in the process tools I recognized from long ago—tools that had belonged to my mother and father in the fifties and—could it be?—a draw knife that once resided in my grandfather's toolshed.

Andrew also had two chain saws, the larger of which sported a thirty-two-inch blade. He used this to cut the first slab of a tree to make a flat surface from which all other vertical and horizontal angles and surfaces could be determined. Andrew referred to this one as Frankinsaw.

I do not recall ever hearing about Andrew lifting a weight or taking to a treadmill to improve himself physically, so I was amazed as he hefted hundred-pound timbers with ease and levered tons of fifteen-foot logs into position for cutting.

One danger we had not adequately anticipated, however, was how unpredictable large trees were when they fell. We had dropped many smaller trees, but when Andrew toppled one twenty-foot tree stump, nearly three feet in diameter at its base, the top snapped the remaining fibers holding it in place, and it came spinning and crashing down. In a split second, many foot tons of energy were transferred to the back end of the tree where Andrew was standing. This log bounced up at an angle, hit Andrew square in the chest, and pitched him like a sack of wheat onto his back in the underbrush. It was Bronco Nagurski versus George Plimpton.

Miraculously (and mercifully), Andrew suffered absolutely no physical damage. Today, we are out of the woods and into the garage with four fourteen-foot plates and beams and four nine-foot posts, all six inches square (more or less), planed, and weighing two hundred to four hundred pounds each. The "rightful work" that remains is making eight corner braces and twelve mortises and tenons each and then raising the whole collection of beams and posts into place, a feat equivalent to lifting our old Simmental bull eight feet in the air. This could call for a party!

Meanwhile, Andrew's shoulder has fully recovered from injuries sustained during his many hours on the working end of the chain saws, and my fever has abated—a fever from the tiny tick that transmits the famous disease that gave our town its name. Oh, and be on the lookout for my forthcoming book, soon to be published by Barns and Gambrel, *Timbering for Lunatics.*

Andrew and logs in forest

This is what a pergola looks like at the outset. (Photo by author)

Pergola 1

The entire structure is held together by four-inch tenons inserted into the same-size mortise (hole). All structural parts are prevented from separating by three-quarter-inch-diameter locust pins. The pins are produced by a committed young couple in Maine who make a living entirely on sales of these items for post-and-beam construction. We asked the ladies at the raising to knock in the pins. Here is Barbara Preston, a friend of many years, pounding in her pin for posterity. (Photo by author)

Pergola

The finished product. (Photo by author)

48

The Crooked Road of Life: "O Death, Won't You Spare Me Over 'til Another Year?"

The morning drive did not begin auspiciously as a slight drizzle and fog precluded viewing the spectacular scenery of western Virginia. The problem was especially bad on mountaintops—of which there were countless more than I had anticipated based on my increasingly useless map of the region. Our GPS had long since lost signal contact with the outer world. We were headed for Clintwood, Virginia, our first stop on "The Crooked Road of Bluegrass," and for the Dr. Ralph Stanley Museum, a tribute to a still-living legend of traditional, old-time American music.

We could not pass up the invitation to participate the day before in the change of command involving a former student, now twenty-four, who would become the skipper of an eighty-seven-foot coast guard cutter out of Little Creek Station near Norfolk. I had persuaded Barb that we should take advantage of the occasion and see something of Virginia's storied westernmost parts, home to much of the country's traditional music and many of its great country and bluegrass musicians.

The first of them were immigrants who came to the new world, bringing with them the traditions of their homelands including their songs, music, and dance. (Later on we would see Josh Gibson, the best clogger in southwestern Virginia, clicking away in his special steel-edged shoes on the hollow concrete dance floor at the Carter Fold, middle of nowhere, Virginia.)

I had just finished reading Ralph Stanley's autobiography, a book I ordinarily would neither have bought nor read. Once I started this book, however, I couldn't put it down. It was about his music and his family, but it was also about how to lead one's life. Furthermore, son Rich and his friend Jocelyn, who had given me the book, had also taken us to hear Steve Martin play the banjo in Carnegie Hall the previous October. The lead group warming up the crowd for Martin was none other than Ralph Stanley and the Clinch Mountain Boys. Martin, better known for his comedy and movies, came on stage first, and in a gracious tribute to Stanley's amazing career, played a single banjo tune to launch the evening.

Now, according to otherwise unhelpful signage, we were motoring in the vicinity of the Clinch River, home of the Clinch Mountain Boys and Ralph Stanley. Stanley and his brother, Carter, had invented much of what we call bluegrass, mountain, or old-time American music today.

Our modern navigation gadget had not found a signal in those dark hollers since shortly after leaving Cripple Creek Cabins that morning. The selection of this B&B had turned out to be such a really good dumb-luck decision that, following a fine breakfast at this immaculate retreat, I had cautiously begun to feel a bit smug about suggesting and planning this venture. My smugness was short-lived.

A trip I had crudely estimated to take two hours was approaching five hours. Rain and slippery, winding roads were a minor part of our difficulties. We had been reduced to asking directions at just about any establishment that was open. The most helpful response was from an

Egyptian in charge of a CITGO station who admitted that he had no idea where we were going or how to get there.

Others sent us confidently into the unknown with vague, ambiguous directions that never coincided with anything we later observed. The pain mounted in my cramped, arthritic hands after countless tortuous downhill curves where we slowed to ten miles per hour to avoid rock outcroppings and oncoming cars.

What we *could* see was a land of considerable misery: farms making do on hardscrabble; sparsely inhabited towns with gray, dirty windows and "For Rent" signs; working coal mines, monstrosities from another era that had not seen a cent of obvious capital improvement since the publication of *Silent Spring*.

In addition to coal, the main industries were hospitals and wellness, rehabilitation, and lung disease centers. Doctors from foreign countries advertised their names and pictures on billboards. The whole area seemed to be up for auction. Rusty, broken equipment was scattered randomly along the road. There was one church for every five houses. One entrepreneur, defying economic gravity, had sold identical carports to every neighbor within two miles of his establishment. Finally, who knew that self-storage would prosper in poor, rural America?

Ironically, there was no lack of money in Virginia—federal money, that is. Four- and even six-lane highways abounded. In western Virginia, the highways all run in a southwesterly (or northeasterly) direction. To reach the heartland of traditional American music, however, one must travel at ninety degrees to these superhighways over endless mountains and twisting roads.

The ride was beginning to take a toll on the car's inmates. We had grown testy. Someone suggested that our second fifty years together was not exactly off to a good start. The needle on the surliness meter, if we had had one, would have been inching toward "palpable." My expectations for the day had sunk like a stone in water. I ventured cheerily, "By the time we get there, the museum will probably be closed."

True enough. When we finally drove into Clintwood, exhausted in every human dimension, and found the museum high on a hillside, there was a handwritten note on the locked door that rudely announced, "Closed—out of power." The whole town of Clintwood was closed, in fact. Only the funeral parlor down the street, which must have had a generator for obvious reasons, still had its neon sign working. A more dismal, hapless, and hopeless situation I cannot recall. We turned to head back to our car. In a matter of seconds, we would be back in our four-wheeled prison for more bickering—or worse, silence.

At precisely that moment, a car approached and parked on the road below us—a black Mercedes with the license plate DRRALF. A white-haired man in a bright purple shirt with pearl buttons got out on the driver's side, a man we had not seen since the night at Carnegie Hall.

Ralph and his wife, Jimmi, had brought two cousins from Tennessee to see the museum. They were as surprised as we were that the museum was closed. Barb and I treated them all to lunch at the local Huddle House just as power was restored; meanwhile, Jimmi worked her cell phone to find someone who could reopen the museum. Ralph had a patty melt and a diet Pepsi and then gave us a personal, three-hour tour of his museum and his life. After all, it was not only about family and music but about persevering through the hard times, staying away from the blues, and keepin' on the sunny side of life.

Dr. Ralph Stanley

Here's what Dr. Ralph Stanley told me in 2011. The Stanley Brothers were big in the early fifties. One day, their friend and the father of bluegrass music, Bill Monroe, asked Ralph and his older brother, Carter, to come to his place and listen to a new record. It was one of Elvis Presley's first recordings. Monroe looked the Stanley boys in the eye and said, "We're finished." Bluegrass and the musicians who delivered it struggled for the next few decades. Many bluegrass musicians got by playing live performances throughout Appalachia where people never lost interest in this genre of music. Carter died in the 1960s, and Ralph had great difficulty getting started again, especially since Carter was the voice of the Stanley Brothers, the emcee, the one who could engage with an audience. Ralph overcame this deficiency not by imitating Carter but in his own low-key way, rarely risking humor but always remaining authentic. Ralph lived a decent life until the movie *Oh Brother, Where Art Thou?* was conceived. The soundtrack was created before the movie. The director wanted Ralph to sing "Oh, Death" with accompaniment, but Ralph insisted that the song should be sung the way it had been sung in churches during the Depression, a cappella. By 2011, 7.9 million copies of the soundtrack had been sold. After decades of sticking with what must have seemed a dying art (Stanley did not call what he played bluegrass or country, just "old-timey American music"), Ralph Stanley had finally struck it rich. (Photo by author)

49

An Expensive Way to Be Insulted

I finished five years of college with good tools to build a career: an engineering degree with heavy emphasis on probability and statistics, and a mini-curriculum of business courses including marketing, accounting, economics, computers, production management, and a new branch of mathematics, operations research (OR). This curriculum choice in the Sibley School of Mechanical Engineering was known as the B option; the A option was for those wishing to specialize in technical matters such as internal combustion engines, materials science, and construction. The B option was the brainchild of the school's dean, Professor Andrew Schultz. This option endured until after I had graduated and the Cornell Business School discovered Schultz's project; the result was that with another year, or six in total, one could emerge with a joint degree, a bachelor's in mechanical engineering and a master's in business.

OR became an occupation in itself. It involved the application of mathematics and computers to solve business problems. (The OR of 1960 could be equated with the quants in today's financial industry.) The business problems I worked on included the optimization of short-term refinery operations and a calculation of the return on long-term investments such as petroleum tankage.

After three years in the air force, I joined the OR department of the Esso Research and Engineering Company in Florham Park, New Jersey. (Esso was Standard Oil of New Jersey, now Exxon.) Our small office offered internal consultants to Esso affiliates around the world. We often worked directly with the heads of those organizations, people many years our senior in every way. We also charged a handsome consulting fee for our work. The more senior managers of Esso joked that OR was "an expensive way of being insulted by an inexperienced person half your age." In short, though we may have offered useful analysis, we lacked an understanding of the decision-making culture in this huge enterprise.

My first assignment at Esso was to apply the probability theory of Markov chains to product inventory in tank storage for petroleum products. The two or three of us working on this problem became known as the chain gang. The proposition was "How much tankage do you need to meet random demand for the product (say, in delivery trucks) and still have enough room before reaching the top of the tank for offloading tankers on their periodic (but somewhat predictable) visits to the port?" The tradeoffs were (a) too little tankage—which would result in empty tanks and unfilled demand, meaning lost sales, or in the extra cost of tankers waiting at anchor (called *demurrage*) until there was enough room (called *ullage*) in the unused capacity of tanks to offload the product—or (b) too much tankage, which was viewed as wasted investment. Worldwide, Esso had a lot of tank space, much of which was not used efficiently, and the problem had attracted a great deal of attention at the senior management level.

I had become something of a specialist in this matter of microscopic importance when a 225,000-gallon spheroidal tank collapsed at Esso's Lago refinery on the island of Aruba. (A spheroid is roughly the shape that a balloon full of water takes when it is placed on a flat surface. The design allowed engineers to build tanks in the shape of spheroids, using the bare minimum of steel.) The question was, should it be replaced? Who could develop the economic case to help make the decision? In

1961, I was dispatched to the Lago refinery on Aruba for a year to assess the case for replacement. The study would cost $100,000; a replacement tank would cost about $2 million.

I developed a computer/mathematical representation of the refinery, the port, and the large tanks, or storage facilities. This model represented crude oil arriving by large tankers from Venezuela and being offloaded into tanks designated for crude oil; the model then showed refinery operations to convert the crude oil into major products including heating oil, diesel fuel, jet fuel, three octane levels of gasoline, and petrochemicals.

The model also represented refinery operations during different seasons. Lago at that time was the largest refinery in the world at 440,000 barrels a day. It was also a swing refinery designed at great expense to be able to move from, say, maximizing heating oil in preparation for winter in North America to maximizing gasoline in preparation for increased consumption during the summer vacation months.

The results of this work were (a) a computer program made up of four thousand IBM punch cards and (b) dozens of overhead charts that demonstrated the accuracy of the model and showed the total costs associated with different volumes of tankage. The task was to measure the annual cost of demurrage (the cost of tankers waiting at sea to take on gasoline, because the gasoline tanks on shore were empty) versus the annual cost (depreciation) of additional tankage. The more tankage, the less in demurrage fees but the more in tankage depreciation. What was the optimum tankage for gasoline storage at the refinery? That was the question with which I had been tasked.

As the day approached for my presentation of the results to management, I had amassed sixty-two slides to tell the full story. A few days before the presentation, my boss, Bob Kahle from Florham Park, flew down for the event. After a dry run of the sixty-two slides, Bob asked if I had a photo of the collapsed tank. Embarrassed, I said I had never even seen the wreckage. We walked out to the tank, took a picture, and made that slide number two, right after the title slide.

On the big day, I checked out the projector, reviewed my slides one more time, and was ready. The auditorium seated about a hundred people and was packed to capacity. Senior refinery management (Bud Murray and Jim Ballenger) and the senior person in the room, the director from Standard Oil of New Jersey headquarters, were gathered in the front row. I led off with the title slide of my presentation on the economic justification for replacing the 225,000-gallon tank. I then placed slide two on the screen, the photo of the collapsed tank. Before I could say a word, the director from New York leaned back and said in his Texas drawl, "No question we got to replace that son of a bitch."

50

The American Dream with a Ukrainian Accent

"Hi, Ron," I said into the phone. "Alexander has been admitted into Cornell, but they offered no financial aid. The total cost for his junior and senior year is $56,000. I was wondering if a bunch of us that knew him well could all put up a little each and see if we can raise enough to get him through the first year at least."

Two and a half years earlier, I had just finished a talk before a group of faculty members at the Kiev State Polytechnic Institute, the MIT of Ukraine, when the only student in the audience came up to me and blurted out in excellent English, "Mr. Shriver, my name is Alexander Ponomarenko, and I want to come live in the United States." We swapped phone numbers, and Sashko, as Alex is known familiarly, visited us at our hotel in Kiev once or twice. Then one day we had a problem: how to get two train tickets to Vilnius, Lithuania, at a time when Lithuania was closed to foreigners, including Americans. We put the problem to Sashko, and within two hours, he returned with the tickets. (One could travel anywhere within the Soviet Union by train without a passport; planes were a different matter.)

On the appointed evening, we went to the train station. Ten minutes before we left, Sashko showed up at our train car with a load of sandwiches and other good things to eat and drink along the way. Sashko had a way of doing these things quietly, efficiently, and with grace. Because there were complications with a US visa and because we hadn't formulated a plan, we left Ukraine that fall with no concrete thoughts about bringing Sashko to the United States.

Six months later, our phone rang. It was Sashko. He was calling from New York, and we invited him out to Connecticut to stay with us.

There was just one problem. He had flown over on a plane full of devotees of the Reverend Sun Myung Moon, all of whom had promised to return to Ukraine after a ten-day orientation (and a heavy dose of Moon's proselytizing). The organizers of the religious trip enforced the return of the group by hanging on to everyone's passport. Sashko had planned this leap to freedom, however, by keeping at least one additional passport, the real one, having given his minders an authentic-looking duplicate.

There was just one problem.

He was very likely, or soon would be, "out of status" vis-à-vis the United States. Barb jumped on this matter instantly and had Sashko enroll in the local community college. The point was not just to perfect his already good English—we joked that when he knew how to use *funky* in polite conversation, he could probably function just about anywhere in America—but to give him a basis to reenter the country, legally. Barb knew the ropes. She bought him a ticket to return to Ukraine, and he took his proof of college enrollment to the US consulate in Kiev and received a proper visa.

There was just one problem.

The day he was to go to Borispol Airport in Kiev, August 24, 1991, was the day the Soviet premier, Mikhail Gorbachev, had been placed under house arrest at his dacha on the coast of Crimea. The road to the Kiev airport was lined with tanks, guns, and soldiers, and it was not at all clear what would happen when Sashko tried to buy a ticket and fly out of Soviet airspace. As it happened, his timing was good, because no one knew what was happening. (It took three days for Ukraine to decide to exit the Soviet Union and become one of the fifteen new independent states.) He went to the airport along the road lined with tanks but failed to get a plane ticket. Luckily, on the second day, he was called over to the ticket counter and received his ticket to the United States. His plane departed according to schedule.

The following January, my brother Sam and I drove up to Cornell University to see a demonstration of how trout could be raised in any reasonable-size basement. Sashko went with us. He liked what he saw, applied to Cornell, and was accepted into the School of Liberal Arts as a junior.

When his acceptance letter arrived at our house, only Barb and Sashko were there, but there was enough singing, dancing, and vodka for a crowd. Two weeks later, we received the response to his application for financial assistance. I had assumed this would be a slam dunk since his family, like the vast majority of families in Ukraine, earned just a bit more than $1,000 per year.

There was just one problem.

When the letter arrived, no financial aid was forthcoming. I called Cornell's financial assistance office to ask why. I was told that the school allowed two hundred foreign transfers each year and that only 10 percent (or twenty out of the two hundred) received financial assistance.

I told Sashko to forget about Cornell. There was no way we could guarantee the $56,000 required. That night, however, I couldn't sleep. The next day, I called our friend and neighbor Ron. I told Ron the story and wondered if he thought a bunch of us could put up some portion of what Alexander needed. Without hesitation, Ron responded, "Dick, put me down for three thousand dollars."

I then wrote up a bond offering document that read something like this: "My name is Alexander Ponomarenko. I am from Ukraine and have been accepted into Cornell University. I need twenty-eight thousand dollars to pay for my junior year. I may be deported after finishing Cornell, but if I am able, I will try to find a job in the United States. If I do, I will repay the amount of this bond within two years of completing my studies at Cornell with 10 percent interest." I printed up a few copies to send to family members and friends and for Sashko to show to other friends and to see what would happen.

Meanwhile, Barb and I headed off on a trip that took us around the world as we laid the groundwork for opening sixteen IESC offices in the former Soviet Union, including six in Russia. I had been hired by the IESC earlier that year as vice president responsible for providing American volunteer know-how to the former Soviet republics.

On this five-week trip, we traversed Russia. Our itinerary included Magadan, one of the central sites of the easternmost Siberian prison camps. We then visited Vladivostok, home port of the Russian Pacific Fleet, where we opened up a large office. We were among the first Americans to venture into this formerly closed city. From there, we went to Irkutsk, a small city at the southern end of Lake Baikal, the world's largest body of fresh water, which contains 20 percent of the earth's fresh water. We took a side trip up the coast of Lake Baikal via a rented Russian coast guard cutter. We had an IESC conference at a rustic campsite that had been reserved for the exclusive use of top communists before the Soviet Union collapsed in 1991.

We took another side trip into Mongolia. There are three parts to Mongolia, each roughly the size of France. One-third is green, mountainous grassland with no fences or power lines. The second and third areas, which we did not see, are home to the mountains and the rivers of northwest Mongolia and the Gobi Desert to the south. We then flew to Krasnoyarsk, a virtually unknown region in Siberia five times the size of France, possessing 10 percent of the world's soft pine. Then we traveled to Yekaterinburg (Sverdlovsk in Soviet times) to open another office right on the border between Europe and Asia. We opened an office in Nizhny Novgorod with the enthusiastic support of its governor, Boris Nemtsov.

Nemtsov, a reform leader and an outspoken critic of Russia's president Putin, was assassinated in 2015. He had predicted his assassination by Putin's thugs. In Moscow, we opened another office. (I didn't think Moscow needed our help, but USAID insisted we have a main office there to be near the US embassy and the USAID office.) Finally, we spent a few days in St. Petersburg where we also opened an IESC office.

We returned to our Connecticut home in early August. Sashko had raised $18,000. I then called a fraternity at Cornell, which I had joined in 1951. The phone was, amazingly, answered by the student in charge of hiring other students to work in the kitchen in return for meals. I asked if such opportunities were still available and if there was room for a Ukrainian student. The voice in Ithaca answered yes to everything, so we chalked up another $5,000. This brought the total to $23,000 for the first year. Sashko then headed off to Ithaca, having paid for tuition and having secured meals in exchange for washing dishes. On one of his first days there, he arranged to speak at Ithaca's weekly Rotary meeting. An old friend of mine was in the audience, but he knew nothing of the association between Sashko and me. He later told me that before Sashko was two minutes into his story, he knew he was going to offer Sashko a room in his house—free. We chalked up the final $5,000, which covered the first year's total need of $28,000.

After his junior year at Cornell, Sashko secured a summer job with CS First Boston. He then wrote up a vastly more detailed and official-looking bond to finance his senior year. This time he used a lower interest rate than the 10 percent I had put in the original bond. He quickly raised the $28,000 for his senior year and later went to work for the likes of Lehmann Brothers and Goldman Sachs (London). He still lived with us during much of that period, but we saw little of him since he arrived home near midnight, often via company-paid limousine.

At one point, Sashko visited each of those who had contributed to his education, repaid everyone in full with interest, and gave each an important personal gift. (Mine was a magnificently packaged bottle of excellent aged Kentucky bourbon.)

Alexander did well enough financially during his first few years to leave Wall Street and to move to California where he obtained a master's in business from UCLA. He then joined a real-estate and mall development firm as chief strategist, planning to settle down and to raise a family with his lovely Uzbek-Russian wife, Sophia.

There was just one problem.

Sophia's mother, back in Moscow, had become ill. Sashko left his job in California, and he and his family moved back to Russia. Sashko was hired to manage a Russian stock portfolio.

Suddenly, there were a lot of problems, but Sashko, in his trademark manner, solved them all to perfection. Now, in his late forties, he is fully retired somewhere back in the United States—comparably a land of milk and honey.

So many countries have their Sashkos, young people who cannot see their futures playing out in countries that stifle individual initiative. Many of them are finding their way to the United States to lead productive lives and to raise their families in relative peace and quiet. Let's hope we don't disappoint them.

Ponomarenko

Alexander Ponomarenko, born and raised in Kiev, Ukraine, USSR, has led an extraordinary life. After reaching age twenty-one while attending Kiev Polytechnic Institute, he came to the United States where he lived with us in Westport, Connecticut. After a year at Norwalk Community College, he attended Cornell University, graduating after two years; he joined the Sigma Phi fraternity. All his fraternity brothers attended his wedding in Moscow to his beautiful Russian bride, Sophia. Alexander (Sashko is the Ukrainian or Russian familiar) went to work in the US securities industry. He excelled in this work and earned enough money to take a break, get an MBA from UCLA, and go to work in Southern California in the real-estate and mall development business. In a short time, Sophia's mother, back in Moscow, fell sick. Sashko moved his family to Moscow where he took another job in finance, this time overseeing a Russian equity portfolio. Today, Sashko is fully retired and living somewhere in the southeast United States. (Photo by author)

51

Back to Work!

2009

The recession gave me an idea. I should go back to work!

As the psychological barriers to applying for a barista position at the local Starbucks began to recede, I recalled my association in the early nineties with the International Executive Service Corps, a foreign assistance agency whose mission then was to send American volunteers, mostly retired, to faraway places to lend their expertise to fledgling economies and fragile democracies. These older Americans often had health difficulties, and some had become enormously adept at forging a medical certification of readiness to be deployed or were good at hiding infirmities of all kinds. I had somehow reached the age of those retirees and was dealing with medical issues of my own.

The IESC was once active in Kharkov, the largest city in eastern Ukraine. In 1993, one American volunteer, a doctor, went there to assist the local hospital. On his first day on the job he had a mild stroke and lost his short-term memory, and we had to evacuate him. In those days, getting someone on an airplane from Kharkov to Kiev in response to an emergency was no small task. We chartered a plane *price fixe*, but ticket agents, baggage handlers, and anyone else in a position to block this emergency exodus received their obligatory bribes. Given the serious nature of the medical situation, these were substantial. It was not until our patient was on the plane, however, that we learned what a real bribe was: the pilot, emerging from the cockpit, announced in Russian, "Everybody getting paid extra for this trip—plane doesn't fly without pilot."

The next volunteer into Kharkov was on the job for three days before his leg began to swell due to an acute and painful case of phlebitis. Another evacuation was required, but this time, we knew the drill.

Then we sent Franklin to Kharkov. Franklin was brilliant and would eventually make a great contribution. He had been there just a few days, however, when our local director, Nikolay, called me from Kharkov and said, "Dick, did you know Franklin is blind in one eye and has less than 30 percent vision in the other?" Though I had participated in several meetings with Franklin, I had to confess that I had failed to notice this point. Nikolay told me it wasn't safe for Franklin to be lunging down the dark corridors of Kharkov and dodging the reinforcing iron poking out of Soviet concrete pavements everywhere. Franklin was reassigned to Kiev, a safer place where he did indeed change the world.

After such a rash of medical difficulties with our retired volunteers in Kharkov, I was a bit gun-shy when trying to fill the next request from the city. Our recruiters had identified Bob, from Rhode Island, as the man for the job. I rarely got to see volunteers before they went overseas, but in this case, I decided to make an exception and invited Bob to meet with us in Connecticut.

Meanwhile, our country director in Kiev had sent me a message that read, "The volunteers are, in general, quite good, but PLEASE, NO MORE SICKIES!"

At the appointed time for our meeting, Bob limped into my office. We had a nice conversation, but toward the end I said, "Bob, when you came in, I couldn't help but notice that you have a limp. Kharkov is not an easy place to get around—"

Bob interrupted, "Dick, this leg only needs hard work. Give me a fourth-floor walk-up, anything; I can do it." Bob was persuasive; we bought him a ticket to Kharkov.

Two days after Bob arrived in Kharkov, I received a phone call from Nikolay. "Dick, did you know Bob's right arm is paralyzed?"

"That's impossible," I replied.

"No," said Nikolay. "His right arm has been paralyzed for years." I thought back to how Bob must have shaken hands with me, somehow holding his right arm with his left, doubtless a weak handshake.

"So what's the problem?" I asked. Nikolay said that during the night Bob had had difficulty with his toilet, which began to overflow. Since all the operating plumbing was visible, all he had to do was use one hand to hold a lever at the top and use the other hand to simultaneously pull a plunger at the bottom. With one arm paralyzed, he couldn't do this. Bob had gotten the fourth-floor walk-up he wanted and had flooded the three floors below.

I reflected on all this after a good friend, John, had run into an embarrassment of riches in Washington. He had bid on several government contracts, hoping to get one, but won them all. Could I come help right away? Well, it wasn't the best of times for me, but I agreed. I had a large bandage below my right eye as I waited for a surgeon to graft another part of my anatomy up there, but I thought I could get away with that. I had also been dealing with a sciatic scorcher in my left leg, the pain level alternating between zero when I was seated and a sharp six or eight when I was ambulating. Every now and again I had to sit down to let the pain subside.

So I was off for my first day on the job after nearly two full years of retirement, or at least a period in which I earned no income. Barb drove so I could catch a train from New Haven to Washington the day before I was to start. Along the way, we stopped to see my doctor so she could patch up the hole in my right cheek—or so I thought. She said I was doing such a great job of keeping the wound open that she would like to examine a piece of my left cheek. She punched out the biopsy, put a pressure bandage over the hole, and off I went.

Shortly before the train reached Trenton, I felt blood running down my left cheek. I applied pressure, but it didn't work. The doctor must have forgotten I was on Plavix, a marvelous pill for thinning one's blood to the viscosity of British gin but a major problem when it comes to stopping the blood flow from even the smallest of cuts. I arrived in Washington, DC, around midnight and headed for the hotel. I had brought medical supplies, but somehow bloodstains had shown up on my shirt and pants; I had a change of shirt but had counted on the pants. I took the cellophane wrapper from a clean shirt, filled it with ice, placed it under my cheek and over some towels to induce pressure, and dropped off to sleep—until five thirty in the morning, when I awoke with my face in a modest pool of blood on the towels. I got up, told the front desk to assure the cleaning staff that I hadn't murdered anyone, and caught a taxi to George Washington Hospital's emergency room, hoping I could still be on time for my nine o'clock meeting.

Now, however, even I had become concerned about my appearance, which brought to mind the Phantom of the Opera on a bad day; fortunately or otherwise, my friend John would be away on my first day.

The procedure at the hospital took only ten minutes, but administrative delays had carried us beyond nine. I called the client to tell him I'd be a bit late. I returned to the hotel, cleaned up and, briefcase in hand, limped off to the office, stopping every fifty yards or so, even kneeling on the pavement, until the pain in my leg went away.

I couldn't hide the mess on my face, but I was determined that no one would know I was also temporarily crippled lest someone conclude I was too old and too far gone to be productive. Inspired by the wiles of the old volunteers from my earlier days, I knew I could do it; I would walk normally, no matter how severe the pain, for the short distances required once I was in the office.

The day went well, though I was exhausted by the end of it. I stopped at a store to purchase a new pair of pants.

The following day, my friend John returned from his trip. I had reorganized my face bandages for a more favorable appearance, but I was worried that the shooting pains in my leg might give me away. We had a productive meeting in the morning and headed out for lunch. Since John knew the area, I was in his hands, and I knew him to be an energetic and fast walker. How far would we have to walk to lunch? I was already in considerable pain going down the elevator and dreaded the prospect of walking even a block or so. I knew I couldn't go far without calling a halt and explaining the problem with my leg. As we left John's office building, however, he pointed to a café just steps away and said, "I fell on my knee the other day, and it hurts like hell when I walk. Would you mind if we just ducked in here for a quick sandwich?"

52

The Last Cruise

2008

We had not taken more than an overnight cruise in ten years, but from 1960 to 1995, whenever we had the time, we had enjoyed sailing up and down the East Coast between the Chesapeake Bay and Maine. Now, somewhat retired, we finally had the time again. There was just one problem—or maybe two. The thought occurred to us that in the intervening years we had deteriorated a bit and had less agility, memory, strength, wisdom, and alertness—traits often required on the high seas. Also, perhaps largely as a result of the previous point, my passion for cruising had been somewhat tempered by mental images of hitting another boat or of running our forty-three-foot sloop (with a seven-foot draft) aground. I was also intimidated by the prospect of sailing into a crowded harbor and milling about looking for mooring space or, given the inevitable infirmities of advancing age, of having one of us become incapacitated while under sail.

I was finally able to put these irrational fears aside. In late May, the boat was readied for the year and was delivered to a new mooring just in front of our house—a longtime dream. Barb and I decided to take it for a spin. Barb cast off from the mooring just like in the old days, and we headed out—for thirty seconds. When we tried to turn around in the narrow channel, we ran hard aground. A call to the marina brought a launch out to pull us back into the channel, and once again we were off—a little off, as it turned out. As we made our way slowly down past the boats moored along the channel, a small boat coming up the channel caused me to give way a smidgen, my mistake since we had the right of way. At the same time, wind and tide conspired to cause two large boats to strain in opposite directions on their moorings and close the channel. I was going to hit one or the other, so I made my selection. The boat's anchor raked off part of our starboard railing, yanking out thru-bolts as it went and gouging out large chunks of our varnished (six coats) toe-rail. The sound was chilling. Neither of us said a word as we continued our test drive and I pondered my first accident report.

With the maiden voyage under our belts and everything copacetic with our insurance company, one Saturday in July we headed out to Block Island with our son Andrew, his daughter Emma, and one of her friends. To avoid the Saturday crush for moorings and slip space, I decided to reserve a slip. I called all the marinas save one without luck. The dockmaster at the last marina said he had one slip left, but what was our beam? Beam? Too embarrassed to admit I had forgotten such a key feature of my own boat, I quickly said, "Twelve feet." He said, "That's great because the slip is thirteen feet wide." I hung up and hurried to my files to look up the beam. The boat was fourteen feet wide. I went out to the boat and measured it—and it was still fourteen feet wide. I called the marina back and lied, "Our boat is thirteen and a half feet wide." The voice on the other end said that ought to work. After a fine all-day sail from our mooring to Block Island, we approached the slip. The boat got halfway through and stopped, wedged firmly between two outer pilings, some twenty feet short of the dock. Fortunately, it was not clear who was at fault and no one asked. We were given the only remaining place, right at the head of the pier, likely the best berthing spot on Block Island.

The next day, we motored through dense fog from Block Island to Jamestown, near Newport, Rhode Island. We heard a low rumble and then an ear-clearing foghorn one hundred yards off our port beam. It was the high-speed ferry running between Block Island and Point Judith; neither we nor our World War II radar ever saw it.

A few days later, Barb and I sailed the boat east from Jamestown via Phinney's Harbor, the Cape Cod Canal, Scituate, and then Manchester-by-the-Sea. Midway across Massachusetts Bay, we saw our first pod of whales. After mooring our boat in Manchester, we walked to the train and returned to Old Lyme.

Subsequently, our son Rich joined us for an entire week during which we planned to sail east into Maine, to visit with friends, and then head back. The weather after Isle of Shoals (the border between New Hampshire and Maine) was miserable, however, with wind and rain beating in our faces, and was forecast to remain so all day. We decided to turn around, to go with the wind, and head for home by way of Scituate, Massachusetts. Along the way, we had heavy following seas, and the boat rolled back and forth, so much so that we had to hold on when moving about. Barb was coming up the aft stairs just as a large wave hit. She missed the handrail by an inch and was thrown to the floor with a terrible thump. She picked herself up, and Rich and I watched helplessly as once again she reached for the handrail just as a second wave hit and threw her back into the scuppers with another sickening whomp. Her spirits undiminished, Barb bounced back from this thrashing surprisingly unscathed, though with several bumps on her head and many large bruises.

Meanwhile, I had been experiencing an increasingly severe pain in my left side. In fact, by the time we reached Scituate, I couldn't stand up straight, couldn't pull on a rope or grind a winch, or bend over easily, and had great difficulty even getting to my feet because of muscle spasms— just the kind of hand you need on a sailboat. Leaving Rich in Scituate for the night, Barb and I took a train back to Old Lyme so I could see if my doctor agreed that I had serious kidney trouble. He did not, found the offending pulled muscle ("Ouch!"), and prescribed painkillers, and we were back on board the following afternoon. We made for Phinney's Harbor after a night passage through the Cape Cod Canal.

The next afternoon, we sailed once again into Block Island Harbor, this time knowing how to get a mooring late in the afternoon. As we were relaxing over dinner, a small cannon on the boat next to us suddenly fired—it was now sundown—whereupon a bugler somewhere across the water sounded taps. Barb slowly lowered our ensign.

The following day, we headed home about eight thirty in the morning. The weather forecast called for a nearly perfect day and said that the wind would shift from the north to the west around noon. We set a starboard tack east toward Montauk for about three hours and then tacked north in the direction of Newport, Rhode Island, as the wind indeed shifted to the west. We curled around to the west with a following tide and never touched the sails until we reached the Connecticut River around five in the evening. We had just enjoyed arguably the best day's sail in more than sixty years of this pursuit. The notation in our log for that leg, however, was "Note to self: When approaching infamous tidal phenomena such as the Bay of Fundy, Bermuda Triangle, or 'The Race' [the 'shallow' shelf where nearly all the water in Long Island Sound rushes in from and out to the ocean, a point we crossed at midday], decouple the automatic pilot."

So there she sits, moored out in front of our house, a dream come true at long last—with her stately mast pointing proudly toward the azure sky, with her glistening brightwork (six coats), and with vestiges of new and old electronic paraphernalia attached in strategic locations—mercifully unaware that we have listed her with a broker.

Tern sailboat

I built this boat in a slack year during my three years in the air force. The sails, which were ready-made, were the only material expense, probably $400. We launched the boat (which we named *Ball o'Wax*) in a quarry near Dayton and sailed it on Ohio lakes. According to the boat's log, more than one hundred people had their first sail ever on this craft. Since I had failed to seal the wooden insides below the deck, after ten years this wonderful boat deteriorated. (Photo by author)

Rich Shriver at the helm of *Pyewacket*

We bought *Pyewacket* in 1989, literally days before we had any idea that we would be overseas for most of the next two decades. She was extremely fast. Our son, Rich, became adept at single-handing this 43-foot sloop, without a bow thruster. Over the years, we sailed it between St Michaels, Maryland, and Cundy's Harbor, Maine. (Photo by author)

The Future of the Free World
Lies with Educated Youth

"My granddaughter is studying in Israel for her master's degree in counterterrorism," reported Merlyn, my classmate and good friend from air force flight training in 1957. He and his wife, Anita, were having lunch with Barb and me in New York in November 2015 while on one of their annual trips north from Dallas. I knew the granddaughter was not Jewish. Merlyn's offhand comment almost knocked me off my chair.

On a bad day, my usual optimism may be tempered by a combination of current events and low barometric pressure. My gloomiest thoughts have the United States headed for a civil war at home and toward World War III in the Middle East. In my lifetime, the United States has started at least two wars of questionable justification, Vietnam in 1964 and the war against Iraq in 2003. Such decisions are made initially by only a handful of people, maybe just two or three. I believe presidents Lyndon Johnson and George W. Bush acted honorably in both cases. They were in charge, and for reasons that will be debated forever, may have made unwise decisions. I can't reach that conclusion because I wasn't present when the handful of people involved made those decisions.

Those of us over eighty can't do much to bring about good or to resist bad changes in the world. We can vote, we can speak out, and we can write, but these typically have little effect. I find it increasingly difficult to talk politics with some old friends who view the world from a different perspective, one that is impossible for me to comprehend; as it happens, they have the same difficulty.

Unless they run their own businesses, people have few realistic ways to be productive after reaching retirement age. Knight Biggerstaff, a professor of Chinese history at Cornell, was retired by the university at the mandatory age, but he continued to teach Chinese history pro bono at Ithaca High School until the end of his life. What a lucky bunch of kids! By the same token, however, some of the nation's most successful people don't know when to quit. Woody Hayes, the formidable head football coach of Ohio State University for twenty-eight years, ended his career in a split second at sixty-five when he punched a Clemson player on the last play of the 1978 Gator Bowl game, won by the underdog, Clemson.

Fortunately, the world is increasingly in the hands of younger people. Among those younger people are the cadets at the Coast Guard Academy, where I was privileged to teach from 2008 to 2011, and students from all over Eastern Europe and Asia, such as those who attended ECLA-Berlin. Other students of promise are studying at the Ukrainian Catholic University in L'viv, Ukraine; they cannot graduate from the departments of law, journalism, or business without having drummed into their heads, through explicit programs, the causes, the nature, and the destructiveness of corruption, crime, and totalitarianism.

Seniors in my Coast Guard Academy classes, individually or in small groups, did projects concerning world issues of their choosing. These projects were original and quite diverse. One involved reducing or eliminating diseases in India with medical products unaffordable at the time in that part of the world. Another addressed the lack of clean drinking water in so many parts of the globe. A third analyzed piracy in the Malacca Straits and on the Somali coast. Someday these young officers will be in a position to make good things happen.

One day at the ECLA, students gathered to protest the school's lack of sensitivity toward the environment. Their protest took place in the dining hall some blocks away from my office. When I heard about it, I asked for a meeting to discuss the matter and what we might do about their grievances. They wanted us to recycle the college's waste into four categories offered by the Berlin waste management department; I agreed, and we did it.

I applaud students for their gripes and protests. Each day we progress toward more practical means of reducing greenhouse gases and of eliminating waste in general. We can only hope that these future stewards will do such work by creating incentives motivated by self-interest as opposed to sticks (regulations, laws, and penalties).

Such idealists will rule the world sooner rather than later. An ECLA student from Romania, who graduated in 2004, has already served as the youngest government minister in Romania's history. Another, from Belarus, has become one of the world's more popular gurus on the future impact of the Internet and of cyber warfare. A third is a Harvard Business School graduate and top McKinsey consultant in Poland. Barb and I attended the change-of-command ceremony in Norfolk, Virginia, when one of my students, a 2008 graduate of the Coast Guard Academy, was placed in charge of an eighty-five-foot coast guard cutter and a noncommissioned crew of seven, most of them older than he at twenty-four years.

My four years as teacher and coach at the Coast Guard Academy, starting when I was seventy-five, introduced me to many future leaders of America. One, Margaret Kennedy, was a young officer teaching chemistry. I asked her to help me coach the women's lacrosse team. She became a great coach and we became good friends. I was honored when she asked me to write a letter in support of her nomination by the coast guard to become the military adviser to Vice President Joseph Biden. Though she was not chosen for the job, one day she will make a great commandant of the coast guard if that's what she wants.

Recalling all these developments and more, I believe the positives vastly outweigh the negatives. The US war in Afghanistan, a just war in the view of most, has had huge positive, but largely unreported, results. There are better opportunities for girls, more and better education for all young people, and health literacy for all through satellite radio broadcasts into the deep valleys that defy conventional line-of-sight radio communications. Under the Taliban, about one million young people were enrolled in schools, with fewer than fifty thousand of them girls. Today there are four million K–12 students in Afghanistan, more than one million of them girls.

Sixty percent of Iran's population is under the age of thirty. A poll done around 2009 showed most preferred to return to the era of the shah rather than to continue with the mullahs of Qom in charge. Given the chance, democracy might succeed in a liberated Iran.

Ukrainians under siege by pro-Russian activists have come to realize they obtained their freedom in 1991 too easily. Now, to retain it, they must fight for it. They must fight on the battlefield as well as at the ballot box. They now know they must throw the rascals out, find and elect better people to national and local public offices, and hold them more accountable.

The ramping up of attacks by radical Islam in recent years should motivate the president to draft a national security directive vis-à-vis ISIS. Such a directive would produce a concerted effort, militarily, economically, technically, legally, and in terms of international cooperation, to eliminate ISIS. If this administration does not adopt such a directive, a future president will certainly have to do so.

I cannot believe my great fortune to have worked with so many great patriots. Many appear in this book. The historian Donald Kagan is credited with saying, "Democracy requires a patriotic education." We observed the truth of this statement in much of our work overseas where patriotism was scarce. Patriotism in the United States, though it may wax and wane, can be a formidable force for good and is the envy of many countries hoping to establish democratic forms of government. Patriotism does not coexist easily with autocratic governments. It is nurtured and sustained in the United States mainly by the older generation. I admire those in the younger generation who have developed a sense of patriotism, regardless of which country they are from. If they go into public service, I hope it will be for better reasons than personal gain.

President Truman set the standard for integrity and for the separation of personal and official duties. He paid for his own stamps for personal correspondence. When offered positions on prestigious corporate boards, his reaction was "The office of the US presidency is not for sale." Truman accumulated little wealth during his working years and did not receive a presidential pension until several years after leaving office. After his presidency, however, his personal story had great value as an advance against his biography.

Lennart Meri, Estonia's first post-Soviet president, set a high standard for integrity in public office. I have pictured him sitting with his new cabinet in 1992 and saying, "Now look, folks. Let's spend our time in charge of this country making it a better place for all our citizens. I expect all of you to postpone your pursuit of material wealth until you have completed your time of public service to Estonia." At least that's the way things appeared.

And now I have learned that the granddaughter of a friend of sixty years is studying so that she can help confront what could be her generation's biggest challenge, radical Islamic terrorism.

USCG Lt Matt Borger takes command of the *Albacore*

We were delighted to be invited to attend the change of command for Matt Borger, one of my former students from the Coast Guard Academy, who graduated in 2009. Here, at the Norfolk Coast Guard Station, he has just assumed command of the eighty-five-foot cutter *Albacore*. (Photo by author)

A C K N O W L E D G M E N T S

This book took so long to write that I am sure to have forgotten some person or persons who made excellent contributions to this effort. I am thankful to the many people who encouraged me to keep at it. I feel badly for the two people whom I asked to help me with my earlier attempt to write an academic treatise on the world's major problems. That book will never be. I hope this one is a respectable alternative. Because they played a dominant role in my activities over the past thirty years, I must start with Julie Kidd and Russ Deane, though our work together began so long ago.

Julie Kidd was president of the Christian A. Johnson Endeavor Foundation when we were introduced by David Rockefeller in 1987. Julie invited me to join the board of the Museum of the American Indian, a $1 billion–plus collection of one million items. She provided the leadership to give this collection to the Smithsonian, which established the museum in Washington largely in accordance with her terms and specifications.

When the CIME began its work in the Baltic states in 1990, Julie supported our efforts. When the CIME was asked to establish a private-sector development office in western Ukraine, Julie supported us. When the CIME beat out the German government and the Hudson Institute in the bidding to develop a rule-of-law program for Estonia, Julie provided us with the funds to do the work for ten years. Lennart

Meri, Estonia's president, thanked Julie and honored her family. When the CIME sponsored a conference in Warsaw to persuade the Polish government to waive a ten-dollar customs fee for the million-plus low-income Ukrainian peddlers who crossed the border every year, the Polish government decided to boycott the gathering, giving us only a week's notice. Julie, along with Professor Jerzy Axer, head of the liberal arts program at Warsaw University, helped round up half a dozen prominent Polish leaders to speak at the conference, giving it credibility with the Russian, Belarussian, and Ukrainian leaders attending. By the time Poland joined the European Union, it had dropped the border crossing fee, thus preserving about $1.5 billion in cross-border trade, so important to the poor living in eastern Poland and western Ukraine. Once, as the CIME board was dithering over whether to sponsor a program for the Bulgarian government on the benefits of legalizing farm mortgages, Julie stated emphatically, "Foundations should take risks."

When Julie decided to take on a fragile start-up English-language college in Berlin, Germany, she asked me to serve as its first provost.

Her foundation's website reads, "Founded in 1952, the Christian A. Johnson Endeavor Foundation is a family foundation dedicated to the life of the mind and spirit. It focuses its attention primarily on the field of education, particularly liberal arts education, which can help individuals realize their highest aspirations and fullest human potential."

Russ Deane somehow wound up working for me after I was asked to take over the telephone campaign for the reelection of Richard Nixon in 1972. We spearheaded the recruitment of 140,000 volunteers who called eight million Americans—twice. In February 1991, Russ participated in the CIME conference for the Estonian government, leading the session on the rule of law; his presentation led to a ten-year relationship between the CIME and Estonia that produced an entirely new legal system and new laws. The Estonia Law Center in Tartu, Estonia, was conceived, designed, funded, and established. Estonia's legal system is often credited with being a primary factor in that country's economic success when compared with other republics of the former Soviet Union. Lennart Meri, Estonia's president, gave Russ that country's highest award for a foreigner, the Order of the White Star.

Robert P. Hulburd was my German teacher for two years and my lacrosse coach (the best I ever had) for my last five years in secondary school. He and his wife (my cousin Helen Green) provided me with a home away from home at Middlesex School in Concord, Massachusetts. Bob introduced me to Germany's language and culture, which proved helpful when I worked in that country sixty years later.

Robert Bechhofer was my professor of probability and statistics at Cornell University. I have used this branch of mathematics throughout life. He was as disciplined and pleasant as any person I ever met and certainly among the smartest. A superb and patient teacher, he became my mentor. He was the principal contributor to the mathematical theory of ranking and selection procedures, a statistical approach to optimization, an ideal underpinning the early consulting work of R. Shriver Associates (RSA).

Robert V. Kahle was a year ahead of me at Cornell and, as number one in his class, way ahead of me intellectually. We reconnected in 1959 when we were in the air force and stationed at Wright-Patterson Air Force Base in Dayton, Ohio. Bob then went to work for Esso Research & Engineering in that company's operations research department and asked if I would come to work for him after completing my duties with the air force. I did, and he dispatched me on extended assignments to Aruba, Saudi Arabia, Libya, Sweden, the Netherlands, and throughout Western Europe. Bob provided me with challenging work and extraordinary learning experiences. This background gave me the confidence to start RSA in 1966.

Russell White was a brilliant practical mathematician and knew how to employ computers to solve business problems. He was my first and foremost partner at RSA. I could sell, and he could do. When I joined the Defense Department in 1976, I left a great partnership at RSA.

Thomas C. Reed and I met in 1951 at Cornell where we both studied mechanical engineering, a subject at which he excelled. Tom went on to spectacular achievements in science, nuclear weapons, and politics and became secretary of the air force in 1976. I did consulting for him at the Defense Department in the complex worldwide military command-and-control system. He was later responsible for my being invited to become director of telecommunications and command-and-control systems at the Defense Department. Tom, a man of many parts, started River Oaks Vineyard, which later became Clos du Bois, a popular brand available in most wine stores today. In 1994, I invited Tom to work on an IESC defense conversion project in Kharkiv in eastern Ukraine. There he met former Soviet scientists who were smart and sensible. They introduced Tom to other former Soviet scientists. Tom coauthored *Nuclear Express*, perhaps the definitive work at the time on nuclear proliferation.

Martin R. Hoffmann was a year ahead of me at Middlesex School in Concord, Massachusetts. Our paths crossed from time to time, especially when we worked at the Pentagon while he was secretary of the army. Marty participated in many CIME programs overseas, especially defense conversion programs in Ukraine and Kazakhstan. He also led rule-of-law sessions in L'viv, Ukraine, and in Tbilisi, Georgia. He did his final work on behalf of wounded veterans with traumatic brain injuries; the handling of these cases is a disgrace and a scandal buried by the medical leadership of the US Army and the Department of Veterans Affairs. His former colleagues, including me, continue his work today.

Our partners at L'viv Consulting Group included Hala Dzyadyk, Natalie Bardyn, and Dmytro Symovonyk. They were instrumental in developing more than a hundred substantive clients for LCG in seven years. Among many accomplishments, LCG helped Kiev-Atlantic Ukraine recover $5 million stolen from it by the Ukrainian government; helped create the largest food franchise in Ukraine, Pizza Celantano, with more than a hundred outlets nationwide; helped establish the largest bottled water company in Ukraine through a merger; helped a local textile company add 2,500 jobs to the Ukrainian economy; helped the German wire harness manufacturer Leoni establish a plant in Strih, Ukraine, that now employs five thousand people; helped the owner of five hotels in the traditional, Eastern-style Truskavets spa save the business and five thousand jobs; and helped the governor of the L'viv region develop the L'viv Initiative, a program to make L'viv more attractive to Western investors by reducing excessive regulation and opportunities for corruption.

Finally, I needed much editorial and strategic help on this book. My son Rich labored over the photographs; we worry about the final result, but it won't be for lack of effort and know-how on his part. Joe Haney, a senior editor with AARP, led me through the intimidating process of publishing a book in the first place. Many thanks also to Judy Rogers of Buena Vista, Virginia. Her disciplined approach to spotting and fixing errors in this book was enormously helpful. Charley Holcomb, a friend since 1951, is a craftsman in the business of writing and helped immensely with strategic aspects of this book. Thanks to the sum of their efforts, this is a better book. I am deeply indebted to all four for sharing their extraordinary talent and attention to detail.

Those who went ahead …

Samuel H. and Eleanor R. Shriver, David B. Findlay, Hon. Martin R. Hoffmann, Samuel H. Shriver Jr., Marion K. Shriver

(Photos by author)

A B O U T   T H E   A U T H O R

Richard H. Shriver was trained as an engineer and as a mathematician/statistician. In 1966, after a tour with the US Air Force and six years in capital investment planning with Exxon, he started R. Shriver Associates, which became a nationwide consulting firm. In 1976, he joined the Department of Defense at the level of assistant secretary as director of telecommunications and command-and-control systems. He subsequently became senior vice president and group executive at Chase Manhattan Bank, assistant US treasury secretary, and president of Standard & Poor's Trading Systems. In 1990, he established a nonprofit, the Center for International Management Education, to promote democracy and free enterprise in the Soviet Union.

The CIME has worked on the rule of law and economic and cultural development throughout Central and Eastern Europe, Afghanistan, and, more recently, eastern Africa. Under the leadership of Russ Deane, the CIME led a ten-year effort to rebuild the legal system of Estonia. During this period, Shriver also served as vice president and executive vice president of the International Executive Service Corps with responsibilities for US technical assistance throughout the developing world.

Shriver and his wife, Barbara, created and published *Ukrainian Business Digest*, lived in Ukraine for eight years, teaching market economics and entrepreneurship, and promoted Western investment and mergers and acquisitions for worthwhile projects in Ukraine. These projects involved millions of dollars and the creation of thousands of jobs. The Shrivers then lived in Berlin, Germany, for five years, helping to start a need-blind, English-language liberal arts college.

Shriver has been executive in residence at the US Coast Guard Academy and has been a member of the boards of Oliver Productions (producer of the political talk show hosted by John McLaughlin) and of the Museum of the American Indian. He received the Department of Defense Medal for Distinguished Public Service and the Treasury Department's highest award, the Alexander Hamilton Medal.

"Dick Shriver is a thinking man's patriot who relishes a challenge. His current one: prodding the Defense Department and the VA to stop ignoring brain-injured vets. His observations from seven years in post–Cold War Ukraine, among other places, make fascinating reading."

—Charles R. Holcomb, political writer and coauthor of *Oreos and Dubonnet: Remembering Governor Nelson A. Rockefeller*

INDEX

bold denotes photo; n denotes note

A

Biggerstaff, Knight, 296

Bilorus, Oleg, 16, 17, 18

Blanco, Luis Carrera, 158

bluegrass

    author's visit to Clintwood,
        Virginia for, 267–271

    sessions/tours by author's group,
        192–196

Bob (potential volunteer), 284–285

Boetsch, Elizabeth, **119**

Boetsch, Larry, 115, 117, 118, **119**

Boko Haram, 219

Bolton, John, 140–142

bookkeeping, in Russia, 76–77

Bottstein, Leon, 215

Boyes, Jon, 209, 211

Boyko, Maxim, 75

Bradford, William, 231

Brain Advantage, 252

Brazauskas, Algirdas, **39**

bribes, 22, 110, 117, 127, 182, 284

Bridge of Spies (film), 148

British Petroleum, 76

Brown, George, 207, 208, 209

Brown, Harold, 201

Bush, George H. W., 25, 26, 27, 29, 31,
    225, **227**, 232

Bush, George W., 135, 140–141, 295

C

CAJEF (Christian A. Johnson
    Endeavor Foundation), xv, 40

Capazzola, Christa, **89**

Carroll, Tom, **24**

Carter, Ashton, 70, 218, 230, 254

Carter, Jimmy, 106, 211, 225

Cebu, Philippines, author's visit to,
    173–174, **178, 179, 180**

Center for International Management
    Education (CIME). *See* CIME
    (Center for International
    Management Education)

Cerebrum Health Centers, 252

Chafee, Lincoln, 140

Chambasho, Tanzania, author's work
    in, **184**

Cheney, Dick, 171

chesnikom (garlic), 21

Chester–Hadlyme ferry
    (Connecticut), 241

Chillida, Edurado, 160

Chillida sculpture, **160**

China

    Gravely tractor knockoffs as made
        in, 181, 182, 183, **185**

    as next aspiring hegemon, 234

    technology as supporting economy
        in Africa, 182–183

Chirac, Jacques, 143

Christian A. Johnson Endeavor
    Foundation (CAJEF), xv, 40

Christie, Chris, 237

chronic traumatic encephalopathy
    (CTE), 249, 254

Chubais, Anatoly, 75

Chumachenko, Cathy, 52

Churchill, Winston, 172, 189

CIA, author's experiences with, 197–198

CIME (Center for International
    Management Education), xv,
    xvi, 30, 32, 33, 34, 36, **37**, 39, 48,
    52, 109, 111, 124, 215, 216

Clancy, Carolyn M., 249–250, 251

Clark, William, 28n6

Clash of Civilizations
(Huntington), 191

Clements, William P. (Bill), 207

Clinch Mountain Boys, 268

Cline, Patsy, 192–193

Clinton, Bill, 61, 72

Clinton, Hillary, 61–62, 191

Clintwood, Virginia, author's visit to,
267–271

Coast Guard Academy, 149, 296,
297, 300

Coats, Dan, 147

Cold War, xviii, 2, 4, 8, 27, 31, 67,
148, 232

communism, collapse of, 22

Communist Party, 3, 5, 5n1, 16, 29, 108

Conley, Bob, 205

Connecticut
as penny foolish, 240–242
tax plan of, 237–239

Connors, Jim, 221, 222

Connors, Judith, 221–222

Conrad, Joseph, 1

Cornell University, 124, 152, 153, 155,
156, 272, 276, 278–279, 280,
282, 296

corruption, 67, 76, 104, 108, 116–117,
129, 141, 164, 182, 296

Cosinschi, Lucian, **196**

Costello, John, 146

Costle, Betsy, **38**

Costle, Doug, **34**, **38**

counterterrorism, conference on, 133,
219–220

crime, 111–114

Crimea, author's visit to, 161–166

Cronkite, Walter, 155

CTE (chronic traumatic
encephalopathy), 249, 254

culture, importance of in foreign
assistance, 187, 188, 189–190

D

D'Amato, Al, 25

Dan (musician), 192, 195

Dasha (musician), 192

The Day of New London, 237

Deane, Russ, xv, **32**, **35**, **36**, 106, 107,
109, 124, 125–126, **129**, **131**,
132, 245

Deeley, Pat, 205

Deeley, Walt, 204–205, 206

defense budget (US), 228–230

Defense Science Board, 206n26

Dekeyser, Bobby, 173

Dekeyser & Friends (D&F), 173–174,
176, 180

Demchuk, Steve, 49–54

democracy, conference/talk on, 6, 11,
12, 30

Dikoetter, Frank, 68n11

Dirk (musician), 194

Djilas, Dragana Borenovic, **122**

Donnelly, Tom, 228

Dr. Ralph Stanley Museum, 267

Duranty, Walter, 69n12

Durdaev, Djumamurad, 93, 95, 96, **97**

Durdaev, Kazak, **97**

Durdaev, Shiiki, 93, 95, 96

Durdaev family, 94–95, **97**

Greatest Generation, xviii

Grina, Tony, 29n7

Groark, Eunice, **92**

Gunderson, Jon, 49, 53

H

Haig, Alexander (Al), 133, 134, 220

Hamas, 219

Harch, Paul, 252–253

Hawrylyshyn, Bohdan, 2, 16, 18

Hayes, Woody, 296

HBOT (hyperbaric oxygen therapy), 244–246, 247, 249, 250–253, 254

health care, in Russia, 78–83

Hefsurs, 3, 87

hegemony (of US), 231–235

Hemphill, Jim, 124, **131**, 144, 146

Hemphill, Peggy, 146

Herrmann Equipment Company, 72

Hezbollah, 134, 172, 219

Hinckley, John, 203

Hitler, Adolph, 10, 53, 54, 69, 85, 116, 138, 139

Hoffmann, Florian, **120**, **122**, 173, 178

Hoffmann, Martin R. (Marty), **70**, 71, 198, 243, 244, 245, 246–247, 255

Horner, Melinda, 148

Horner, Pat, **148**, 198

Horyn, Mikhail, **46**

Horyn, Mikola, 111

Hoshovsky, Serhiy, 101

Hudson Institute, 32

Huntington, Samuel F. P., 191

Hussein, Saddam, 147, 219

hyperbaric oxygen therapy (HBOT), 244–246, 247, 249, 250–253, 254

I

IESC (International Executive Service Corps), xvi, 6n2, 24, 40, 67, 70, 72, 74, 84–85, 86, 87, **88**, **89**, **90**, **91**, **92**, 98, 279, 283

Igor, 110

IHMF (International Hyperbaric Medicine Foundation), 252

IMI–Kiev (International Management Institute–Kiev), xvi, 2, 3, 14, 17, **38**, 50, 62, 63

International Executive Service Corps (IESC). *See* IESC (International Executive Service Corps)

International Finance Corporation, 75

International Hyperbaric Medicine Foundation (IHMF), 252

International Management Institute–Kiev (IMI–Kiev), xvi, 2, 3, 14, 17, **38**, 50, 62, 63

Iran

author's visit to, 151–155

nuclear capability of, 149–151

Irina (fictitious name), 115–118

ISIS, 159n19, 172, 211, 218, 219, 298

J

Jakubenaite, Egle, 11

Jalasto, Hans, **36**, 106–108

Jews, 29, 53, 54, 69, 139, 143

Jocelyn, 268

Johns Hopkins Hospital, 247, 252
Johnson, Gregory (Grog), 164, 166
Johnson, Lyndon, xvi, 201, 295
Johnson, Susan, **98**
Jones, Jerry, 167, 168, 172
Jordan
    author's visit to, 167–172
    as respecting individual life, 219
Jose, 157
Juan Carlos (king of Spain), 156,
    158, 159
Juliane (granddaughter), 146

K

Kabul, Afghanistan, author's work in,
    123–132
Kagan, Donald, 298
Kahle, Bob, 274
Kahn, Herman, 32
Kant, Immanuel, 143
Karimi, Abdul Rahim, 124, **129**
Karzai, Hamid, xvi, 127, **131**, 132
Karzai, Hekmat, 127
Kennedy, John F., 147
Kennedy, Margaret, 297
KGB, 197
Khmelnitsky, Bohdan, 7–8n, 102
Khodorkovsky, Mikhail, 76
kickbacks, 110, 182
Kidd, Julie Johnson, xv, 40, **46**, 109
Kidd, Wilmot, 46
Kiev, author and wife's stay in, 2, 16
Kiev Atlantic Ukraine, **47**
Kiev State Polytechnic Institute, 10,
    276, 282
Kindrat, Stepan, 9

Kindrat, Tanya, 2, 9
Kirschenmann, Katherin, **120, 180**
Kitfield, James, 28
Klimek, Bob, 195
Klimkova, Diora, 14–16, 17–19
Kolomayets, Marta, 46
Komsomol, 3
Korzeniowski, Jozef Teodor Konrad
    (Joseph Conrad), 1
Kowalcziek, Natalia, 195, **196**
Kryuchkov, Vladimir, 27
Kuchma, Leonid, 162
Kuchma, Ludmila, 62
Kuleuke, Heinz, 173, 174, 180
Kunanbai-uli, Abai, 188
Kurylko, Bohdan, 51–52

L

Lang, Charles, 194, **196**
Laszlo (musician), 194, 195
Latvia
    countercurrents in, 25
    punishment of by Soviet
        troops, 30
    Russian population in, 33, 35
    Team Latvia, **35**
Lavrov, Sergei, 191
LCG (L'viv Consulting Group), xvi,
    45, 47
Leimann, Jaak, 30, **37**, 215
Lena, 68, 69
Lenin, Vladimir, **91**
Lermontov, Mikhail, 188
Lincoln, Abraham, 203
Lindborg, Nancy, **87**
Linowitz, Sol, xvi

Lithuania
  countercurrents in, 25
  declaration of independence, 7, 25
  punishment of by Soviet
    troops, 30
  question of US recognition of
    independence of, 29
  Russian population in, 33
  as seeking political freedom, 39
  Team Lithuania, **34**
Liv (musician), 192
Livadia Palace, Yalta, author's visit
  to, 161
Longfellow, Henry Wadsworth, 187
Loshko, Andrei, 19
Lubov, 114
Luchma, Leonid, 62
Lugar, Richard, 70
Lundin, Ruth, 84–85, 86, **90, 91**
L'viv, Ukraine
  author and wife's return visit
    to, 147
  author and wife's stay in, 40–44
L'viv Consulting Group (LCG), xvi,
  45, 47
L'viv Polytechnic, 111, 113

M

MacArthur, Douglas, 211
Macdonald, Bruce, 145
Macdonald, Sunny, 145
Magruder, Jeb, 15
Malloy, Daniel P., 237–238, 240–242
Mandelbaum, Michael, 49–50n8
Maney, Caroline, 245
Maney, T. Patt, 245

Mantle, Mickey, 80–81
Mao Zedong, 68n11
*Mao's Great Famine: The History
  of China's Most Devastating
  Catastrophe* (Dikoetter), 68n11
Maria (musician), 192
Marik, Bob, **34**, 198
Martin, Steve, 268
Marx, Karl, 91
Massoud, Ahmad Shah, 132
Maxwell, Kay, **92**
McDonald, Robert A., 249, 250
McGraw-Hill International Advisory
  Council, 2
McKinley, William, 203
McLaughlin, Christina, 162
McLaughlin, John, 80, 161, 162,
  164, **166**
Medvedev, Dmitri, 36
Mellon, Andrew, 75
men, impact of collapse of
  communism on, 22
Mencken, H. L., 199
Meri, Lennart, 26, 32, **109**, 299
Merkel, Angela, 104
Merlyn (friend), 295
Metro (Moscow), 58–59
Michel, Larry, **91**
Mikhael, Admiral, **166**
militant Islam, 135, 136, 298, 299.
  See also Muslim extremists/
  terrorists
military, civilian control of, 207–212
military service, xviii
military-industrial complex, 230
Monroe, Bill, 192, 195, 271

S

CPSIA information can be obtained
at www.ICGtesting.com
Printed in the USA
LVOW12s0327260717
542519LV00001BA/265/P